PREPARE *to* THRIVE

A SURVIVAL GUIDE

FOR CHRISTIAN STUDENTS

Prepare to Thrive

SKU 10-2-539

ISBN: 978-1-9844-1033-7

For more information write: Answers in Genesis, PO Box 510, Hebron, KY 41048

Cover design and interior layout: Michaela Duncan

Editors: Ryan Freeman, Evonne Krell

Cover images: Getty Images and Unsplash

Printed in the USA

TABLE of CONTENTS

FOREWORD

"Fake news" is a buzzword in our culture, and examples on both sides of the political spectrum abound (and, sadly, the "fact checkers" often can't be trusted to check beyond their own biases and presuppositions). Well, fake news isn't confined to social media or news media. Every day, professors preach fake news in the classroom to thousands of impressionable students. Their murky false narrative and wrong interpretation of the data can be difficult to sift through, and many students swallow it, hook, line, and sinker. Sadly, these students include many Christians who hear clever-sounding arguments and are slowly dragged away from their sincere and pure devotion to Christ and belief in his Word. But it doesn't have to be that way.

Students must be taught critical thinking skills and equipped with biblical literacy and apologetics so that they can see through the subtle lies and half-truths of the enemy. These skills don't arise on their own—we must be intentional about coming alongside the next generation and discipling them in the Lord, helping them apply a biblical worldview to the shifting sand of the humanistic secular worldview dominating the classroom and the culture.

But how do we do that? What's most effective? Patricia Engler lays out a tested and highly practical method for how Christians can survive higher education with their faith not just intact but deeply rooted and how other Christians can be part of grounding younger believers in their faith. We desperately need such an approach, and I'm thrilled this new book is available for students, parents, pastors, mentors, and others.

As you read this book, keep five big-picture principles in mind:

1. Satan seeks to steal, kill, and destroy (John 10:10). The world, including higher education, is not neutral toward your faith (Matthew 12:30) or the faith of those you love. Satan is actively opposing you and trying to destroy you and your faith. You're in a battle (but—spoiler—Christ has the ultimate victory).

2. For parents, pastors, and others—universities might not be what you remember them to be! What do I mean? Well, when I went to a university in the 1970s, there wasn't the antagonism toward Christians there is today (the Western world was much more Christianized). I could even mention creation in my assignments and wasn't penalized for it! But that's not the way things are on college campuses today. These institutions are very antagonistic toward

Christianity and biblical truth (sadly, even many Christian colleges won't stand for biblical truth in certain areas), and so now Christian students desperately need survival tools to navigate, survive, and thrive in colleges that hate God, hate his Word, and won't stand biblical truth. We can't send students in unarmed!

3. Satan will use the same attack that he used on Eve (2 Corinthians 11:3) to try to cause you to doubt God's Word: "Did God actually say?" (Genesis 3:1). Watch out for arguments crafted to undermine God's Word in subtle ways. That attack is not an accident. It's intentional on the part of our enemy to undermine, weaken, and destroy faith.

4. There are answers! When, as a young person, I came to my godly father with questions he couldn't answer, he would tell me that just because we don't know the answer doesn't mean there isn't one. It just means we don't know the answer yet! If you encounter an argument that contradicts God's Word and can't find a satisfactory answer, don't throw away the Word of God. It is eternal (Isaiah 40:8) and will outlast any argument that raises its lofty head. Let God be true, but every man a liar (Romans 3:4).

5. For parents, pastors, and other Christians—you've been called to make disciples. And that doesn't just mean convert people. Listen to Jesus' words: "Go therefore and make disciples of all nations, baptizing them in the name of the Father and of the Son and of the Holy Spirit, teaching them to observe all that I have commanded you" (Matthew 28:19–20). We're to teach people the Word of God, discipling them in the truth. Don't just abandon your youth when they head off to post-secondary education. Maintain strong relationships whenever possible, being available to answer questions and grapple with difficult subjects. And help those young people, whenever possible, to get plugged in with a strong Christian community at their college campus. We're built for relationship, and young people need those relationships to ground them.

As you read this book, be encouraged—God's Word is true. It has stood the test of time, questions, and persecution in the past, and it will continue to do so until Christ returns. Stand firm and believe his Word and the gospel message!

Ken Ham

CEO and cofounder of Answers in Genesis, the Creation Museum, and the Ark Encounter

Dedication

If you're a Christian young person reading these words, or a parent, pastor, or mentor supporting a Christian young person, then this book is dedicated to you and to Jesus, our Creator, with love.

1 Corinthians 16:13–14

Introduction

WELCOME TO THE BATTLEFIELD

Staring at the email, I could only wonder what I'd gotten myself into.

Sure, the letter sounded friendly enough. But did that central sentence really mean what it seemed to mean? Pulse quickening, I read the missive again.

Yep . . . no mistake there. My professor's letter gently—but explicitly—suggested that students who didn't believe humans evolved "from the tiniest mammals 150 million years ago" needed to rethink joining the upcoming anthropology class.[1]

Interesting.

I'd heard that higher education might be this way. Rumor had it that the university is an ideological battlefield where scary professors with laser eyes (or was it laser pointers?) roved in search of dissidents. Their favorite targets? Nice Christian students. Upon a single glance into a scary professor's eyes, a nice Christian student may never be seen again.

"Scary professors with laser eyes"

But that was just a rumor . . . right?

Closing the email, I knew I might soon find out. I'd already survived one semester as a Bible-believing Christian, and none of the professors I'd met so far brandished laser vision. Besides, I had another motive for joining classes like this one.

That motive had seeded in my mind years earlier when I'd learned about the consequences of two related beliefs: *earth is millions of years old* and *humans evolved from apelike ancestors*. As we'll explore in the next couple of chapters, these ideas shattered many Westerners' trust in God's Word, driving Western cultures to largely reject Scripture—and scriptural morals—as irrelevant.

Today, it's no secret that this rejection of Scripture remains more rampant than ever, unfolding not only in society but also in countless individual lives. Research has linked Christian youths' unanswered questions about evolutionary ideas to the reality that two-thirds of churched teens are leaving their faith by young adulthood.[2] After all, why should any young person (much less an entire society) believe the Bible if science shows it to be about as reliable as a guide to identifying tooth fairies?

With these consequences in mind, I wanted to find out how Christian students can keep their faith during evolutionary education. But to do so, I had to become one of those students. That's why after 12 years of homeschooling, I enrolled in a science degree at a secular university.[3] And despite my professor's ominous email, I began the anthropology class.

THE PROBLEM: A BATTLE OF WORLDVIEWS

There and in other classes, I discovered that my instructors weren't so much scary professors as friendly human beings—albeit with much different worldviews than mine. Typically, the worldview that Western societies embrace is secular humanism, an atheistic belief system which claims that humans evolved to become the godlike masters of their own morality.[4] But does that idea seem compatible with the gospel, which explains that humans sinned against their Creator's perfect moral standards and therefore need a Savior? No way!

If secular humanism is true, then the gospel is irrelevant. But for humanism to be true, evolution must be true because humanists must explain their existence without a Creator. Messages touting evolution as an undeniable fact, therefore, often *saturate* Western public education, together with other humanistic messages claiming that truth is ours to decide. So while most universities (hopefully) don't harbor laser-eyed warlord professors, campuses can nonetheless be treacherous worldview battlefields. In fact, universities field one of the highest-stake wars imaginable: a war to coronate human reasoning above God's Word as the supreme authority ruling the beliefs—and therefore decisions—of entire generations.

"It's like being a double agent."

During the four years I spent on secular campuses, I fought recurring messages falling like missile after missile to rattle the foundations of my faith: *intelligent design is "totally wacked," evolution is indisputable, Christianity is a cultural construct, and humans created God*.

I wrote home during my first year: "It's strange arguing in quizzes, exams, and assignments for a paradigm I disbelieve (evolution). . . . I'm being conditioned to fight against a worldview I stand for. It's like being a double agent by training as a cadet for an opposing army."

My story represents only one life among countless students who are being taught to deny a Creator. In diverse studies ranging from anthropology to zoology, students worldwide face a barrage of evolutionary messages enforcing secular humanism. At any cost to culture and the church, these messages are pervasive, persistent, and persuasive.

They're artillery in a spiritual battle for the hearts and minds of students—students who represent society's future.

KEYS TO SURVIVING THE BATTLE

Naturally, no one expecting to survive a battle can enter the front lines armed with only sweatpants and a water gun. Warriors need equipping. They need to have the right weapons, strategies, tactics, and timing to survive and be effective. And students on the battlefront of humanistic education are no exception.

As one of those students myself, I realized the importance of having strong personal foundations for knowing, defending, and living out the truth of God's Word at a secular university. While these foundations helped *me* survive the battlefield, I wondered what strategies were helping *other* Christian students navigate evolutionary education systems worldwide.[5] So, soon after graduation, I embarked on an investigative globe-trekking mission to find out. My plan? To backpack 360° around the world in 180 days documenting how Christian students keep their faith at universities (more on that adventure in chapter 5).

As I interviewed students, pastors, and campus ministers across 17 countries, I noticed recurring themes which wove these Christians' stories into one overall message. Christian students worldwide need three types of strong personal foundations:

---

1. **Spiritual foundations:** a close personal walk with God, including frequent prayer, consistent Scripture study, and biblical literacy.
2. **Intellectual foundations:** training in critical thinking and apologetics, the field of study which examines why the Christian faith makes rational sense.
3. **Interpersonal foundations:** a Christian support network including family, peers, and mentors.

This discovery not only confirmed my own student experiences but also showed me that, while the challenges Christian students face often vary with culture, the solutions are largely the same. Therefore, if families, churches, and ministries focus on these solutions, the results could make a difference for equipping future Christian generations around the world.

THE RIGHT KINDS OF TOOLS

One of these solutions—intellectual foundations—involves arming students with apologetic answers to defend their faith against culture's myriad lies. But no matter how many answers students memorize, they will always have more questions because there will always be new information. So students need to learn how to think like apologists. They need accessible tools to process any faith-challenging information without panicking, deal with each component, and handle remaining questions, all without draining valuable study time.

Imagine what a toolkit like that could mean for Christian students around the world. Best of all, think of how those tools could benefit not only Christians in secular classrooms but also any Christ followers in broader secular society. After all, persuasive-sounding messages that oppose God's Word don't just rain like mortar fire at a university. Statements that life evolved over millions of years also pervade museums, zoos, aquariums, movies, books, nature shows, kids' media, news stories, magazines, science centers, and national parks. All Christians who engage with their culture, therefore, are bound to encounter convincingly presented "facts" that challenge a biblical worldview. And as society accelerates away from a biblical worldview, equipping disciples to navigate secular classrooms and cultures without compromising their grip on God's Word is growing more important than ever.

"Think like apologists."

A SURVIVAL GUIDE FOR THE REAL WORLD

Equipping disciples this way might sound nice in theory, but how does that theory translate into action? What tried-and-true techniques will strengthen believers' foundations for following Christ in secular schools and societies? How can Christian students prepare for—and survive—the worldview battle in real classrooms?

That's what this book is about.

Drawing on biblical principles, scientific research, personal experience, and insights from campus Christians worldwide, this book is a field-tested survival guide for Christ followers who want to stand on the authority of God's Word from Genesis to Revelation in secular classrooms and cultures. It exposes unignorable facts about atheistic, evolutionary education, outlines preparatory strategies for youth planning on attending a secular university, and offers tactical tools for students in the trenches of humanistic teaching.

EQUIPMENT FOR EVERYONE

While this book is written to Christian students on secular campuses, it's not only for these students. Here are a few other reasons to pick up this survival guide:

If you're a parent, grandparent, pastor, youth leader, campus minister, mentor, friend, or anyone else who is supporting a current or future student . . .

The best-case scenario is for families, churches, and students to be learning this material together. That way everyone is on the same page when it comes to helping students thrive. Ideally, everyone understands the challenges students will likely face, the preparation they'll need, and the support they'll require. And everyone will be doing their part in response.

If you're a student pursuing a Christian education . . .

Is this book still relevant to you if you're not attending a secular university? Absolutely. As we'll see in chapter 3, evolutionary teachings (and potentially other unbiblical messages) impact many Christian institutions, as well. And temptations to compromise your biblical convictions are not restricted to secular campuses. Even if you never end up facing a single challenge at your university, this book will help you to support friends who are encountering such obstacles and prepare yourself for the battlefield of secular culture beyond the classroom.

If you're a student pursuing an online education . . .

With more schools and programs going digital, you may be anticipating unique sets of challenges and opportunities associated with online learning. For example, while you might not need to stroll through campus hallways papered with unbiblical messages, you may have a tougher time finding the type of in-person fellowship a campus ministry could offer.[6]

Despite such differences, many pressures of secular university—like evolutionary teachings coming from persuasive-sounding professors—exist online as well as on campus. As a digital learner, you must still be ready for spiritual battle.

If you're any other Christian engaging with secular culture . . .

What if you don't know any Christian students and don't plan on going (or returning) to a university yourself? The same principles that help Christian students navigate secular college also apply to any Christian navigating secular culture or other challenging contexts. The same principles that apply to thinking through evolutionary courses also apply to thinking through any other unbiblical message. And as we'll see in chapter 14, the same foundations that apply to surviving a university also apply to impacting culture.

"Navigate secular culture."

READY FOR BATTLE

Ultimately, whether you're a current student, future student, parent, pastor, mentor, or any other Christian engaging with secular culture, this book is for you. As a student myself, I've had the opportunity to test the tools in this book during four years of intensive evolutionary coursework. Speaking from experience, I encourage you that students can survive the battlefield of humanistic education, keep their biblical worldview intact, and emerge not only as Christians but stronger ones.

Let's find out how.

Endnotes

1. What's the big deal about believing in human evolution? We'll see in the next two chapters why a consistent biblical worldview can't accommodate evolutionary origins the way my professor was asking us students to.
2. Ken Ham, Greg Hall, and Britt Beemer, *Already Compromised* (Green Forest: Master Books, 2011).
3. The word *secular* is often used to mean "religiously neutral." But because whoever is not for Christ is against him (Matthew 12:30), there is no real neutral ground. That's why many ideas promoted in secular classrooms and cultures are not just nonreligious but *anti*-biblical.
4. You can find out more about the atheistic nature of humanism in chapter 3, including a definition of humanism from a global humanist organization that states, "[Humanism] is not theistic, and it does not accept supernatural views of reality" (IHEU Minimum Statement on Humanism, Humanists International General Assembly, 1996, https://humanists.international/what-is-humanism).
5. I'll share more about what I experienced in secular university, and how God helped prepare me with foundations for withstanding the battle, in chapter 4.
6. For ideas about connecting with fellow Christians at a university, see chapter 8.

HOW TO USE THIS BOOK

When I'd pick up a new book as a time-crunched student, I'd skim the back cover, contents, foreword, preface, introduction, and the first one or two chapters. Then I'd put the book down, needing to tackle an assignment. The next day would bring new demands, however, and nonrequired readings rarely made it into my hands again. So if you're anything like me, you might like to approach this book from a different angle.

Let me explain.

This book is a survival guide, a spiritual army handbook for students to keep their faith alive in the trenches of evolutionary education. If you were lost in the desert behind enemy lines, you probably wouldn't pick up a survival guide to read every page. Rather, you'd flip to the sections that were most relevant to you—like how to navigate with a compass, avoid land mines, and find water. Later, you could benefit from reading the other chapters when your situation stabilized.

On the other hand, if you were at home munching pretzels on your couch before the army sent you on your desert mission, you'd be wise to grab that survival guide and read enough of it to help you keep from getting lost in the first place. You'd likely want information about what challenges to expect from desert environments, what to pack in a desert survival kit, and what to do in case of different emergencies. In the same way, this book contains theoretical, preparatory, and practical information for Christian students facing a *spiritual* survival situation—the battlefield of secular education.

HERE'S HOW THIS SURVIVAL GUIDE WORKS

Part 1: Analyze

Part 1, "War Stories," **analyzes** the realities of evolutionary education. We'll uncover evolution's role in Western cultures' free fall from Christianity, documenting how evolutionary education contributes to an anti-biblical agenda to secularize youth. Later, we'll see that while this agenda is an international problem, the solutions students are adopting to combat that problem work internationally, too. Along the way, stories from my own university experiences—and those of other Christian students worldwide—will reveal what youth can expect to encounter in secular higher education.

Part 2: Strategize

Part 2, "Boot Camp," **strategizes** how students can effectively prepare for a secular university. Backing scriptural truths with insights from real-life student experiences and scientific research, we'll examine why spiritual, intellectual, and interpersonal foundations are vital. We'll also explore practical ways to begin building these foundations now, anticipate possible attacks against them, and outline action plans for maintaining all three foundations throughout a secular education.

Part 3: Mobilize

Finally, part 3, "In the Trenches," **mobilizes** Christian students with hands-on tools, tips, and tactics for countering evolutionary indoctrination in real time. We'll cover strategies you can start using right now to recognize propaganda, separate fact from interpretation, spot logical fallacies, and combat the brainwashing conditions which are common on campuses. These resources follow the "seven checks of critical thinking" system for processing any faith-challenging information, based on techniques which helped me as a Christian student in evolutionary classes. At the back of the book, you'll also find appendices with more information to help you practice thinking through real textbook messages, counter fallacies, and find answers to any remaining questions.

Ultimately, if you're a time-crunched student wanting to jump straight to these later chapters, go for it—on one condition: no matter what section you head to afterward, it's essential to first understand the concepts in chapters 1–2. Why? Because without knowing why molecules-to-man evolution poses such a problem for a biblical worldview, you'll have no basis for fighting evolutionary education with the tools outlined in the rest of the book. So I'd recommend making sure you're familiar with the concepts in the first couple of chapters before you choose your own adventure from there. I'd also encourage you to peruse part 2, "Boot Camp," even if you're already in a university, because these chapters will help you strategize ways to keep your faith's foundations strong for the long haul.

Ready?

Let's get started.

Part 1

WAR STORIES

Uncovering the realities of humanistic education

THE FOUNDATION OF OUR FAITH

1

I never saw it coming.

Then again, what 14-year-old would expect a single homeschool conference seminar about creation to have such a radical effect?

Honestly, despite growing up in a Christian home, I'd never cared much about creation, evolution, or Genesis. To me, creationists' enthusiasm for fossils, ark models, and rocks from Noah's flood seemed cute but irrelevant. Give me a talk on justice causes, the gospel, or the church's future. Something important. But my entire perspective—and life—shifted at age 14 when I heard a seminar by Ken Ham, the founder of Answers in Genesis.

From the seminar's opening, the message hit me hard. I saw image after image of European churches transformed into restaurants, shops, and night clubs, evidence of how Western nations are growing less Christian every year. I learned how the erosion of Christianity's influence (not to mention moral values) in Western society traces back to a long series of attacks on Genesis 1–11. And I realized that these chapters represent the foundation of the whole Christian worldview—including the gospel.

Even the justice causes I cared about ultimately hinged on Genesis. After all, real justice depends on objective morality, objective morality depends on absolute truth, and absolute truth depends on God. Without a Creator whose character supplies the source of absolute morality, and whose Word distinguishes good from evil, how can anyone consistently say what's absolutely right or wrong? Who decides those moral standards? And if humans are just by-products of natural evolution, why should the moral guidelines we invent objectively value every human life?[1]

"I knew what I wanted to do with my life."

After learning these concepts at the conference, I knew what I wanted to do with my life. If everything I'd known to be important depended on God's Word being trustworthy from its first verse, then I needed to defend the truth of Genesis. And since the story of human evolution is one of culture's go-to frameworks for attacking Genesis, I decided to learn more about evolution by studying science at a secular university.

WAIT, WHAT KIND OF EVOLUTION?

Before getting any further into this story, I'd better explain what I mean by evolution. Textbook references to biological evolution are often just talking about patterns of genetic variation that show up within different kinds of living things over time, thanks to processes like mutation and natural selection. (We'll cover these more in chapter 7.) This kind of evolution explains why finches with long beaks can give rise to finches with short beaks. But it can't explain how finches could evolve from a totally different kind of animal—like dinosaurs.[2]

That's where another kind of evolution comes in, the "big picture" evolutionary origins story which people rely on to try explaining all life's existence apart from God. While Christians have different interpretations of how God created humanity, it's still a central tenet of Christianity that we exist because the God of the Bible created us in his image.[3] However, it's a central tenet of secular humanism that people evolved from scum—no God required. That's what I mean by evolution.

A complete evolutionary worldview includes four types of supposed evolution.

---

1. **Cosmic evolution** tries to explain how the universe came to be the way it is.
2. **Geological evolution** tries to explain how the earth came to be the way it is.
3. **Chemical evolution** tries to speculate how the first life appeared from nonliving chemicals.
4. **Biological evolution** tries to explain the history of all living organisms.

Together, these types of evolution compose the big picture of history according to secular humanism. And this is the origins story being taught as the exclusive truth to millions of students worldwide.

WHY DO ORIGIN BELIEFS MATTER?

To show why culture's beliefs about origins are such a big deal for society and the church, let me tell you my version of the message Ken Ham shared when I was 14. Doing so will take a couple of chapters, but it's vital to establish why equipping Christian students to defend their worldview against evolution—which is the purpose of this book—is so important.

To start, I'd like to invite you on a tour of a typical university in my home country, Canada. Everything I'm about to describe is based on what I personally saw at Canadian campuses during my travels to document Christian students' university experiences worldwide.

WELCOME TO THE UNIVERSITY

Stroll through the corridors where students stream like ants between their classes, and you'll notice posters on the walls promoting everything from Bible studies to Eastern spirituality to nightclub crawls. Messages that scream an extremely secular view of human sexuality paper the hallways, complete with free fliers, pamphlets, and paraphernalia. As you head outside, you'll notice political propaganda rioting on the nearby bulletin boards, including a poster telling students to join Canada's Young Communist League.

Try walking into the science building. Those glass displays of fossils labeled as millions of years old look impressive, don't they? There's a staircase just around the corner; if you head up into the maze of faculty offices, you can find cartoons mocking Christianity posted outside professors' doorways. One drawing, for example, shows Moses parting the sea while Jesus walks on the water. At the bottom, a penciled-in caption reads, "When fables collide."

"Cartoons mocking Christianity"

Why not explore the religious studies building? It's the old brick one across campus with the heavy wooden doors and the stained-glass window. Inside, a glass case exhibits faculty-authored books claiming that God used evolution to create humans, that Adam wasn't real, and that the Apostle Paul made a mistake by claiming that Adam literally existed.

Now you come to the university chaplaincy center. See those pentagrams on the business cards posted inside? You didn't misread them; that's the number you can call for spiritual guidance from the Wiccan campus chaplain.

Clearly, a short stroll across campus is all it takes to glimpse how Canadian culture has abandoned God's Word as its source of authoritative truth.

WHAT ELSE YOU'LL FIND IN WESTERN CULTURE

Of course, you don't need to visit a university to see how far Western cultures like Canada's have wandered from biblical values. Just read the headlines. In 2018, for instance, news sites buzzed that Trinity Western University, a Canadian Christian university, lost its law school accreditation in a Supreme Court ruling.[4] Why? Because the school upheld the biblical definition of marriage rooted in Genesis.[5]

Or take another topic which often makes headlines: abortion. I'll never forget the bioethics class I attended in the third year at my university, when our professor—one of Canada's most influential bioethicists—stated, "I don't know if you know this, but I am [a] reason why Canada has no abortion law." Did you know Canada is (as I'm writing this) the only democracy in the world with no laws about abortion? Any woman in any province can legally abort any pregnancy for any reason, right up to full-term live births.

My bioethics professor also played a role in Canada's decision to decriminalize euthanasia in 2016. Within just 30 months, euthanasia became responsible for over 1% of all reported deaths in Canada, with 6,749 Canadians killed by "medical assistance in dying" (MAID).[6] By 2020, the death toll had already skyrocketed to more than 13,000.[7] And in 2021, Canada passed a bill offering death not only to people diagnosed with terminal sicknesses but also to those struggling with mental illnesses.[8] Tragically, these examples show how quickly my home country is normalizing assisted suicide and euthanasia.[9]

A GLOBAL PATTERN

Altogether, the evidence is clear that Canada is turning further away from biblical values by the year. But it's not just Canada—or even North America. The next stop in my investigative globe-trekking mission was Australia, where locals told me their country is growing less Christian every year. Journeying farther to New Zealand, I learned that this nation's nonreligious population keeps rising every year while its religious (including Christian) population keeps falling.[10] I later visited Holland, where for the first time in history, more people identify as nonreligious than religious.[11] When I reached France, a Christian student told me, "I remember a guy saying, 'I cannot imagine that Christian people still exist.' This guy knew there were Catholic churches, but he couldn't believe that other people his age still believe in God."

Altogether, I thought a Christian student in Germany aptly summed up what's happening in Western cultures worldwide. "Most people are not interested in Christianity anymore," she told me, "like it doesn't have anything to do with their lives. Culture influences church more than church influences culture."

SO HOW DID THIS HAPPEN?

How did so many nations which once built cathedrals, birthed revivals, and brought up missionaries fall so far from God in just a few generations?

Let me tell you a story.

Not long ago in Malaysia, there stood three apartment buildings called the Highland Towers. Behind the towers rose a hill which construction workers were developing, exposing the soil to erosion. An over-pressured water pipe system burst on the hill, triggering a landslide which careened into one of the towers, piled against its foundation, and began pushing the foundation forward millimeter by millimeter. Eventually, locals noticed cracks spreading around the building. But nobody did anything about it—until the structure collapsed, taking 48 lives.

So how does this tragedy in Malaysia relate to Christianity in the West?

Imagine that the Christian worldview is like a building, with God's Word as our foundation. That foundation is the basis for our Christian doctrines, which are the basis of our Christian morals; together, all these components provide the basis of our Christian lifestyles and ministries.

For the rest of this chapter, let's look at this building in a little more detail. First, we'll zoom in on the foundation and see what God's Word teaches about the world's history. Next, we'll see how our doctrines, morals, and ministries are based on that history. Then we'll be ready to spend the next chapter investigating what happens when something

The 7 C's of History

Creation

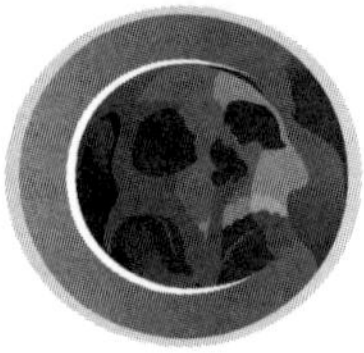

Corruption

Catastrophe

Confusion

Christ

Cross

Consummation

compromises this whole structure at a foundational level, like the landslide did to the building in Malaysia.

All set?

Let's dive in.

THE UNIVERSE ACCORDING TO GOD: A WHIRLWIND TOUR OF HISTORY

Looking at our foundation, God's Word, you'll notice that the Bible talks about both heavenly things of the spiritual world and earthly things of the physical world. Because Scripture is consistently true, both are important. As Jesus said to Nicodemus, "If I have told you earthly things and you do not believe, how can you believe if I tell you heavenly things?"[12]

In this context, Jesus was describing earthly phenomena—like the wind—as metaphors for spiritual realities. These verses remind us that Jesus understands how physical and spiritual realities work because he created them. Since he designed (and therefore completely comprehends) the universe, his Word must be the ultimate authority for the truth about everything that exists, both physical and spiritual. So it makes sense that God's Word reveals a history of the universe which covers both heavenly and earthly realities.

Because this history provides the foundation for our entire Christian worldview, let's take a minute to understand Scripture's big picture by walking through what Answers in Genesis calls the 7 C's of biblical history. Even if this biblical history is a review for you, these 7 C's can help you share the whole message of the gospel with others—a message that stretches from Genesis to Revelation.

"A message that stretches from Genesis to Revelation"

1: Creation

The first C is Creation. History began when God spoke the universe into existence, creating everything in it over six days. And Genesis isn't the only book which says so! Crack open Exodus, and you'll read, "For in six days the LORD made heaven and earth, the sea, and all that is in them."[13] That's a statement about cosmology—the origin and age of the cosmos—and the order of creation.

Genesis also describes the history of life, repeating 10 times in chapter one that God created living creatures to reproduce "according to their kinds." This implies dogs produce dogs, finches produce finches, and squids produce (you guessed it) squids. And that's a statement about biology. The Bible doesn't say that God created one original cell and declared, "Let the cell gradually diversify into unlimited kinds of plants and animals over millions of years." He could have said that, but he didn't. So while we do see variation within kinds of created things, like different finch varieties in different environments, we know that offspring will always be the same kind of creatures as their parents.

Speaking of looking like parents, Genesis describes human origins, too. A straightforward reading of Genesis reveals that in one actual, literal day, God fashioned one actual, literal guy, Adam, and one actual, literal woman, Eve. As Genesis 1:21 puts it, "So God created man in his own image, in the image of God he created him; male and female he created them." That's a statement about anthropology.

So far, so good—literally. The end of creation week arrived, and God repeatedly described everything he'd made as "very good."[14] (Hold that thought; it's important!)

2: Corruption

You know what happened next. Within this very good creation, God gave humans a boundary: "You may surely eat of every tree of the garden, but of the tree of the knowledge of good and evil you shall not eat, for in the day that you eat of it you shall surely die."[15] And what did Adam do? He crossed the one line drawn for him, rejecting God's authority in the first human act of sin.

When there's sin, something has to die.[16] It's cause and effect. God is the giver of life, so when we separate ourselves from him through sin, we cut ourselves off from life, hope, and peace, leaving death, hopelessness, and chaos—in other words, the effects of sin.

"In Adam we fell."

The problem for humanity is that since we all descended from Adam, we were all figuratively in Adam when we fell. Like a genetic disease, sin infects all its first possessors' descendants. So sin's consequences, which include both physical death and spiritual separation from God, affected not just Adam but all humans because we're all related to Adam.[17] But the consequences didn't stop there. Sin corrupted not only all humans but also all creation because God placed humans in charge over his physical creation. Ever since Adam's fall, as Romans 8:22 puts it, "the whole creation has been groaning together in the pains of childbirth."

If you need evidence of creation's groaning, try tap-dancing barefoot through a thistle field. Doesn't feel "very good," does it? That's because according to Genesis 3, nastiness like thorns, thistles, and increased pain in childbirth originally didn't belong in God's "very good" creation but resulted from sin's curse. In fact, even carnivory apparently wasn't part of God's original plan for creation. Check out Genesis 1:29, and you'll notice that God initially ordained humans, animals, birds—everything that has the "breath of life"—to be vegetarian. But now, intense pain, bloodshed, death, and suffering are par for the course in our sin-broken universe.

3: Catastrophe

Eventually, creation grew so corrupt that God, in his holiness, couldn't bear it any longer. So he reset the world with a global flood, sparing Noah, his family, and the animals they brought on the ark, which God had told Noah to construct. And here's the thing: because a global flood destroyed every land-breathing, air-dwelling creature not on the ark, we'd expect to see a geological record of that all over the world. We'd expect to find, as I can still remember Ken Ham saying, "billions of dead things buried in rock layers laid down by water all over the earth."

"*He reset the world.*"

Moreover, we'd expect those dead things (fossils) to show a record of the sin and destruction which brought on the judgment of the flood. We'd expect to uncover fossil evidence of death, killing, disease, thorns, struggle, and suffering. And in fact, that's just what we find in the fossil record, including plants with thorns, bones with diseases, and tons of examples of carnivory. We've found fossil dinosaurs with bird bones in their stomachs[18]—and fossil mammals with dinosaur bones in their stomachs![19] (So, long before *Jurassic Park* claimed dinosaurs evolved into birds or were replaced by mammals, these animals were already, um, interacting.)

Altogether, the fossil record shows a history of the effects of sin and judgment by a global flood, which is exactly what we'd expect to find if the Bible's geology were true. And that brings us to the next C of history, Confusion.

4: Confusion

When the flood subsided, God told humans to spread throughout earth. But instead we decided to get together and build a tower to heavens. God confused that plan when उहाँले हामीलाई बभिन्नि भाषाहरू दनिुभयो जसले हामीलाई फैलाउन र मानसिहरूका बभिन्नि समूहहरू हुन बाध्य तुल्यायो।.

(That's Nepali for, "He gave us different languages, which forced us to spread out and become different people groups," in case you didn't catch it. At least, that's what my language translation app assures me.)

Notice, though, that the Bible doesn't teach that we're different races—we're just different people groups which all descended from Adam.[20] And all along, God had a plan to redeem from sin Adam's descendants in every nation. That's why God sent his Son, Jesus.

5–6: Christ and Cross

Remember that when there's sin, something has to die. This reality set the basis for the Old Testament's sacrificial system, with lamb after lamb being slaughtered to temporarily cover for sin. The New Testament, however, talks about another sacrifice, Jesus, the Lamb of God,[21] who bore on the cross the physical and spiritual death penalty for Adam's sin.

Remember how the fossil record shows the effects of sin, including extreme pain, death, killing, disease, thorns, struggle, and suffering? When Jesus became sin for us, he took those effects on himself. He underwent excruciating pain. He experienced death. He let himself be killed. Isaiah says he bore our disease.[22] He wore a crown of thorns. He endured struggle and suffering to reverse the effects of sin, give life to those who put their faith and hope in him, and one day reconcile all creation to himself—the final C of history.

7: Consummation (Restoration of Creation)

Because of Christ's redeeming work on the cross, God promises to prepare a new creation restored to its original "very good" state. As John described in Revelation 21,

> Then I saw a new heaven and a new earth, for the first heaven and the first earth had passed away, and the sea was no more. . . . And I heard a loud voice from the throne saying, "Behold, the dwelling place of God is with man. He will dwell with them, and they will be his people, and God himself will be with them as their God. He will wipe away every tear from their eyes, and death shall be no more, neither shall there be mourning, nor crying, nor pain anymore, for the former things have passed away."[23]

THE FOUNDATION FOR THE CHRISTIAN WORLDVIEW

These 7 C's provide an outline for the complete history of the universe, laying the foundation for the rest of our biblical worldview, including Christian doctrines, morals, and ministry. For example, if the Bible's history is true, then God really created humans in his image, supporting the doctrine that every human life has value. If that doctrine is true, then we need to protect the unborn. That's the basis for the church's moral stance on abortion. If Christian morals are founded on truth, then Christian ministries like pregnancy care centers are significant. We want to protect the unborn because life has value, which we know because God's Word is true.

Or think about another Christian doctrine, marriage. God established marriage as a family union between a man and woman at creation. So if that history is true, then God's institution of marriage has meaning. As Jesus said when questioned about marriage, "Have you not read that he who created them from the beginning made them male and female, and said, 'Therefore a man shall leave his father and his mother and hold fast to his wife, and the two shall become one flesh'?"[24]

"Why does life matter?"

Jesus was citing Genesis to prove the meaning of marriage. If marriage has meaning, as Jesus taught, then we should protect the institution of family as God designed it. That's why ministries that help build relationships and family counseling are valuable.

Ultimately, our whole worldview depends on the truth of God's Word beginning in Genesis. Think about any major Christian doctrine, and you'll find that it's directly or indirectly founded in Genesis. How can you tell? Because you can't answer key questions about those doctrines without resorting to concepts first established in Genesis. Why does life matter? Why does marriage matter? Why did Jesus die? What is sin? Why is there death and suffering in the world? Why do we need a new heaven and a new earth? Genesis provides the foundation for understanding all these concepts. It's the foundation for our faith.

Now let's think about what happens to our whole worldview structure—and to a society at large—if we allow just one compromise at a foundational level.

Endnotes

1. For more on why objective morals depend on the truth of God's Word beginning in Genesis, see https://answersingenesis.org/morality.
2. While we won't have time to dive deep into the science of why natural selection and mutation can't drive Darwinian evolution, entire books, articles, and videos already exist to show just that. You can find some of them listed in appendix A.
3. While salvation does not require a literal interpretation of Genesis, in chapter 2 we'll see some of the major theological and consistency problems with the idea that God used evolution or millions of years.
4. Kathleen Harris, "Trinity Western Loses Fight for Christian Law School as Court Rules Limits on Religious Freedom 'Reasonable,'" Canadian

Broadcasting Corporation, June 15, 2018, https://www.cbc.ca/news/politics/trinity-western-supreme-court-decision-1.4707240.

5. Genesis 2:24, quoted by Jesus in Matthew 19:5 and Mark 10:7.

6. Heath Canada, *Fourth Interim Report on Medical Assistance in Dying in Canada* (Ottawa), 2019, https://www.canada.ca/en/health-canada/services/publications/health-system-services/medical-assistance-dying-interim-report-april-2019.html.

7. Department of Justice Canada, "Government of Canada Proposes Changes to Medical Assistance in Dying Legislation," media release, February 24, 2020, https://www.canada.ca/en/department-justice/news/2020/02/government-of-canada-proposes-changes-to-medical-assistance-in-dying-legislation.html.

8. Bill C-7, An Act to Amend the Criminal Code (Medical Assistance in Dying), 2nd sess., 43rd Parliament, 2021, https://parl.ca/DocumentViewer/en/43-2/bill/C-7/royal-assent.

9. In assisted suicide, patients give themselves their own lethal medicine, whereas in euthanasia, a healthcare worker personally ends the patient's life. Out of over 5,000 deaths reported in Canada outside Quebec, Northwest Territories, Yukon, and Nunavut from 2016 to 2018, only six occurred by assisted suicide; instead, nearly all those thousands of Canadians died by euthanasia (see endnote 6).

10. McCrindle Research (commissioned by the Wilberforce Foundation), "Faith and Belief in New Zealand," 2018, https://nzfaithandbeliefstudy.files.wordpress.com/2018/05/faith-and-belief-full-report-may-2018.pdf.

11. Hollandse Hoogte, "Over Half of the Dutch Population Are Not Religious," Statistics Netherlands, October 23, 2018, https://www.cbs.nl/en-gb/news/2018/43/over-half-of-the-dutch-population-are-not-religious.

12. John 3:12

13. Exodus 20:11

14. Genesis 1:31

15. Genesis 2:16–17

16. Romans 6:23

17. Romans 5:12

18. E.g., Jingmai O'Connor, Zhonghe Zhou, and Xing Xu, "Additional Specimen of Microraptor Provides Unique Evidence of Dinosaurs Preying on Birds," *Proceedings of the National Academy of Sciences* 108, no. 49 (2011): 19662–19665.

19. E.g., Yaoming Hu, Jin Meng, Yuanqing Wang, and Chuankui Li, "Large Mesozoic Mammals Fed on Young Dinosaurs," *Nature* 433, no. 7022 (2005): 149–152.

20. For more on what the Bible (and science) teaches about human "races," see https://answersingenesis.org/racism.

21. John 1:29

22. Isaiah 53:4 (Note: In some versions of the Bible, *disease* or *sickness* is translated as "*griefs*" or "*sufferings*" here.)

23. Revelation 21:1–4

24. Matthew 19:4–5

THE ASSAULT ON SCRIPTURE

2

Fortunately, Genesis isn't supposed to be confusing. You don't need a degree in ancient Hebrew to understand it; you don't need to squint at the pages a certain way, change the words, or even pronounce them with a spiritual-sounding vocal quaver. The ancient Israelites, New Testament writers, and Jesus himself regarded Genesis as literal history, so all you need to do to understand Genesis is to read it, trusting that God said exactly what he meant to when he revealed earth's history to Moses.[1]

When you do that, you'll find Genesis couldn't have been much clearer in explaining that God created everything in six days—the kind of day with an evening and morning attached. But we know that many humans eventually decided the universe created itself instead, a feat requiring millions and billions of years (not to mention a few broken laws of nature[2]). So even if we don't exactly want to, we might feel obligated to try adding this idea of millions of years into our biblical worldview's foundation, Genesis.

"That might not seem like a big deal."

That might not seem like a big deal. But if we're going to accept millions of years, then we need to accept man's word over God's Word in several major areas.

WAIT, "MAN'S WORD"?

By "man's word," I'm not talking about "dad jokes" or other sayings that necessarily come from literal guys. I'm talking about ideas based on human reasoning, especially when those ideas conflict with what God has already said is true. God doesn't make mistakes, but people do. In other words, man's word is fallible, but God's Word is infallible—and it's the only sure foundation for our thinking in every area of life. Yet when we treat human ideas as if they're more correct than the Bible's teachings, we're making man's word our authority for truth instead of God's Word. That's what ends up happening whenever we try to incorporate millions of years into the historical account God provides us in Genesis. Even if we don't mean to, we're basically saying the Bible is wrong.

For instance, if the universe is billions of years old, with the sun and stars forming before the earth, then the Bible is wrong about cosmology. Biological evolution would also require millions of years. But if everything evolved from one cell instead of God designing creatures to reproduce according to their kinds, then the Bible's biology is wrong. What about anthropology? If humans evolved from apelike ancestors instead of God creating a literal Adam and Eve in his image, then the Bible's anthropology is wrong. And geology? Let's face it—if the majority of those fossils and rock layers were laid down slowly over millions of years instead of rapidly in a global flood, then the Bible's geology is also dead wrong.

Cosmology, geology, biology, anthropology—these are earthly things, physical things, real-world things. And man's word tells us that what the Bible says about the real world is wrong. So if the Bible is wrong about the real world, where do most students (including ones from Christian homes) learn about the real world instead? School! School is where kids go to learn "real history," while church is where they go to learn "Bible stories." As one of my own university textbooks said,

> Those who accept a creationist doctrine on the origin of the human species as recounted in sacred texts or myths do so on the basis of religious authority, conceding that such views may be contrary to genetic, geological, biological, or other explanations.[3]

In other words, my textbook is saying that the Bible is wrong about the real world, so students need to read the textbook. But is that true? Do the Bible's teachings apply only to the heavenly things of the spiritual world but conflict with the earthly things of real-world science?[4] That's a key question, so before we go on to examine what happens if we try to work millions of years and evolution into our worldview foundation, we need to think about what science really is. And when we do that, we see two basic types of science.

"But is that true?"

OBSERVATIONAL AND HISTORICAL SCIENCE

The first is observational science, which makes measurements in the present. It involves repeatable experimentations and observations about what we can see going on right now. Observational science is how we develop medicines, create new technologies, and describe animals' anatomy. It's what I did in my university labs—the kind of science that helps us identify what species a fish fossil is or measure a gun barrel at a crime scene. But observational science can't tell us exactly how the fish became a fossil or who shot the gun. Those events happened in the past, so we can't observe them directly in the present. That's where historical science comes in.

Historical science draws conclusions about the past based on facts we can observe in the present. That requires us to use assumptions, speculations, and educated guesses to fill in for gaps in the facts as best we can. Those assumptions, however, are going to be influenced by our worldviews. So the worldviews we start with ultimately help determine the conclusions we end up with. But we can't directly test those conclusions because we can't rewind history. It's gone.

Think, for example, about a crime scene. If you were investigating a murder, you'd go to the scene of the crime to make observations. (You might go, anyway. I'd stay home because I'm a squeamish wimp.) There maybe you'd unearth fingerprints, footwear impressions, or even a discarded gun. Those are the facts of the case. So your observations about those facts constitute (you guessed it) the observational science in your investigation. You'd then take those observations to court where different attorneys would interpret the same facts to present different stories about the past.

"Think about a crime scene."

Prosecution: Cleah-ly, the finguh-prints on the murdah weapon indicate that our culprit is [*insert dramatic music here*] Mr. Butlah!

Defense: No, no, they merely indicate that Mr. Butler was framed by the real culprit, who was clever enough to wear gloves but not clever enough to avoid leaving footprints—footprints the size of Mrs. Cook's shoes!

So the debate rages on as different sides, beginning from different starting points, use historical science to draw different conclusions about the past based on different interpretations of the same observations.

Now let's think of another event from the past: human origins. Where did we come from? To try to find out, we could make observations about facts in the present. By observing human genetics, anatomy, physiology, and behavior, we might conclude that humans have an intelligent Creator who wrote the language of DNA and engineered our biology. But the conclusion I heard from my professors is that we're the result of unguided evolution from scum.

We could debate this all day and even lay out some pretty intelligent arguments pointing to some kind of Creator. But we wouldn't know for sure who that Creator was or what exactly happened at the beginning of time because we weren't there to see it. In this case, however, we have eyewitness testimony to make up for the gaps in our data: we have the Word of God, who is the only one who has always been there, who knows everything, who cannot lie, and who reveals the history of human origins in his Word.

TWO PAIRS OF WORLDVIEW GLASSES

Ultimately, it makes a huge difference whether our authority is God's Word or man's word when we're considering observational science. That's because, as we observe things in the present, we'll draw different conclusions about the past based on our worldview assumptions.

Remember, a worldview is the set of beliefs we use to explain the world around us, like a set of glasses. We really only have two pairs of glasses to pick from: man's word or God's Word. No matter which set of glasses each of us chooses, we all look at the same world—the same rocks, same plants, and same fossils. So we all observe the same facts. But we interpret those facts differently thanks to our separate worldview glasses, which give us distinct biases. Take, for instance, the following scene:

> **Person 1:** *(Examines a fossil)* Wow! That's great evidence of something happening quickly in a global flood!
>
> **Person 2:** *(Examines the same fossil)* Wow! That's great evidence for something happening slowly over millions of years!

See what's happening here? By looking at the same fact through different worldview glasses, both individuals are appealing to separate explanations from historical science to interpret the same fact from observational science. The resulting disagreement isn't a conflict between science and religion but between two worldviews, leading to different interpretations of the same evidence.[5]

MILLIONS OF YEARS: THE EXPLANATION FROM MAN'S WORD

All too often, however, culture teaches kids—even in Christian families—to draw only evolutionary conclusions by observing real-world facts through the glasses of man's word. That's what kids' media taught my brother and me to do, even while we were growing up in a Christian home.

When we were five and seven years old, I remember exploring a riverbank where my brother picked up a fossil and exclaimed, "This is millions of years old!"

"Whoa," my dad responded, "that's not what the Bible says!" But even at an early age, we had already been indoctrinated to view real-world facts like fossils through the glasses of man's word.

So where did this incredibly widespread idea that earth is millions of years old come from, anyway? Although different cultures throughout history have believed in millions (or billions) of years, these ideas didn't gain much traction in Western countries until the 1700s. In the 1800s, geology enthusiast Charles Lyell popularized old-earth beliefs even further, arguing that the sedimentary rock layers we see all around the world show that our planet must be extremely ancient. According to Lyell, every one of those sliver-thin rock layers represents a little bit of time, with wind or water laying down each layer over months or years. Every year would add more layers of sediments. So after thousands of years, we'd see thousands of layers. After (supposedly) millions of years, we'd see millions of layers.

Lyell's arguments shaped his beliefs about the ages of different fossils found in these rock layers, too—and about the entire history of life on earth. Lyell and other old-earth advocates speculated that as living things die, sediments gradually build up around the bones to create fossils. When these layers accumulate, the resulting geologic column must chronicle the fossil history record of death and extinction over millions of years.

"After (supposedly) millions of years, we'd see millions of layers."

This concept of millions of years opened the way for belief in evolutionary origins rather than creation. Without those long geologic ages, biological evolution wouldn't have time to happen. But by saying that most fossil-bearing layers piled up over millions of years rather than during the Genesis flood, Lyell's followers—including a young naturalist named Charles Darwin—could begin viewing fossils as creatures which lived, died, and evolved over eons.

Interestingly, Lyell's personal letters show that he proposed his ideas in order to "free the science from Moses."[6] In other words, he deliberately set out to explain geologists' observations apart from the flood which Moses recorded in Genesis. Lyell's motives highlight the fact that the conflict between Genesis and ideas like millions of years isn't really a battle of faith versus science. Instead, it's a battle of historical science based on man's word versus historical science based on God's Word. Both types of historical science vie to explain the same facts—in this case, fossils and rock layers—from observational science.

CAN MILLIONS OF YEARS FIT INTO THE BIBLE?

Before people like Lyell fought to explain geology using man's word instead of God's, Westerners typically accepted that most fossil-laden rock layers formed during Noah's flood.[7] However, both explanations for those rocks and fossils can't be true. So why does it really matter which explanation we believe? Can't we just fit millions of years into the Bible?

Well, let's try it. Maybe by comparing the versions of history that God's Word and man's word teach, we can figure out how to mash these two origin accounts together.

According to man's word, the sun happened to form 4.6 billion years ago, followed by a molten earth, dry land, oceans, and eventually sea creatures. Finally, plants and animals colonized land and continued evolving. Dinosaurs, for instance, slowly gave rise to birds.

"We can't consistently believe both."

On the other hand, God's Word clearly explains that he first fashioned a watery earth, and then he separated the sea from the land, and he created land plants on day three. Then he formed the sun a day later, followed by sea creatures and birds on day five and land animals, including dinosaurs, on day six.

Wait a minute. Those two versions of earth history give a totally different order of events. We can't consistently believe both. But it's usually God's Word that we humans compromise to conform it with man's word, isn't it?

There are different ways we could go about that. We could suggest, for instance, that maybe there's an invisible gap of millions of years wedged between the first verses of Genesis. Or maybe the "days" in Genesis really describe long ages. Maybe God even used evolution to create humans.

If you want to dive into some of the technical problems with these ideas, resources listed in appendix A can help you get started. For now, let's look at a heftier theological issue that these reinterpretations of Genesis share—besides the fact that they all esteem fallible man's word as the authority over God's Word.

A DEATHLY DILEMMA

Remember how man's word teaches that rock layers formed slowly over millions of years, showing a fossil history record of death, thorns, and the effects of sin? If we want to accept man's word as our authority by trying to stuff millions of years into Scripture, where are we going to put those millions of years? We can't fit them after Adam because genealogies in Genesis record an unbroken line of real people from Adam to Abraham, which later scriptures pick up all the way to Christ. Eon-sized gaps won't fit in those Genesis genealogies because they document historical details, like each father's age at his son's birth. So the only place to jam millions of years into Genesis must be in creation's six days, most of which occurred before God created humans in his image on day six.

But hang on a second. If most of the rock layers that supposedly show that the earth is millions of years old existed long before God created humans, then the fossils in those rock layers also existed long before humans. That would mean all the animals' pain, death, killing, disease, thorns, struggle, and suffering happened during God's creative process leading up to humans. If the earth is this old, death must be just a normal, natural, necessary part of life.

That's completely backward to what the Bible teaches: death and suffering are not a normal part of God's "very good" creation but a result of human sin. From God's originally creating animals and humans to be vegetarian[8] to his slaying of an animal to clothe Adam and Eve in Genesis 3:21, followed by the countless sacrifices slaughtered throughout the Old Testament to the Lamb of God who bled on a cross, Scripture links physical death—including animal death—to human sin. But if we try squeezing millions of years into the Bible, we have to say that all the fossil history of death, thorns, and the effects of sin that Jesus died for must have occurred before Adam sinned. Yet effect never comes before cause.

"Effect never comes before cause."

Besides throwing aside the history of redemption outlined in God's Word, placing millions of years of death before sin affects our view of God's character. Have you ever heard someone ask, "How could a loving God create a world with so much death and suffering?" Well, Genesis shows us that he didn't.

God created a universe which he called very good, a world without death, carnivory, or other downers that we wouldn't expect to find in the new heaven and new earth he's promised. In fact, that's why we need a new heaven and earth—this one is broken! Yet if someone asks how a loving God could create a world with death and suffering, and we want to fit millions of years into the Bible, then we don't have a logical answer that defends God's revealed character. Instead, we have to say death and suffering were the means God used to create the world he called very good. But that's morally and intellectually inconsistent.

Even my third-year evolutionary biology textbook pointed out that evolution can't be compatible with a competent, benevolent Designer. Calling natural selection "the very epitome of waste and seeming cruelty," the textbook continued,

> Indeed, when Darwin proposed his theory for the cause of evolution, it was widely rejected just because people found it so distasteful, even horrifying, to contemplate. And, of course, this process often does not preserve species in the face of change: more than 99 percent of all species that have ever lived are extinct. Were those species the products of an incompetent designer?

Ultimately, by undermining God's character, compromising Scripture's redemptive timeline, and treating God's Word as less trustworthy than man's word, writing millions of years into the Bible affects our proclamation of the gospel. The significance of Christ, who Paul calls the last Adam,[10] hinges on the reality of the first Adam. As Paul wrote in 1 Corinthians, "For as by a man came death, by a man has come also the resurrection of the dead. For as in Adam all die, so also in Christ shall all be made alive."[11]

"And the atheists know it."

Paul is citing a historical Adam to make a case for the gospel. There had to be a real Adam who committed real sin leading to real physical and spiritual death for all humanity. That's why Jesus died a physical death to give life to all the descendants of Adam who put their faith and hope in him. The gospel is founded on Genesis.

And the atheists know it.

Look at how clearly the American Atheists explained, in a Christmas campaign, that the truth of the gospel hinges on the reality of Genesis:

> Chances are, if you're reading this, you don't believe in the fable of Adam and Eve and the talking snake. You probably think it's a story, created out of ignorance, to explain the origin of life. You probably don't believe that Adam literally ate a fruit, resulting in God expelling him and Eve out of the idyllic Garden of Eden.
>
> In other words, you know that's a myth.
>
> Right so far? So if Adam and Eve and the Talking Snake are myths, then Original Sin is also a myth, right? Well, think about it . . .
>
> - Jesus' major purpose was to save mankind from Original Sin.
> - Original Sin makes believers unworthy of salvation, but you get it anyway, so you should be grateful for being saved (from that which does not exist).
> - Without Original Sin, the marketing that all people are sinners and therefore need to accept Jesus falls moot.

All we are asking is that you take what you know into serious consideration, even if it means taking a hard look at all you've been taught for your whole life. No Adam and Eve means no need for a savior. It also means that the Bible cannot be trusted as a source of unambiguous, literal truth. It is completely unreliable, because it all begins with a myth, and builds on that as a basis. No Fall of Man means no need for atonement and no need for a redeemer. You know it.[12]

A GOSPEL ISSUE

Clearly, the accuracy of Genesis is no teensy side issue. But here's something important: it's true that you don't need to believe in a literal Genesis to be saved. Teaching that you need anything besides Jesus to be saved would be heresy. So a literal Genesis is not a salvation issue, but it is a consistency issue and an authority issue. Is our authority man's word, which is fallible, or God's Word, which is infallible?

If we accept man's word as the authority, we're basically showing that we think God's Word is inaccurate and untrustworthy at its very foundation. That might not affect our salvation, but it could affect the salvation of those around us, who don't yet know why the Bible (and its salvation message) is trustworthy. So Genesis, because it's the root of the gospel, is a gospel issue.

A MORAL ISSUE

Remember the story of the Highland Tower collapse from the last chapter? That tragedy happened because nobody responded to the cracks appearing around the building's foundation. In the same way, by ignoring the cracks of compromise in our worldview's foundation, we allowed a crack in our doctrine. So we can't really be surprised when that fissure keeps spreading to affect our moral values. After all, if the Bible is wrong about real-world history and real-world science, then who cares what it says about morals?

If God's Word is wrong, that leaves us with man's reasoning. Without a God who created us in his image, humanity gets to invent all its own rules. We can decide what it means to be human. In fact, we can decide everything about what it means to be human—including human meaning, value, moral standards, and ethical concepts. We can decide what personhood is, what family means, and what human rights should look like. All truth is open-ended, up for humans to interpret and define, if man's word is the authority.

For example, if man's word is the authority and we can define personhood however we want, then we get to decide who legally counts as a person and who doesn't—like the unborn. That's how we end up with fully legalized abortion. If man's word is the authority, we can also define family, gender, and marriage however we want. That's how we end up with situations like one in Newfoundland, Canada, where a court ruled that a trio of adults in a three-way relationship could all legally be one child's parents.[13] Similarly, if man's word is the authority and we can define rights however we want, that's how we end up with policies to extend "the right to die" by euthanasia, not only for terminally ill adults but also for minors and individuals with mental illnesses.[14]

A JUSTICE ISSUE

These are just some of the things we start to see happening in culture when we make man's word our authority instead of God's Word, which should be our authority in every area. If the history that God's Word teaches is true and humans are created in his image, that means God defines our meaning, value, morals, personhood, rights, and everything else on which justice depends. So not only is Genesis the ultimate foundation for all of Scripture's doctrines, as the last chapter showed, but it's also the ultimate foundation for justice.

Compromising that foundation has cost more than we ever imagined. Ignoring the cracks turned out to be a life or death issue, like at the Highland Towers in Malaysia. Only this time the consequences include not only earthly deaths but also eternal deaths as people reject God's Word as no longer trustworthy because of its cracked foundation.

A BATTLE FOR THE FUTURE

The cracks in our worldview's foundation also affect Christian missions and the future of the church. Why would we invest in missions to preach a message that's founded on myth? Why would anyone want to believe it? Why would kids growing up in the church want to keep believing it? After centuries of compromises, little fractures in our

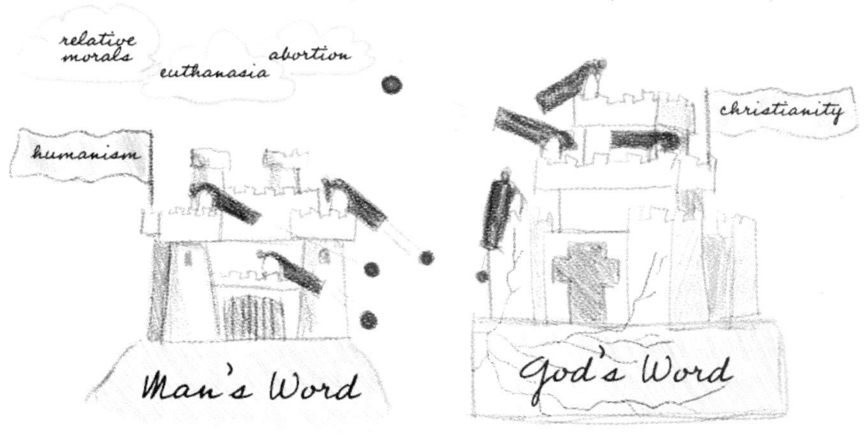

When I first heard Ken Ham explain these concepts when I was 14, he showed an illustration that summarizes everything I've been saying. It's the picture that made me get it, kindling my conviction to become an apologetics speaker.

The illustration shows two castles, representing two worldviews that stand or fall based on the strength of their foundations. On the right is the castle of Christianity, which has the authority of God's Word as its foundation. The castle on the left is the worldview of secular humanism, which makes man's word its foundation.

These two worldviews are in a battle for the hearts and minds of the culture. Issues like abortion and euthanasia are springing up from the secular castle because those things are symptoms of making man's word the authority. The Christians are aiming their guns at these topics because we know how important they are to fight. But we won't make much headway by just fighting such issues because they're only symptoms of a deeper problem—basing our authority on the wrong foundation.

Instead of aiming our guns at the foundation of man's word, some of us are firing at our own foundation by compromising on the authority of God's Word. Many are firing at each other in denominational wars, shooting at random cultural topics off in the distance, or dozing in the watchtowers. But the secularists are highly strategic in specifically firing at our foundation, the authority of God's Word. And they attack the Bible in Western culture for the long-term by attacking the accuracy of Scripture in the minds of Western youth, knowing the youth represent the culture's future.

REBUILDING THE FOUNDATIONS

All this shows why equipping Christian youth to defend their worldview from foundation-level attacks, such as evolution and millions of years, is so urgently vital. Protecting the foundation of Genesis is a gospel issue, a moral issue, and a justice issue.

When churches, families, and ministries can stand uncompromisingly on the authority of God's Word, and when they disciple students to do the same, we can rebuild our worldview foundation instead of ignoring its cracks (and even adding to them). But it's going to take work. It's going to take prayer. And it's going to take strategy.

Part of that strategy involves understanding how the secular castle is tactically undermining God's Word in the minds of youth through intensive evolutionary education. Just what do these tactics involve?

Let's find out.

Endnotes

1. You can find out about the apostles' and Jesus' views of Genesis in several helpful books, including Ken Ham's *Six Days: The Age of the Earth and the Decline of the Church* (Green Forest: Master Books, 2013), or through online resources, such as Terry Mortenson's chapter "Did Bible Authors Believe in a Literal Genesis?" from *The New Answers Book 1* (Green Forest: Master Books, 2010), https://answersingenesis.org/genesis/did-bible-authors-believe-in-a-literal-genesis, and Simon Turpin's "Who Is Jesus and What Did He Believe About Creation?" December 24, 2015, https://answersingenesis.org/jesus/what-did-jesus-believe-about-creation.
2. E.g., the law of biogenesis, which states that life-forms come only from preexisting life-forms (not nonlife), or the first and second laws of thermodynamics (see Danny Faulkner, "The First and Second Laws of Thermodynamics and the Origin of the Universe," February 19, 2019, https://answersingenesis.org/physics/the-first-and-second-laws-of-thermodynamics-and-the-origin-of-the-universe). You can also read more about what natural laws are and why spontaneously producing genetic information to generate life breaks known laws; see Dr. Werner Gitt's book In the Beginning Was Information (Green Forest: Master Books, 2006), which is available online for free at https://answersingenesis.org/answers/books/in-beginning-was-information.
3. William Haviland et. al., Anthropology: The Human Challenge, 14th ed. (Belmont: Wadsworth, 2014), 16.
4. John 3:12
5. Since the Bible is true, you'd expect observational science to confirm it. Entire books document how. Some of these books are listed in appendix A.
6. See chapter 11 in Katherine Lyell, ed., Life, Letters, and Journals of Sir Charles Lyell, Vol. 1 (Cambridge: Cambridge University Press).
7. What we know from observational science confirms this biblical explanation, as you can find out from resources listed in appendix A.
8. Genesis 1:29–30
9. Douglas Futuyama, Evolution, 3rd ed. (Sunderland: Sinauer Associates, 2013), 640.
10. 1 Corinthians 15:45

11. 1 Corinthians 15:21–22

12. American Atheists, "Christmas," http://atheists.org/content/christmas (original article no longer available), as cited by Ken Ham, "I Agree with the Atheists!" Answers in Genesis, June 1, 2011, https://answersingenesis.org/blogs/ken-ham/2011/06/01/i-agree-with-the-atheists.

13. Michael McDonald, "3 Adults in Polyamorous Relationship Declared Legal Parents by N. L. Court," Canadian Broadcasting Corporation, June 14, 2018, https://www.cbc.ca/news/canada/newfoundland-labrador/polyamourous-relationship-three-parents-1.4706560.

14. Department of Justice Canada, "Government of Canada Proposes Changes to Medical Assistance in Dying Legislation," media release, February 24, 2020, https://www.canada.ca/en/department-justice/news/2020/02/government-of-canada-proposes-changes-to-medical-assistance-in-dying-legislation.html.

THE ATTACK ON YOUTH

3

It's time for a thought experiment. Let's say you wake up one morning, pull on your socks, and decide to take over the world. Being the strategic sort, you figure it's best to begin by taking over your own home culture. You'll usher out its old belief and value systems, replace them with the worldview you've invented, and change the planet from there. How will you get started?

Let's think about it. Every culture consists of three basic age groups: seniors, the middle-aged, and younger students. All these people hold beliefs, and their beliefs and actions influence other persons around them—especially within families. To change your culture's beliefs, you'll need to target the age groups within families differently.

Take seniors, for instance. With more life experience than anyone else, seniors have had the most time to decide what they believe. Likely, that means they'll be the strongest in their beliefs. However, they also have the least lifetime left to influence upcoming generations. So what you'd want to do is marginalize the seniors. Let them talk amongst themselves but meanwhile promote the message that seniors aren't relevant to the rest of society—and especially to the youth.

"Foster complacency..."

What about the middle-aged people? They'll probably be somewhat set in their beliefs; they're also the most responsible for raising the next generation. So you'd be wise to try mellowing their beliefs. Foster complacency in the parents, keep them busy, and tell them that society will help take responsibility for training their kids.

And the kids? They're the ones who represent society's future. Today's students are tomorrow's leaders, teachers, parents, and politicians. Youth are also the least set in their beliefs—and the easiest to influence *en masse* through media and public education. So you want to use those channels to shape youth's beliefs, ensuring a future society built on the values you've created.

If you want to be really strategic, you'll also leverage media and public education to launch an attack on the family unit. That's because family is where discipleship happens, with parents and grandparents passing beliefs onto their young. So you need to do whatever you can to fragment, redefine, and undermine families.

Now you can sit back to admire your efforts. Look at the students championing the slogans you've programmed into them through classes, videos, and literature, harnessing their youthful energy to advance your cause. Look at the parents working by themselves, upswept in spheres of their own. See how youth and parents interact less as you make family seem more irrelevant. And look at the elders, sidelined in isolated clusters to whisper of forgotten days.

Congratulations.

You're well on your way to changing the world.

A RECURRING THEME

Flip through history's pages, and you'll notice how often world changers in the past have operated this way—including Marx, Lenin, and Stalin. This strategy is also how secular humanists have maneuvered over the last century to build Western societies founded on man's word instead of God's, as part of the worldview battle we investigated in the last chapters. In those chapters, we also saw how evolutionary ideas play a key role in that battle by undermining Genesis, the foundation of our biblical worldview.

Today, it's no secret that public education—the primary system shaping the minds of each new Western generation—tends to exclusively teach evolution (and other unbiblical ideas) in the name of religious neutrality. Jesus said, however, that whoever does not stand with him stands against him,[1] so there is no such thing as religious neutrality.[2] Instead, as we're about to uncover, secular education is really religious education, training Western youth in the religion of secular humanism.

"You're well on your way to changing the world."

THE BIBLICAL BASIS FOR EDUCATION

Does all this mean that education itself is an unbiblical concept? Not at all.[3] In fact, a biblical worldview provides the consistent philosophical foundation for making education possible in the first place. After all, education involves the transmission of knowledge, based on principles like truth, logic, and scientific reasoning. But as many scholars have explained in detail,[4] the absolute basis for knowledge, truth, logic, and scientific reasoning requires an absolute, all-knowing, logical Creator who does not lie.[5] Because a rational God fashioned a rational universe and created humans in his image as rational beings, we have a meaningful basis for discovering, reasoning about, and communicating how our world operates.

Newton, Linnaeus, Pasteur, and many other early Western scientists understood this, enabling the development of modern science.[6] A biblical worldview also enabled the development of modern education worldwide, as research has documented a strong historical link between the presence of Protestant missionaries and the rise of mass education in the countries they visited.[7] Ultimately, while many secularists may idolize education,[8] the principles of education rest on a Christian foundation. Yet the world has co-opted these biblically grounded principles to promote decidedly unbiblical ideas like human evolution, creating a secular society.

Now, to see how youth are the focus of this battle for society's future, let's uncover seven facts about evolutionary education.

FACT 1: EVOLUTIONARY TEACHING IS A HUMANIST SPIRITUAL AGENDA.

Before we can unmask the spiritual agenda behind evolutionary education, we need to understand evolution's role in secular humanism. What exactly is secular humanism, anyway? Essentially, it's the worldview which claims that (to quote one of my professors) "God did not create people; people created God." According to Humanists International, a top-gun global organization which envisions creating a "humanist world,"[9]

> Humanism is a democratic and ethical life stance, which affirms that human beings have the right and responsibility to give meaning and shape to their own lives. It stands for the building of a more humane society through an ethic based on human and other natural values in the spirit of reason and free inquiry through human capabilities. It is not theistic, and it does not accept supernatural views of reality.[10]

In other words, humanism is an atheistic worldview which sets man's word, or human reasoning, over God's Word as the ultimate authority for truth, meaning, and ethics. As sinful humans, we often don't want to recognize that the basis for absolute truth is God's Word. If we did, we'd have to face the fact that we're morally accountable to our Creator. Like Jesus observed, "The light has come into the world, and people loved the darkness rather than the light because their works were evil."[11]

If we don't want to admit that humanity has a Creator, how can we explain human origins? That's where evolution comes in. Evolution is such a core belief of humanism that the American Humanist Association's latest manifesto states, "Humans are an integral part of nature, the result of unguided evolutionary change."[12]

The *Secular Humanist Declaration*, which the Council for Secular Humanism published in 1980, also lists evolution—and education—among its 10 main points. While saying that creationists have "freedom to express their viewpoints in society," the declaration states,

> There may be some significant differences among scientists concerning the mechanics of evolution; yet the evolution of the species is supported so strongly by the weight of evidence that it is difficult to reject it. Accordingly, we deplore the efforts by fundamentalists (especially in the United States) to invade the science classrooms, requiring that creationist theory be taught to students and requiring that it be included in biology textbooks. This is a serious threat both to academic freedom and to the integrity of the educational process. . . . In our view, education should be the essential method of building humane, free, and democratic societies.[13]

Three years after this declaration's release, humanist John Dunphy[14] famously penned these words in an essay entitled "A Religion for a New Age":

> I am convinced that the battle for humankind's future must be waged and won in the public school classroom by teachers who correctly perceive their role as the proselytizers of a new faith: a religion of humanity that recognizes and respects the spark of what theologians call divinity in every human being. These teachers must embody the same selfless dedication as the most rabid fundamentalist preachers, for they will be ministers of another sort, utilizing a classroom instead of a pulpit to convey humanist values in whatever subject they teach, regardless of the educational level—preschool, daycare, or large state university. The classroom must and will become an arena of conflict between the old and the new—the rotting corpse of Christianity, together with all its adjacent evils and misery, and the new faith of humanism, resplendent with its promise of a world in which the never-realized Christian ideal of "love thy neighbor" will finally be achieved.[15]

Decades later, we don't have to look far to see how well this strategy has worked to create a thoroughly post-Christian culture. As another famous humanist, Charles Francis Potter, foresaw back in 1928:

> Education is . . . a most powerful ally of humanism, and every American school is a school of humanism. What can a theistic Sunday school's meeting for an hour once a week and teaching only a fraction of the children do to stem the tide of the five-day program of humanistic teaching?[16]

FACT 2: EVOLUTION IS LINKED TO OTHER MAN-MADE TEACHINGS, INCLUDING EASTERN MYSTICISM.

Education is humanism's chief battle strategy to build a society based on man's word instead of God's. So it's no shock that today's humanistic Western education systems often push not only evolution but also related ideas from man's word, like Eastern mysticism. Just try typing mindfulness, meditation, or yoga into your search engine alongside words like *public education* and any Western country's name, and you'll discover how quickly Eastern practices have flooded Western education from preschool to doctoral studies. Even one of my own psychology classes promoted Buddhist-based mindfulness and Zen meditation.

While at some levels, these practices may seem harmless or be endorsed as healthy, there's no sidestepping the spiritual bases for even their secularized forms. The founder of one popular American meditation center, for instance, describes the secular mindfulness classes they offer in public schools as "stealth Buddhism," packaging Buddhist instruction within secular vocabulary.[17]

Why do supposedly secular Western schools seem so enamored with Eastern spirituality? Some would suggest it's because the idea that we're nothing but soulless biological machines (and accidental ones at that) can't satisfy us spiritually, since God hardwired humans for a relationship with him. So many people crave a teaching that tickles their need for spirituality without requiring them to give up belief in evolution—or to recognize their accountability to the Creator revealed in Scripture. Enter Eastern mysticism.

"Stealth Buddhism"

Eastern mysticism, which includes belief systems like Hinduism, Buddhism, and New Age, took the West by storm after Darwin published *On the Origin of Species*. That's because Darwin's ideas shook many Westerners' trust in the Bible but fit well with Eastern worldviews which, like secular humanism, are founded on man's word instead of God's. Swami Vivikananda, the mystic who helped popularize yoga in late nineteenth-century America, even argued, "The idea of evolution was to be found in the Vedas [ancient Hindu scriptures] long before the Christian era; but until Darwin said it was true, it was regarded as a mere Hindu superstition."[18]

Another famous figure to blend Darwinism with mysticism was Pierre Teilhard de Chardin, an influential forerunner of New Age.[19] A priest, paleontologist, and ardent evolutionist, Chardin taught that evolution would advance humanity to an "Omega Point" of attaining godlike consciousness. Interestingly, one of the most prominent evolutionary biologists of the twentieth century, Theodosius Dobzhansky, concluded his book *The Biology of Ultimate Concern* with a chapter extensively quoting Chardin's spiritualistic ideas.[20]

The *Encyclopedia of New Age Beliefs* called Chardin "perhaps the man most responsible for the spiritualization of evolution in a global and cosmic context."[21] But Chardin wasn't alone in deeming evolution an engine of spirituality. For example, Helen Blavatsky, who founded a twentieth-century cult known as Theosophy, wrote, "Evolutionary law compelled the lunar 'Fathers' to pass, in their monadic condition, through all the forms of life and being on this globe. . . . These 'Forms' are called 'Sons of Yoga,' because Yoga [union with Brahma[22] exoterically] is the supreme condition of the passive infinite deity."[23]

In other words, Blavatsky thought that evolution provides a way for living things to reach their full divine potential—to become gods. Another famous Theosophist (and social Darwinist[24]), Annie Besant, echoed this idea, teaching that Eastern spiritual practices help evolution make people "like God":

> That which we know as Yoga is the method by which evolution is quickened in the individual, and all the powers of the Self, up to the threshold of divinity, may by it be brought into manifestation in the man of the present. That is why Yoga training was necessary for the ancient scientist; he must develop in himself the three aspects of God, if he were to understand them as manifested in the universe around him.[25]

Such spiritual spinoffs of Darwinism have (pardon my language) "evolved" over the decades but certainly haven't gone out of style. Today, for example, people who promote a movement called transhumanism believe that humans will, through technological innovations, evolve godlike traits, including immortality. As influential transhumanist Ray Kurzwiel declared,

> Evolution moves towards greater complexity, greater elegance, greater knowledge, greater intelligence, greater beauty, greater creativity, and greater levels of subtle attributes such as love. In every monotheistic tradition God is likewise described as all of these qualities, only without limitation. . . . Evolution moves inexorably towards this conception of God, although never quite reaching this ideal. We can regard, therefore, the freeing of our thinking from the severe limitations of its biological form to be an essentially spiritual undertaking.[26]

Did you catch that? Evolution is supposed to make us become like God. But wait, doesn't the line "You will become like God" sound familiar? It's the same lie the serpent sold Eve in Eden, a lie which surfaces in countless cults and false religions to this day. It's also the root deception of secular humanism. After all, if we evolved apart from a Creator, we *must* be gods, responsible for defining our own "truth." Ultimately, evolutionary humanism and Eastern mysticism go together like mac and cheese—especially in Western public education—because they both make man's word the authority, enthroning human reasoning in God's place.

FACT 3: THIS ISN'T JUST A "SECULAR SCHOOL" ISSUE.

Given that evolution is a core belief of humanism—a grenade fired at the Genesis foundation of the Christian worldview and a reincarnation of the lie that you can be like God, we might expect that intense evolutionary teaching happens only in secular schools.

Certainly, America's Research Group found otherwise by surveying over 200 evangelical colleges.[27] At each campus, the president, vice president, science department head, and religion department head reported three things: how old they thought the earth is, how literally they viewed the Bible (including Genesis), and how they taught evolution.

In *Already Compromised*, the book which documents this study, Ken Ham and Dr. Greg Hall revealed that, curiously, while nearly 8 out of 10 *religious* department heads believed the earth is millions of years old, only about 1 in 3 *science* department heads agreed. So students studying religion may be even more prone to learning a compromised view of Genesis than students studying science! And that's at evangelical colleges in America, where rates for public belief in evolution already rank among Western nations' lowest.[28]

Even globally, Christian education seems to embrace evolution like a long-lost relative. Two years before *Already Compromised* came out, for instance, the *Christian Higher Education Journal* (CHEJ) published an article called "Evolutionary Creation: Moving Beyond the Evolution Versus Creation Debate."[29] Now, this wasn't some cutesy opinion essay. The CHEJ is an international, interdenominational publication that goes out to every school associated with the Christian Council for Colleges and Universities—a network of 180 institutions around the world.

"Embrace evolution like a long-lost relative."

Calling evolutionary creation a "conservative Christian approach to evolution,"[30] the article admits that throughout history, most people who based their thinking on God's Word (including New Testament writers and Jesus himself) treated Genesis 1–11 as literally true.

However, the article also claims that the Bible's science is outdated—like, by thousands of years. So the article suggests that Christians shelve Genesis 1–11 as ancient poetry, dismiss the New Testament's literal interpretations of Genesis because the apostles didn't know better, and assume that "the Image of God and human sin were gradually and mysteriously manifested" during human evolution.[31]

When we banish a real Genesis, real Adam, and real fall this way, what happens to the gospel? I'll let an evolutionary creationist answer that:

> God does not send Jesus to die. God does not require Jesus' death in order to forgive humanity's sin. . . . As a demonstration of God's immense love and compassion, God takes on flesh and bone. . . . He experiences torture, humiliation, and isolation on the cross. In the end, Jesus experiences death. And in so doing, Christ connects to humanity in a new and powerful way.[32]

Whoa, whoa. Hang on. This writer is claiming that *the purpose of Jesus' death has nothing to do with paying for sin,* which spread through Adam to all humans. That totally goes against historical Christianity, the core salvation message of Scripture, and the doctrines which entire New Testament chapters, like Hebrews 10, clearly teach about the purpose of Jesus' incarnation. Cutting Adam, sin, and the fall out of Genesis cuts the heart out of the gospel. And for what? It's all to accommodate man's ideas about evolution. As the writer summarizes, "The view sketched above does not require a historical Adam and Eve or a traditional concept of original sin, making it more compatible with evolution."[33]

"Whoa, whoa. Hang on."

Did I mention that the author teaches philosophy at a Christian university?

Let the buyer beware. Going to a Christian school does not exempt you from needing to defend your faith against evolutionary doctrines that contradict the gospel.

FACT 4: EVOLUTIONARY TEACHING HELPS EXPLAIN WHY SO MANY YOUTH ARE LEAVING CHURCH.

Okay, so evolution clearly opposes the Bible. If evolution is true, then the Bible is wrong. And if the Bible is wrong, why would anyone schedule their Sundays around learning what it teaches?

This question hints at a trend which researchers have known about for over 20 years: young people are draining out of Western churches. Back in 2000, George Barna figured that 6 out of 10 church-raised teens were evacuating the pews by young adulthood.[34] Study after study has uncovered similar findings since then, showing that up to 90% of youth from some denominations abandon church altogether.[35] Now in my home country, more than two-thirds of all 18–34-year-olds who still attend weekly services for any religion were born in other nations,[36] reflecting how youth fallout rates are highest among native Westerners.

So why are Western churches losing youth like air escaping from a punctured life raft? That's what Ken Ham and Britt Beemer of America's Research Group wanted to investigate, documenting their findings in the book *Already Gone*.[37] Released in 2009, this study of 1,000 ex-churchgoer twentysomethings across America revealed that most (nearly 9 in 10) individuals left church before college. Universities, although a hotbed of unbiblical indoctrination, are therefore not where most students end up abandoning their faith. The fade-out begins long before, with almost 90% of young adults who left church reporting that their first doubts about God's Word surfaced during middle school or high school.

Meanwhile, teens who grew up attending Sunday school were ironically even more likely to leave church. After all, Sunday schools often teach the Bible as "stories" rather than true events grounded in real science and history. It's not surprising, then, that Barna Research reported in 2018 that nearly half (49%) of American churchgoing teens agreed with the statement, "The church seems to reject much of what science tells us about the world."[38]

To repeat the words of humanist Charles Francis Potter, "What can a theistic Sunday school's meeting for an hour once a week . . . do to stem the tide of the five-day program of humanistic teaching?" The answer, suggest the authors of *Already Gone*, lies in churches, families, and ministries equipping students of all ages with answers to defend their Christian worldview against unbiblical beliefs in the culture—like evolution and millions of years. That's especially important because evolutionary teaching is everywhere, bringing us to the last three facts.

FACT 5: EVOLUTIONARY TEACHING IMPACTS (PRETTY MUCH) EVERY SCHOOL SUBJECT.

Like we saw earlier, evolution is a key belief of secular humanism, the worldview which tends to rule Western education. You can't accept secular humanism without evolution any more than you can wear sunglasses without some kind of frame. And like sunglasses, secular humanism tints everything viewed through its lens—hence the word *worldview.* So humanistic education systems are naturally bound to teach every subject through an evolutionary framework.

The most obvious school subject where evolution often shows up is biology. From amoebas to zebras, everything that moves, breathes, or squeaks supposedly does so thanks to evolution. Do ghost crabs growl by vibrating "teeth" in their stomachs? Evolution did that. Do nine-banded armadillos always have quadruplets? Evolution did that too. If I had a $100 for every biology professor or textbook who quoted Theodosius Dobzhansky's famous line, "Nothing in biology makes sense except in the light of evolution," the total might have funded my classes.

But that's just biological evolution. Biological evolution would require millions of years to happen, and that's where geological evolution—changes in earth over long ages—comes in. Take a secular geology, minerology, or earth and oceans science class, and you're just about guaranteed to learn that different rock layers (and the fossils in them) formed evolutionary eons ago.

Of course, an old earth means an old universe. And the universe, according to man's word, looks the way it does because of cosmological evolution. So most first-year astronomy, planetology, and meteorology classes will work long ages and evolutionary processes into the exam material, too. Ultimately, whether astronomy, geology, or biology, many science classes are bound to be packed with references to unbiblical ideas.

So does that mean nonscience students are off the hook from learning evolution? Hardly. As part of a secular worldview, evolutionary interpretations color everything. Like evolutionary biologist and humanist Sir Julian Huxley (grandson of "Darwin's Bulldog," Thomas Huxley) put it:

> The concept of biology was soon extended into other than biological fields. Inorganic subjects such as the life-history of stars and the formation of the chemical elements on the one hand, and on the other hand subjects like linguistics, social anthropology and comparative law and religion, began to be studied from an evolutionary angle, until today we are enabled to see evolution as a universal and all-pervading process.[39]

In other words, evolutionary beliefs change how we look at everything—including ourselves. By saying "We are not created beings," evolution makes a statement about human nature, which affects our approach to everything that has to do with being human. Human psychology, anthropology, sociology, philosophy, history, music, and art all take on evolutionary explanations.

To see for yourself how many school subjects evolution infiltrates, just type "evolution" into the course listings webpage of your nearest university. When I tried this myself, over 16 courses with explicitly evolutionary titles popped up for faculties, including earth and ocean science, astronomy, psychology, anthropology, and (no surprise) biology. When I searched for evolution in course descriptions, another 40 classes showed up, covering topics like cosmology, stellar astrophysics, animal behavior, biological anthropology, geography of plate tectonics and energy cycling, biogeography, algae (wait—there's an entire class on algae?), invertebrates, vertebrates, flowering plants, land plants, whale conservation, paleobiology, microbiology, neurobiology, mycology (the study of fungi), osteology (the study of bones), ichthyology (the study of fish), entomology (the study of insects), and glabrorycteropology (the study of hairless aardvarks).

> "Evolutionary teaching is everywhere."

Okay, so I just made up that last class. (But it sounds like it'd be a great elective.) The point is, evolutionary teaching is everywhere, affecting not only multiple school subjects but also every grade level. And that just happens to be the next fact.

FACT 6: EVOLUTIONARY TEACHING IS FOR ALL AGES.

Of course, exactly which evolutionary ideas schools teach at different grade levels varies by each region's education system. In North America, different provinces, states, and territories have their own science education standards. Many places amp up the evolution lessons in both middle and high school, but public education (not to mention secular media) often plants evolutionary seeds in kids' minds long before that. In Canada, for example, a report from 2015 listed all the evolutionary ideas in each province's science curricula, with teaching about evolution and millions of years beginning as early as kindergarten.[40]

K–12 educational frameworks that promote evolution are overtaking America, too. One of them, the Next Generation Science Standards (NGSS), includes biological evolution as one of its "Disciplinary Core Ideas" for life sciences. The NGSS requires middle schoolers to explain everything ranging from the fossil record to supposed similarities between animal embryos as being evidence for evolution.[41] As I'm writing this, at least 20 states have adopted the NGSS framework, while another 24 base their own education standards on it.[42] That means the NGSS influences 71% of American K–12 students.

While kindergarten might not seem like the likeliest place for kids to become Darwinists, thinking up ways to spoon-feed kindergarteners (and even preschoolers) evolutionary doctrines has practically become a sport among some education researchers. Using storybooks, animal figures, colorful pictures, and cutting-edge knowledge of how kids' brains work, these "learning interventions" teach concepts like natural selection to convince youngsters that everything alive belongs to one evolutionary family.[43, 44]

But here's something remarkable: according to the researchers who study how to teach evolution to children, kids intuitively tend to see *design*, not evolution, in nature. Researchers trying to "correct" such thinking in American 5–8-year-olds put it this way: "These reasoning biases include tendencies to teleologically assume that . . . the natural world is agentive and operates in intentional, designed, and purpose-driven ways."[45]

"The likeliest place for kids to become Darwinists"

Basically, that's a science-y way of saying that kids recognize the universe is designed. And education experts in America aren't the only ones working to wipe that kind of thinking from kids' minds. In Germany, for instance, the organization EvoKids aims to mandate evolutionary teaching throughout all levels of German primary school instead of just beginning in grade 10.[46] In France, where evolutionary teaching holds a central place in the national curricula, schools ingrain evolution and millions of years into students from age 9.[47] Look up the education standards for almost any Western country you like (and many non-Western nations, too), and you're bound to find evolution among the core learning requirements. That brings us to the last fact.

FACT 7: EVOLUTIONARY TEACHING IMPACTS COUNTLESS STUDENTS WORLDWIDE.

To show how vehement global education powers can be about vacuuming any thoughts of divine creation out of students' heads, let me tell you about a document called Resolution 1580. In 2007, the Parliamentary Assembly of the Council of Europe (PACE), which sets the legal agenda for 57 nations, passed this resolution, dubbing it "The Dangers of Creationist Teaching in Education." You can find the whole resolution—and its even more anti-creationist draft report[48]—online, but here's just a sample:

> If we are not careful, creationism could become a threat to human rights, which are a key concern of the Council of Europe. . . . The Parliamentary Assembly therefore urges the member states, and especially their education authorities, to . . . firmly oppose the teaching of creationism as a scientific discipline on an equal footing with the theory of evolution and in general the presentation of creationist ideas in any discipline other than religion [and to] promote the teaching of evolution as a fundamental scientific theory in the school curriculums.[49]

Wow. The PACE is urging its member nations to hammer home a core doctrine of secular humanism which undermines the gospel. The resolution continues,

> The Assembly welcomes the fact that 27 academies of science of Council of Europe member states signed, in June 2006, a declaration on the teaching of evolution and calls on academies of science that have not yet done so to sign the declaration.[50]

Just what declaration are they talking about? It's a document called the IAP Statement on the Teaching of Evolution,[51] with IAP standing for InterAcademy Partnership—a network of government-supported organizations which oversee nations' official education standards. This statement declares that "scientific evidence has never contradicted" supposed events like human's evolution from life-forms that "appeared on Earth at least 2.5 billion years ago." No fewer than 68 national and international science education foundations around the world have signed this statement, from Albania to Zimbabwe.

As part of the spiritual agenda to build humanist societies founded on man's word instead of God's, this global push for evolutionary teaching has been a long time coming. Remember Sir Julian Huxley, who called evolution a "universal and all-pervading process"? Besides being an evolutionary biologist, Huxley served as president of the British Humanist Association. He was also the first director-general for the United Nations Educational, Scientific, and Cultural Organization (UNESCO). While he began in this office in 1946, he didn't publish the framework he originally proposed for UNESCO until 1979,[52] stating,

> The general philosophy of UNESCO should, it seems, be a scientific world humanism, global in extent and evolutionary in background. . . . The unifying of traditions in a single common pool of experience, awareness, and purpose is the necessary prerequisite for further major progress in human evolution. Accordingly, although political unification in some sort of world government will be required for the definitive attainment of this stage,

unification in the things of the mind is not only also necessary but can pave the way for other types of unification.

A LONG WAR TO WIN THE YOUTH

Sir Huxley's goals for the world's most powerful educational organization unmasks evolutionary education for what it is: a key strategy in the worldview battle to make man's word—not God's—the authority for a global society. The battle for the hearts and minds of culture wages chiefly in the hearts and minds of youth. And like anyone who's recently tried taking over the world probably knows, whatever enters youths' minds today will shape society's values, morals, and belief systems tomorrow. We're in a war for our culture's future.

Right now, every day, around the world, classrooms teaching any subject at any grade level—even in many religious schools—represent the front lines of this war to enthrone humanity above our Creator as definers of our own truth. It's a war that has raged ever since Eden, fueled by the ancient lie, "You will be like God." And if the rocketing rates of youth leaving church are any indication, it's already a war with countless casualties.

But here's the good news: youth can absolutely survive this war. They need training, equipping, and backup for the trenches—and with God's grace and his people's support, they can do it. I know, because I was one of those youths. Let me tell you what I experienced on the front lines of evolutionary education at my university.

Endnotes

1. Matthew 12:30
2. Ken Ham, *The Lie: Evolution/Millions of Years* (Green Forest: Master Books, 2012).
3. Notably, *the mass public education specifically of children* is not mandated in the Bible compared to discipleship within families (e.g., Deuteronomy 11:19). Still, the principles behind the general concept of education (like truth and the importance of sharing it) are founded in a biblical worldview.
4. E.g., Jason Lisle, *The Ultimate Proof of Creation: Resolving the Origins Debate* (Green Forest: Master Books, 2009); C. S. Lewis, "The Self-Contradiction of the Naturalist," in *Miracles*, rev. ed. (London: Fontana Books/Collins, 1960).
5. Numbers 23:19
6. "The Creationist Basis for Modern Science," Answers in Genesis, January 24, 1998, https://answersingenesis.org/creation-scientists/the-creationist-basis-for-modern-science.
7. Robert Woodberry, "The Missionary Roots of Liberal Democracy," *American Political Science Review* (2012): 244–274.

8. For instance, the Council for Secular Humanism listed education among 10 core principles of humanism in *A Secular Humanist Declaration* (1980), https://secularhumanism.org/a-secular-humanist-declaration.

9. Importantly, youth explicitly factor into Humanist International's strategies to build a humanist planet. For instance, one of the points in their "2018–2020 Strategy" is that "we will have a successful youth section," clearly showing the secularists understand that youth are the key to winning the future. ("2018–2020 Strategy," Humanist International, accessed January 4, 2021, https://humanists.international.)

10. "IHEU Minimum Statement on Humanism," Humanists International General Assembly, 1996, https://humanists.international/what-is-humanism.

11. John 3:19

12. *Humanism and Its Aspirations: Humanist Manifesto III, a Successor to the Humanist Manifesto of 1933*, American Humanist Association, 2003, https://americanhumanist.org/what-is-humanism/manifesto3.

13. *A Secular Humanist Declaration*, Council for Secular Humanism, 1980, https://www.secularhumanism.org/index.php/11.

14. Mr. Dunphy and I later struck up a friendly correspondence over email; while *A Religion for a New Age* had a far-reaching impact, his more current views are expressed in "Dunphy: A Church Without Collection Plates," *The Telegraph*, March 20, 2018, https://www.thetelegraph.com/opinion/article/Dunphy-A-church-without-collection-plates-12768212.php.

15. John Dunphy, "A Religion for a New Age," *The Humanist*, 43, no. 1 (1983): 23–26. Full essay is available at https://medium.com/@johnjdunphy/a-religion-for-a-new-age-f812839c4cb8.

16. Charles Francis Potter, *Humanism, A New Religion* (Simon and Schuster, 1930), 128.

17. Candy Brown, "Mindfulness Meditation in Public Schools: Side-Stepping Supreme Court Religion Rulings," December 5, 2014 (updated December 6, 2017), https://www.huffpost.com/entry/mindfulness-meditation-in_b_6276968.

18. Swami Vivekānanda (1896), as cited by Dermot Killingley, "Yoga-sūtra IV, 2–3 and Vivekānanda's Interpretation of Evolution," *Journal of Indian Philosophy* 18, no. 2 (1990): 151–179.

19. For more information about Chardin, the evolutionists he influenced, and other links between Darwinism and New Age, see Dr. Henry Morris, *The Long War Against God* (Green Forest: Master Books, 2000).

20. Theodosius Dobzhansky, *The Biology of Ultimate Concern* (New York: New American Library, 1967).

21. John Ankerberg and John Weldon, *Encyclopedia of New Age Beliefs* (Harvest House Publishers, 1996), 661.

22. The creator deity of Hinduism

23. Helen Blavatsky, *The Secret Doctrine: The Synthesis of Science, Religion, and Philosophy, Vol. II: Anthropogenesis* (London: Theosophical Publishing Company, 1888), 115.

24. Social Darwinism is the idea that some humans are less fit and should be eliminated or prevented from having children. This thinking helped spawn the eugenics movement of the twentieth century and related atrocities in Nazi-occupied Europe (Jerry Bergman, "Darwinism and the Nazi Race Holocaust," *Journal of Creation* 13, no. 2 [1999]: 101–111, https://answersingenesis.org/charles-darwin/racism/darwinism-and-the-nazi-race-holocaust). Darwinian mystics, including Annie Besant, believed yoga aided the evolution of the "mother race," which eugenicists meant to promote (Mark Singleton, "Yoga, Eugenics, and Spiritual Darwinism in the Early Twentieth Century," *International Journal of Hindu Studies* 11, no. 2 [2007]: 125–146).

25. Annie Besant, "First Lecture: Ancient and Modern Science," in *Four Lectures Delivered at the Twenty-third Anniversary Meeting of the Theosophical Society at Adyar, Madras, 1898*, 2nd ed. (London: Theosophical Publishing Society, 1900), 20.

26. Ray Kurzweil, *The Singularity Is Near: When Humans Transcend Biology* (New York: Penguin, 2005), 389.

27. Ken Ham, Greg Hall, and Britt Beemer, *Already Compromised* (Green Forest: Master Books, 2011).

28. Jon Miller, Eugenie Scott, and Shinji Okamoto, "Public Acceptance of Evolution," *Science* 313, no. 5788 (2006): 765.

29. Dennis Lamoureux, "Evolutionary Creation: Moving Beyond the Evolution Versus Creation Debate," *Christian Higher Education* 9, no. 1 (2009): 28–48.

30. Ibid., 28.

31. Ibid., 28.

32. Joseph Bankard, "Substitutionary Atonement and Evolution," BioLogos, June 9, 2015, https://biologos.org/articles/series/atonement-and-evolution-a-biologos-conversation/substitutionary-atonement-and-evolution.

33. Ibid.

34. Barna Research Online, "Teenagers Embrace Religion but Are Not Excited About Christianity," January 10, 2000, www.Barna.org.

35. James Penner et. al., "Hemorrhaging Faith: Why and When Canadian Young Adults Are Leaving, Staying, and Returning to Church," *commissioned by The EFC Youth and Young Adult Ministry roundtable,* 2011.

36. "A Spectrum of Spirituality: Canadians Keep the Faith to Varying Degrees, but Few Reject It Entirely," Angus Reid Institute, April 12, 2017, http://angusreid.org/religion-in-canada-150.

37. Ken Ham and Britt Beemer, *Already Gone: Why Your Kids Will Quit Church and What You Can Do to Stop It* (Green Forest: Master Books, 2009).

38. George Barna, "Atheism Doubles Among Generation Z," Barna, January 24, 2018, https://www.barna.com/research/atheism-doubles-among-generation-z.

39. Julian Huxley, "Evolution and Genetics," in J. R. Newman (ed.) *What Is Science?* (New York: Simon and Schuster, 1955), 272. Cited in Henry Morris, *The Long War Against God* (Green Forest: Master Books, 2000).

40. Anila Asghar et. al., "Biological Evolution in Canadian Science Curricula," *Reports of the National Center for Science Education* 35, no. 5 (2015): 1.1–1.21.

41. Bertha Vazquez, "A State-by-State Comparison of Middle School Science Standards on Evolution in the United States," *Evolution: Education and Outreach* 10, no. 1 (2017): 5.

42. "About the Next Generation Science Standards," National Science Teaching Association, accessed January 4, 2021, https://ngss.nsta.org/about.aspx.

43. E.g., Natalie Emmons, Kristin Lees, and Deborah Kelemen, "Young Children's Near and Far Transfer of the Basic Theory of Natural Selection: An Analogical Storybook Intervention," *Journal of Research in Science Teaching* 55, no. 3 (2018): 321–347.

44. E.g., Johanna Frejd, "If It Lived Here, It Would Die: Children's Use of Materials as Semiotic Resources in Group Discussions About Evolution," *Journal of Research in Childhood Education* 32, no. 3 (2018): 251–267.

45. Natalie Emmons, Hayley Smith, and Deborah Kelemen, "Changing Minds with the Story of Adaptation: Strategies for Teaching Young Children About Natural Selection," *Early Education and Development* 27, no. 8 (2016): 1,205–1,221.

46. "Das Evokids-Projekt," EvoKids, accessed January 4, 2021, https://evokids.de.

47. Marie-Pierre Quessada and Pierre Clément, "Evolution Education in France: Evolution Is Widely Taught and Accepted," in *Evolution Education Around the Globe* (Cham: Springer, 2018), 213–233.

48. Brasseur, Anne, "The Dangers of Creationism in Education," Parliamentary Assembly of the Council of Europe, Committee on Culture, Science, and Education, September 17, 2007, https://assembly.coe.int/nw/xml/XRef/X2H-Xref-ViewHTML.asp?FileID=11751&lang=EN.

49. "Resolution 1580: The Dangers of Creationism in Education," Parliamentary Assembly of the Council of Europe, Committee on Culture, Science, and Education, October 4, 2007, http://assembly.coe.int/nw/xml/XRef/Xref-XML2HTML-EN.asp?fileid=17592&lang=en.

50. Ibid.

51. "Inter-Academy Panel (IAP) Statement on the Teaching of Evolution," Inter-Academy Panel, 2006, http://www.interacademies.org/13901/IAP-Statement-on-the-Teaching-of-Evolution.

52. Henry Morris, *The Long War Against God* (Green Forest: Master Books, 2000), 57.

53. Julian Huxley, "UNESCO: Its Purpose and Its Philosophy," Preparatory Commission of UNESCO, 1946, https://unesdoc.unesco.org/ark:/48223/pf0000068197.

MEMOIRS FROM THE FRONT LINES

4

My experiences in a secular university

First, let me just say that some of the years I spent in a university were among the best in my life.

Sure, it was a ton of work. Sure, there were times when I suspected that if I had to solve one more equation, plot one more graph, or memorize one more evolutionary "family tree," my sanity might shatter like a beaker dropped during chemistry lab. But as I share my experiences on the battlefields of evolutionary education, I don't want to give the impression that a university is solely a dark and deadly dungeon of tumultuously terrible tortures. My professors were friendly; my classmates were friendly; and my textbooks' authors sometimes even wrote like they were friendly, too. So before I unpack the pressures I faced at college (for the first half of my science degree) and university (for the last half), let me describe the bright side of undergrad life.

THE BEST PART OF A UNIVERSITY

In a university, like everywhere else in life, the people you're around can make all the difference between having an awful or awesome experience. So looking back over my own undergrad years, I praise God for surrounding me with truly fabulous people—like my best study buddy in college. Whether creating goofy mnemonics for our exam notes, studying over waffle brunches, or laughing ourselves half comatose during Thursday-night physics lab, we turned whatever we did into a blast. Then there were the golden times in university—like hiking with Christian students every Friday morning, meeting my roommate on the local pier for sunsets, or praying, jamming, and road-tripping with campus ministry members. We didn't have long together, but we made the most of it.

All the while, I was learning. I didn't just learn science-y stuff like how plants grow or how tides work or how far frog eggs can squirt when a professor accidentally squeezes a female *Xenopus laevis*, whose posterior happens to be facing a student. I also learned valuable life lessons. I learned to solve problems, think critically, and communicate ideas like never before. I learned to depend more on God, bringing him any concerns ranging from *Wow, sandwich meat is pricey* to *How am I going to pass this calculus exam*? I even learned that spaghetti strainers can melt into impressive abstract art forms when left unsupervised near temperamental hot plates. Yes, the university helped me become stronger, wiser, and nerdier. But it wasn't a Sunday school picnic. How did I, as a Bible-believing homeschooler, prepare for the battlefield that I'd heard secular university could be?

GETTING READY

Ever since listening to Ken Ham's seminar at age 14, I'd known I wanted to study science, learn how to refute evolution, and become an apologist. The faith-based universities where I lived militantly taught evolutionary creationism,[1] so my family and I decided that at least in a secular university I'd know that any unbiblical ideas I heard in class wouldn't sound like they came from a Christian perspective. Plus, navigating a public university would help me learn firsthand how to help other Christian students keep their faith at secular schools.

"If you really want to study science," my mom said, "you should connect with a local Christian biologist, Dr. Margaret Helder. Why don't you email her?"

"And say what?"

"Just ask if you can bring her a list of science questions and talk about biology."

I wasn't convinced a random teenager and an educated stranger could spontaneously connect. But what did I have to lose by asking?

A few emails later, I stood on Dr. Helder's porch, a wide-eyed adolescent clutching a notebook of questions. With that, I found a mentor. She patiently answered my questions, showed me apologetics resources, and encouraged me to come again. I did! A few times every year, we'd meet to discuss the Bible and science all throughout the rest of my homeschooling and into the university.

Meanwhile, I pumped myself up with apologetics training to learn about defending my biblical worldview. I attended every seminar I could, stockpiled books, volunteered at conferences, browsed biblical creation-vs.-evolution websites, and sweet-talked my family into visiting the Creation Museum in Kentucky. Finally, after nearly five years of preparation, the time approached for me to enter the door I believed God had opened: attending a little college over 800 miles from home.

Before moving there for good, I took a scouting trip with my parents to spy out the school, connect with the campus ministry leader, and meet a local pastor. Because the college didn't have dorms, I was also praying for a Christian home to stay in. God answered those prayers only weeks later!

Finally, the moment arrived. At just shy of 19, I left my home, family, and wisdom teeth a time zone behind, ready (I hoped) to face whatever lay between me and a paper bearing the letters *BSc*.

What happened during those four unforgettable years?

Well, since you asked . . .

FIRST IMPRESSIONS OF COLLEGE: WHAT HAVE I GOTTEN MYSELF INTO?

Oh, first year. The memory still leaves a certain taste in my mouth—something between peanut butter and cold pizza. Having never been to college (or any traditional school) before, I felt like the planet's biggest faker the first time I walked into class among all those calm-looking freshmen who'd probably been sitting in classrooms their whole lives. But my nerves quieted when the professor announced, "Welcome to college! This isn't high school anymore. You actually have to work now—to take your learning into your own hands."

Great, I thought, *that's what I've already been doing for years!*

And *work* it was.

So trapped did I feel beneath the crushing weight of homework (never mind its evolutionary content), I remember calling my parents to confess I'd considered leaving school, buying a unicycle, and peddling across Canada as a nomadic busker. They said that if I did, they'd still be cheering for me—but that I shouldn't give up yet.

"Now, let me bring you behind the classroom doors."

Being caught in this avalanche of assignments made me realize how important it had been for me to build up a solid defense of my biblical beliefs *before* college. I certainly didn't have time for much apologetics research anymore, beyond looking up occasional questions on biblical creation websites. Even if I didn't have time to read a whole article, just seeing that a thoughtful answer existed helped.

Meanwhile, other measures I took to keep my faith strong for the long haul included keeping up with church, attending campus ministry nights, and writing semesterly newsletters to let praying friends and family know what I was going through—especially in my more evolution-heavy classes.

Now, let me bring you behind the classroom doors of just five such courses.

1. FIRST-YEAR BIOLOGY

To get a feel for what first-year biology is like, picture perching atop a hard, wooden stool at a lab bench cluttered with binders, pencils, notebooks, rubber gloves, and pipettes. To the left is a wall of assorted biological bric-a-brac, including bones, shells, taxidermized heads, and jars of whole pickled amphibians. To the right, all you can see are shelves upon shelves of files, textbooks, and at least one skinless plastic torso. And there at the front, between the whiteboard and the resin human skeleton, a professor is declaring 10 weighty words:

"There is not a single piece of evidence against evolution."

At least, that's what *my* first-year biology instructor said. And my textbook, one of the best-known introductory biology books around, apparently agreed. Right in the first chapter, under the heading "The Core Theme: Evolution Accounts for the Unity and Diversity of Life," the text stated, "There is consensus among biologists that evolution is the core theme of biology. The evolutionary changes in the fossil record are an observable fact."[2]

Later in the book, a section headed "Evolution Is Supported by an Overwhelming Amount of Scientific Evidence"[3] also listed nine evolutionary evidences we had to memorize for the exam.[4] I soon realized, however, that I was being trained not only to think like an evolutionist but also to oppose creationists. For instance, an exercise in my textbook asked me to critique (in the sense of *counter*) an argument about protein complexity from the "anti-evolutionary" (in other words, "anti-science") Intelligent Design movement. I felt dissonant, like a double agent learning how to fight in an enemy army. And that feeling only intensified the next semester when physical anthropology class began.

"I felt dissonant, like a double agent."

2. FIRST-YEAR ANTHROPOLOGY

Physical anthropology—it seemed like a good idea at the time. I wasn't wildly excited about "the study of human physiological traits and their origins," but since it was a prerequisite for another class I'd been considering, I signed up. That's when I got the email.

The professor's first letter, which I mentioned in this book's introduction, gently cautioned that students who didn't accept human evolution should rethink taking the class. But since I figured it would be a great chance to learn what students are taught in evolutionary classrooms, I headed to the lecture anyway.

The Story I Was Told

"Because a 'theory' in science is backed by a well-established body of evidence . . .," the professor reiterated once the classroom door had clicked shut, "if your worldview cannot accept evolution, this is really not the best course for you."[5]

I held my peace as the lecture morphed into an eloquent evolutionary storytelling session. As the professor described mysterious ancestral beings rising upright for the first time, migrating across distant deserts, fashioning weapons, developing speech, domesticating animals, and inventing culture, art, and religion, I couldn't help but notice how poetic his story sounded. Clearly the topic fascinated him. And he made it all seem so . . . true!

As the course progressed, I found references to the "rise of religion" the most unsettling. The story I heard went that as primitive humans struggled through the cosmic accident called life, they gazed up at the stars and searched for meaning. From there, according to my study notes, religion "probably developed as a way to cope with agricultural uncertainties. When faced with problems beyond control of technology or better organization, people tended to resort to magic or the supernatural." Allegedly, this quest to control nature, explain the unexplainable, and generally make sense of life caused the evolution of all religion from primitive cults. Or as my professor put it, "At the root of every institutionalized religion is shamanism."[6]

Judeo-Christian religions specifically, he told us, emerged as a reflection of Middle Eastern pastoralism, where a patriarchal male leads flocks of people and sheep around the desert. Throughout the centuries, these religions continued thriving because of human sociology, psychology, and politics. Still, the professor implied, churches eventually reached their intellectual "best before" dates thanks to advancements from science.

Faith: "No Match for Science"

As a supposed example of when faith started succumbing to science,[7] the professor explained how Galileo advocated that the earth is round, contrary to the Catholic Church's stance at the time that the earth is flat.[8] "Since then," he added, "the church has mostly stepped back from science—unless you're in one of those whacked-out tea party movements like Intelligent Design."

Other ruffling remarks included times when the professor implied that biblical geology is good for laughs, outright questioned Jesus' existence, or stated that science shows earth is *certainly* more than 6,000 years old. When nobody responded to the age-of-the-earth comment, he explained that back in the day, people *used* to think earth is roughly that old because of the Bible. Then again, people once held (in his perspective) many other strange beliefs supposedly from Scripture, too.

"When dinosaur bones were first discovered in North America," he said, "people had different ideas about them because, of course, dinosaurs aren't in Genesis. Or in the Old Testament. Or in the New Testament. So some people decided that the devil must have put the bones there in order to turn humans away from God and to claim their souls."

Naturally, a chuckle rippled through the classroom around me.

"But other people," the professor continued, smiling, "thought that the bones meant that prehistoric animals had been living there. Occam's razor says that whatever idea is the most straightforward, with the fewest premises, is the one to go with." Counting down on his fingers, he continued, "Now the first idea required (1) that there be such a creature as Satan, (2) that he has anything to do with humans, (3) that he's out to get their souls, and (4) it presupposes the existence of a God. The second idea simply says there would have had to be dinosaurs."[9]

Clearly, religious notions are "no match for hard science." At least that's the idea the classroom was getting. And not just from lectures! The textbook, too, framed evolution and creation as a conflict of science versus faith instead of a worldview battle that pits historical science based on man's word against historical science based on God's Word. As the book said,

> It is important to distinguish between scientific theories—which are always open to challenges born of new evidence or insights—and doctrine. A doctrine, or dogma, is an assertion of opinion or belief formally handed down by an authority as true and indisputable. For instance, those who accept a creationist doctrine on the origin of the human species as recounted in sacred texts or myths do so on the basis of religious authority.[10]

Ironic, I thought, *that here I am, being formally handed down by authority figures the humanistic religious doctrine of evolutionary origins as true and indisputable.*

Subtle Indoctrination

Sometimes, though, evolutionary indoctrination was subtler than this. For instance, I noticed our textbook dedicated its entire second chapter to evolutionary biology, followed by another whole chapter about primates. This way, the course layout psychologically primed students to think about everything else they learned in the context of evolution. Similarly, the third chapter's front page featured a picture of two female chimps engaged in a sexual act, conditioning students to view human sexuality through an evolutionary lens.

Reading those chapters, I sensed what David might have felt upon glimpsing Goliath. Here I'd come face-to-face with the giant of humanist education, champion warrior of secular camps, defying the armies of the living God. Its taunts weighed down my spirit; its boots left imprints on my soul.

It's too big, Lord. I thought. *How can anyone slay a giant?*

Then I remembered David's slingshot. Where did that little guy get those mad slinging skills, anyway? Simple. He was faithful to the task God called him to: watching his father's sheep. Literally counting sheep for a living probably felt mundane at times, but David kept defending his flock, combating carnivores, and honing his slingshot abilities, all out of a commitment to God and his family. That's how by being the best shepherd he could be, David developed the skills necessary to overcome Goliath when the time came. In the same way, God reminded me that by being faithful to the task he'd called me to—being the best student I could be, he'd help me cultivate the skills required to battle this giant, too.

> "It's too big, Lord, I thought. How can anyone slay a giant?"

3. SECOND-YEAR CRITICAL THINKING[11]

Besides anthropology, another course where I could practically smell the secular giant's breath was critical thinking—a philosophy class that covered logic, fallacies, and how to argue like a pro. Now don't get me wrong, I loved learning these topics. But as other students tell me often happens in humanities classes, the professor relished weaving leftist views into the course wherever possible.[12] These included comments about "terrible" arguments for Intelligent Design and "right-wing fundamentalist" (aka evangelical) stances on issues like abortion, as well as assignment questions that made students argue against fictional creationists. In fact, the textbook featured an entire chapter called "Judging Scientific Theories," complete with a blatant, five-page-long attack on biblical creation.[13] While we ran out of time to cover the chapter in class, the professor strongly encouraged us to read it. I did.

The chapter began tamely enough, seeming to offer a balanced look at both biblical creation and evolution. But soon, the textbook whipped off its objective Mr. Nice Guy mask and pounced savagely—teeth bared, claws flexed, slobber flying—at creation. Brace yourself for some excerpts:

> [An evolutionary] sequence is exactly what scientists see time and time again. Creationism, however, has not faired as well. Its claims have not been borne out by evidence. In fact, they have consistently conflicted with well-established scientific findings. The latter point means that creationism fails the criterion of conservatism—it conflicts with what we already know.[14]

To illustrate creation's "failure," the book claimed that science supports an old earth and denies a global flood, offering as evidence not findings from scientific research but rather two quotes from the militantly evolutionist US National Academy of Sciences. For good measure, the book also quoted Dobzhansky's mantra,"Nothing in biology makes sense except in the light of evolution."[15] The chapter then continued,

> Creationism is not a fruitful theory. . . . Creationism has zero scope. . . . On every count, [creationism] shows itself to be inferior. Scientists then are justified in rejecting creationism in favour of evolution—and this is exactly what they do.[16]

Whew. I still remember sitting in the university library, top floor, pencil in hand, filling these pages' margins with notes as I worked through each section using the critical thinking techniques outlined in part 3 of this book. By the time I had to leave for my next class, I felt slightly pummeled yet strangely encouraged. After all, I'd just studied a hit-'em-with-our-best-shot critique of creation by critical thinking experts. Yet God had provided me tools to work through it with my biblical worldview unscathed. And did those tools ever come in handy for other courses, too—like third-year evolution.

4. THIRD-YEAR EVOLUTION

To be honest, I hadn't planned on taking an entire evolutionary biology class. *Why walk into another lions' den?* I figured. But while registering for third-year courses, I was having a terrible time trying to choreograph my academic schedule. So when I accidentally clicked the evolution course and noticed it (amazingly) fit my timetable, I thought, *hmm*.

When I learned that a friend at that campus had also signed up for evolution, I thought, *hmmmmmm*.

Then, when I told some Christian friends in another province that I'd likely be taking the class and they lent me an older edition of that class' textbook which they'd randomly found in a dumpster (true story), I thought, *hmmmmmmmmmmmmm!*

Prayerfully, I headed to the first lecture.

On the way, I couldn't help wondering what kind of professor to expect. Would I end up being swallowed alive by an acerbic atheist, like what happens to Christian students in church movies? Pleasantly, however, I walked into class to meet not a raving anti-creationist but rather a grandmotherly researcher who liked plants. I did once land in her office on the verge of tears, but that was only because she'd described a method of enzyme analysis by protein electrophoresis which struck me as so beautiful, I was touched. (Did I mention college made me nerdier?)

Navigating the Course

While I did end up buying a new textbook for this class, the dumpster edition my friends had lent me provided a useful preview of what to expect—like an entire chapter critiquing all types of creationism, including Intelligent Design.[17] In the book's words,

> The historical reality of evolution—the descent, with modification, of all organisms from common ancestors—has not been in question among scientists for well over a century. It is as much a scientific fact as the atomic constitution of matter or the revolution of Earth around the Sun.[18]

Well then.

Although we didn't cover the chapter in class, this quote illustrates a tactic I noticed popping up throughout the course: blurring observational science with origins science.[19] Here the book claimed that a fact we can observe in the present (earth's orbit) is equal to a conclusion about the past which we can't directly observe—the story of all life's supposed evolution.

Along the same lines, the textbook often cited cases where we can observe natural selection working in the present to remove genetic variety from kinds of living things God created. As chapter 7 will unpack, this kind of process can explain variations we see *within* kinds of living things, like stickleback fish. But it can't create the new genetic information required to change primordial sludge into a professor. That's a conclusion about the past from historical science, and what we know from observational science just doesn't support it.

By keeping observational science and historical science constantly in mind, I finished the semester only to realize that the course had never really offered a watertight example of one kind of living thing evolving into another. Maybe I'd missed something. To see whether another course might present a more convincing case for evolution (and because I liked the professor who would teach it, and the course would even fit my timetable), I signed up for round two: molecular evolution.

5. FOURTH-YEAR MOLECULAR EVOLUTION

Looking back, a main memory I recall from this class is how expensive the textbook was. And we barely even read it! Of course, I still checked out what the writer had to say about creation, finding this gem in the book's introduction:

> If genes, genomes, and organisms were created by a benevolent intelligent designer, the problem of theodicy[20] would never have arisen, and departments of pediatric oncology would never be needed.[21]

Basically, the book is saying, "If there were really a loving Creator, there wouldn't be evil, death, and suffering in the world, and kids would never get cancer." That goes back to the second C of biblical history we saw in chapter 1, Corruption, and to the reality that trying to fit millions of years (and millions-of-years-old dates for fossil evidence of cancer) into Genesis undermines the character of God. However, we didn't talk about any of this in the lectures.

Instead, we spent the first half of the semester without really examining evolution in the sense of "change between kinds of living things" at all. Rather, most of the course dealt with population genetics, which looks at the math behind how individual mutations become established in a gene pool. This type of study can describe how a population of flying beetles could lose genetic information for wings to become a population of flightless beetles. But it doesn't explain the origin of new information for evolving beetles or wings in the first place.

"I didn't walk out of class an evolutionist."

For that type of change, the story goes that duplicating a gene (say a HOX gene, which codes for part of the body plan during an animal's development) and letting the gene mutate further might eventually lead to the evolution of useful new structures. But duplicating and mutating a gene doesn't communicate useful new information any more than repeating part of a sentence and deleting some letters does repeating art of a sentence and deeting some etters doe.

Interestingly, we didn't even really discuss evolution in the sense of "change between kinds of living things" until the very last lecture—just 90 minutes out of a four-month semester! And even then the discussion was highly hypothetical, based on speculative interpretations from historical science. I didn't walk out of class an evolutionist.

HOW I SURVIVED (AND CAME OUT STRONGER)

So how did I navigate all these classes without my biblical worldview changing? Let me pretend to be super artsy and mysterious by answering with an old legend.

Once, back in the days before animal welfare associations, a farmer heard a pitiful braying sound from a dry well. Running to peer down the well, he saw his aged donkey gazing up at him. As hard as the farmer wracked his mind, he couldn't figure out how to retrieve the donkey safely from where it had fallen. So resigning himself to the animal's loss, he grabbed a shovel to fill in the well lest anything else fall in.

Thump.

The first load of dirt hit the donkey's back. But getting buried apparently didn't factor into the animal's afternoon plans. Instead of letting the soil cover him, the donkey shook off each shovelful and stepped up onto the accumulating dirt pile.

Thump.

Shake it off.

Step up.

Thump.

Shake it off.

Step up.

Eventually, this sequence continued until the dirt reached the top of the well—and away the donkey trotted.

In the same way, every shovelful of evolutionary teaching that hit me in school left me two choices. Either I could let the growing weight of unbiblical messages bury my beliefs, or I could deal with each message as it came using the techniques I'll explain in part 3, surrender any remaining concerns to God, and step up to face the next message. In the end, the number of messages I encountered stacked up to a finished degree, and away I went with my faith still very much alive. Not that I'm calling myself a donkey.

During this whole process, how did I handle practical situations like answering evolutionary exam questions? How did I respond to professors' unbiblical remarks in class? What helped me the most to survive the university with my faith intact?

Whoa there. One question at a time! How each Christian student handles individual situations that come up in class will vary by the person and circumstance, requiring individual attention to the convictions of the Holy Spirit. But below are the general approaches I took.

Handling Exam Questions

What is the age of the earth?

A. 13.8 billion years
B. 6.4 million years
C. 4.6 million years
D. 6,000 years

Six thousand is the biblical answer, I knew, pencil poised above the bubble sheet during my first-year biology exam. *But 4.6 million years is the answer we heard in class.*

The test wasn't asking whether I agreed with the material—just whether I'd learned it. So when deciding how to answer questions like this, I'd try to keep the *kind* of question in mind. Multiple choice questions don't let students explain whether or why they agree with something, and busy professors or grad students probably won't analyze exactly which questions students circled "wrong" on a 50-item bubble test anyway. So for those types of questions, I've personally circled the expected answer knowing it was false. But I'm not suggesting this will always be the right thing for students to do in every instance.

Essay questions are a bit different. Whoever marks the exam is going to see each individual response, but students also have flexibility to answer however they want. They can write the expected information but also cite issues with that answer or indicate why they disagree. Personally, I often prefaced essay questions with statements like "It's commonly believed that" or "Some researchers interpret this to mean" to show I understood the material without treating it as objective truth.

Responding to Professors

What about when lecturers made remarks I couldn't agree with? Did I ever stand up and argue with professors right in class?

Personally, I didn't usually feel compelled to openly challenge a lecturer, though in some cases that might be necessary. Most of the time, I felt that standing up and announcing my dissent wouldn't have been helpful. Whether or not it's important to speak up at a given time, of course, will vary by the situation, so if you're in a classroom where God is convicting you to say something specific, it's important to obey! After all, we are called to speak the truth, to do so in love (Ephesians 4:15), and not to skimp on the salt.

Wait, salt?

Yep. In Colossians 4:6, Paul said, "Let your speech always be gracious, seasoned with salt, so that you may know how you ought to answer each person."

The salt, most commentators think, refers to speech that is wholesome, pleasant—even savory. It's the kind of speech Jesus used when responding to his many opponents. He often posed questions to get people thinking, and in school, I found it useful to do the same thing.

"Wait, salt?"

One time, for instance, a professor was talking about Neanderthals and humans as belonging to separate evolutionary branches. "So if you killed a Neanderthal," I asked, "would that be murder?" The professor agreed that it would be, showing that he accepted Neanderthals as being ethical persons. This fits a biblical view that Neanderthals were just ancient people.

Another time, a professor asked our class whether there is any difference between parents teaching their kids about Santa Claus and about Jesus. I did answer that. Knowingly telling kids a fairy tale is a far cry from communicating a worldview which the parents (rightly) hold to be true. And the professor conceded the point.

The Most Important Things I Needed to Survive a University

Through all these experiences at a secular university, I learned firsthand the importance of three personal foundations I'd been building as a Christian young person.

1. Spiritual Foundations

No Christian student can keep their relationship with God strong throughout university life without having an individual relationship with him in the first place. That's where the importance of strong spiritual foundations come in. Spiritual foundations involve building and maintaining a close personal walk with God, including frequent prayer, consistent Scripture study, and biblical literacy. One way I found that helped me fortify these foundations as a student was to turn challenges I encountered at school into opportunities to draw closer to God.

Right after my first anthropology lecture, for instance, I walked outside, headed to a nearby forest, and listened to worship songs. As the course continued, I wrote journal entries addressed to God, telling him how the class irked me. In turn, he encouraged me with truths from his Word. Following up on my course content by bringing it to God not only maintained my spiritual foundations for a secular university but also strengthened those foundations.

2. Intellectual Foundations

As important as spiritual foundations are, they only count if that spirituality is true. That's why I don't know if my faith would have survived college without intellectual foundations, which involve two components: apologetics training and critical thinking skills. The apologetics information I'd been learning since my early teens proved invaluable for helping me stay confident in my beliefs and answer specific questions, especially about evolution. But even with all the apologetics training I'd taken, my classes always raised new information, leaving me with new questions.

For instance, while I'd researched a fair bit about evolution in general before college, I hadn't spent much time specifically learning about the human evolution concepts in my anthropology class. Fortunately, I only had four courses that semester, leaving me time to read an apologetics book that lent biblical perspectives (and scientific observations that weren't in the textbook) about what I was learning.

"My classes always raised new information, leaving me with new questions."

Still, because my usual course load didn't leave much time for apologetics research, I needed to learn how to think like an apologist myself using the critical thinking tools in part 3 to evaluate every message I encountered.

3. Interpersonal Foundations

The final key which helped me survive a university as a Christian student was having interpersonal foundations—a strong Christian support network, including family, peers, local church, and mentors. For instance, knowing that my own mentor, Dr. Helder, was always available to answer my questions freed me from feeling like I had to grapple with the unbiblical information in my classes alone. Meanwhile, attending church, campus ministry events, and a student Bible study connected me to consistent encouragement, prayer support, and the reminder that many other people—both on campus and in the community—shared my biblical beliefs.

And I always knew I could tell my family about any struggle I was facing, confident they'd offer support, prayer, and biblical advice. Before every anthropology lecture, for instance, I'd text my dad, asking him to pray. Both of us understood the nature of the battlefield my class represented. But we also knew that one of our greatest weapons was prayer.

While these three foundations helped me keep my faith in a secular university, I realized they wouldn't mean much beyond myself unless they could also help other Christian students survive the worldview battle. So after I graduated, I began to wonder how other Christian students kept their faith in secular education. How did my experiences at a university compare to those of other Christian students in Canada and around the world?

I didn't know it yet, but that question was about to launch me on the wildest adventure of my life.

Endnotes

1. The idea that God used evolution to create
2. Jane Reece et. al., *Campbell Biology,* Canadian ed. (Don Mills: Pearson Canada, 2014), 493.
3. Ibid., 493–500.
4. More on these in chapter 11
5. Incidentally, the story of evolutionary origins is inconsistent with much observational data, so it does not live up to the title of a "theory," as this article discusses: "Evolution: Not Even a Theory," Answers in Genesis, https://answersingenesis.org/theory-of-evolution/evolution-not-even-theory.
6. We'll look at how to think about these types of explanations, along with any other faith-challenging messages you might hear in secular classrooms and culture, in part 3 of this book. You can also find related critical thinking practice exercises and follow-up resources in appendix C. Stay tuned!
7. Remember, while many people are taught that faith conflicts with science, the real battle is not faith versus science but historical science interpretations based on the religion of man's word versus historical science interpretations based on God's Word.
8. This idea didn't come from the Bible so much as from Aristotle, whose words the church had begun to view as being roughly equal with Scripture. For more information, see Thomas Schirrmacher, "The Galileo Affair: History or Heroic Hagiography?" Answers in Genesis, April 1, 2000, https://answersingenesis.org/creation-scientists/the-galileo-affair-history-or-heroic-hagiography.
9. Certainly, the idea that Satan interfered with fossils doesn't come from the Bible. In fact, biblical history provides the best explanation for fossils, including dinosaurs (see the resources in appendix A for more information). And compared to the idea that everything including dinosaurs happened to arise naturalistically, the explanation that we have a Creator who doesn't lie *is* more straightforward. For more on evaluating explanations, see Patricia Engler, "The First Test of a Logical Explanation," Answers in Genesis, March 10, 2021, https://answersingenesis.org/blogs/patricia-engler/2021/03/10/first-test-logical-explanation, and "Five Criteria for Discerning the Best Explanation," Answers in Genesis, March 17, 2021, https://answersingenesis.org/blogs/patricia-engler/2021/03/17/five-criteria-discerning-best-explanation.
10. William Haviland et. al., *Anthropology: The Human Challenge,* 14th ed. (Belmont: Wadsworth, 2014), 16.

11. Technically, I took this course as an elective in my third year, but it was a second-year level class.

12. This liberal bias in Western universities is not just hearsay but has been confirmed by scholarly research. See Eric Kauffman, "Academic Freedom in Crisis: Punishment, Political Discrimination, and Self-Censorship," Center for the Study of Partisanship and Ideology, March 1, 2021, https://cspicenter.org/reports/academicfreedom.

13. Chris MacDonald and Lewis Vaughn, "Judging Scientific Theories" in *The Power of Critical Thinking,* 4th Canadian ed. (Don Mills: Oxford University Press, 2016), 393–435.

14. Ibid., 407.

15. Theodosius Dobzhansky, "Nothing in Biology Makes Sense Except in the Light of Evolution," *The American Biology Teacher* 35, no. 3 (1973): 125–129.

16. MacDonald and Vaughn (2016), 408–410.

17. Intelligent Design isn't the same as biblical creation, which identifies who the Designer is, and how he created, according to Genesis. See Terry Mortenson, "Intelligent Design or Designer?" Answers in Genesis, March 1, 2020, https://answersingenesis.org/intelligent-design/intelligent-design-or-designer.

18. Douglas Futuyama, *Evolution,* 3rd ed. (Sunderland: Sinauer Associates, 2013), 631.

19. For more on the difference between observational and origins science, see chapter 2.

20. Theodicy refers to explaining why a loving God would allow death and suffering in his creation. (See Terry Mortenson, "Christian Theodicy in Light of Genesis and Modern Science," Answers in Genesis, November 11, 2009, https://answersingenesis.org/reviews/christian-theodicy-in-light-of-genesis-and-modern-science.)

21. Dan Graur, *Molecular and Genome Evolution* (Sunderland: Sinauer Associates, 2016), 2.

GLOBAL PROBLEMS, GLOBAL SOLUTIONS

5

Insights from my investigative globe-trekking mission, 360° in 180

The idea didn't strike at once, like a burning comet. If it did, I probably would have tossed it, still smoldering, onto the "Sounds Fun but Also Impossible" pile, together with notions like building a helicopter from recycled paperclips or riding a live *Brontosaurus*. Instead, the plan took shape in fragments as I pondered the age-old question students wonder, *Is there life after graduation*?

Certainly, I wanted to do apologetics ministry, writing resources to help other Christian students in secular education. But for as long as I could remember, another dream had been tugging at my mind, too—a relentless, indelible drive to explore other places. Go on missions. Have the kinds of adventures with God I'd read about in missionary biographies.

I could still remember feeling that tug at age 11, strapped into the backseat of our minivan about to embark on a family mission trip to Mexico. Before we even left the driveway, I journaled that I was born to be on the road and on the mission field—whatever that meant.

"Could it really work?"

Over the next dozen years, I kept talking about moving overseas. I even earned a diploma for teaching English as a second language, thinking I might work abroad while speaking about apologetics to whoever listened. Still, I didn't want to commit to teaching in just one country for a whole school year.

"There are so many places to go," I told my mom one evening. "If I could just backpack for a while, connect with different ministries and Christian students, write about their stories . . ."

"Well, why don't you try it?" she asked.

Hmm. Could it really work?

CHARTING A COURSE

To research where to go, I grabbed a red marker and printed off two papers: a world map and the IAP Statement on the Teaching of Evolution.[1] I hoped to document Christian students' experiences in secular universities, so nations whose education systems had pledged to teach evolutionary origins as fact seemed like strategic destinations. After shading these nations in red, I held up the map.

The red band wrapped all the way around the world!

Obviously, I reasoned, *I can't travel that far!*

Over the following days, however, the idea refused to leave me. I could legally be away from Canada for six months before losing residency benefits. What if I tried backpacking 360° around the world solo in 180 days, researching how Christian students keep their faith at universities?

It sounded ridiculous. But I gave the idea for the project, 360° in 180, to God. If it was his idea, he'd bring it to pass. He'd open the doors, provide the means, and take care of any troubles that might occur along the way. That's what makes the surrendered Christian life an adventure.

Prayerfully, I began knocking on doors, emailing overseas organizations, and researching visa requirements. I soon secured confirmation to meet contacts in Australia, Japan, and Thailand, though I didn't know exactly when. I also didn't know where else to travel. In other words, I had no idea what I was doing.

But legally, that was okay. To enter most countries on a one-way ticket, I'd only need to produce another ticket proving I'd leave. Therefore, I'd need to plan only one country ahead at any given time, relying on God for every next step—and for provision.

"I'm glad you asked."

I'll travel on savings leftover from my summer jobs since high school, I decided, *and if I run out of cash except for the cost of a ticket back, I'll have to go home*. If this was God's plan, he'd see it through. So late one night with wildly frizzy hair, I booked a one-way flight to Australia.

Launch date loomed only three months away: September 17, 2018.

What happened in those 180 days of investigative globe-trekking? What did I learn about the challenges Christian students are encountering worldwide? How do other students' experiences relate to the spiritual, intellectual, and interpersonal foundations I already found so essential in my university experience?

I'm glad you asked.

360° IN 180: AN OVERVIEW

To test-drive my research methods, I began exploring campuses, interviewing students, and collecting baseline data in Canada before heading to Australia. From there, my massive green backpack and I journeyed to New Zealand, the Philippines, Japan, Thailand, two nations which local Christians' security prevents me from naming, the United Arab Emirates, Turkey, Greece, Switzerland, Germany, Holland, Belgium, France, and Great Britain.

Originally, I hadn't planned to visit many of these places. During my final weeks overseas, in fact, I often didn't know which country I'd enter next—or even where I'd sleep some nights. But whether I ended up staying at ministry bases, mission stations, or with friends of friends (of friends), God always provided. Meanwhile, I lived simply, flying budget airlines, eating inexpensive groceries, and sleeping more in airports than in hotels. And like I experienced in university life, I was learning all the while.

In the Philippines, for instance, I learned that smartphones don't mix with waterfalls. In Greece, I learned that fish market floors have less traction than a whale on a waterslide—and that fish scales can cling undetected to human shins for over 20 minutes. I also learned to never wholly consume any pepper the locals call "Atom Bomb."

Perhaps the finest learning moment of all, however, happened before I flew from Istanbul to Athens. Upon reaching Istanbul's Asian airport, I discovered my flight was leaving from the airport across the Bosporus Sea, on the city's European side. I'd just showed up for a flight not only at the wrong airport—but also on the wrong continent! The next hour's white-knuckle taxi ride cost more than my flight, but pushing 105 mph in a cab is an excellent way to boost blood circulation. And I did catch my plane.

"Thanks, Lord, I thought. I see what you did there!"

Experiences like this taught me to confront every problem by praying, "Thank you for this opportunity to trust you—please help!" And whether I found myself lost, stranded, soaked, homeless, covered in fish scales, missing valuables, or any other predicament, God always somehow did help.

His faithfulness shone on the drearier days, too. Once, as I trudged through a New Zealand rainstorm, a Christian stranger not only offered me a lift but welcomed me into her home for two nights. Another time, when grocery prices prompted me to (figuratively) pray for daily bread, someone handed me *two whole loaves*!

Thanks, Lord, I thought. *I see what you did there!*

The day that bread ran out, someone else randomly offered me another loaf of bread! Ultimately, witnessing God's provision let me glimpse how God is greater than we imagine him to be, and life is simpler than we think it is, because the Bible is truer than we often live like it is.

WHAT 360° IN 180 UNCOVERED

In between gleaning vagabond life lessons, I prioritized finding campus Christians to interview. God creatively answered my prayers to meet the right contacts, connecting me with students, campus ministers, university chaplains, pastors, and retired Christian professors. Often I met interviewees through churches, friends, or student groups. And almost always, I'd ask four key questions.

---

1. What are the challenges of being a Christian student here?
2. What are the opportunities?
3. What advice would you give a first-year Christian student?
4. How can churches effectively support students?

Not surprisingly, students' answers to the first two questions often varied by culture. After all, a Buddhist-born student who converted to Christianity in a communist country would encounter quite different challenges from a church-raised student in rural New Zealand. Yet even across vast distances and diverse cultures, Christians' answers to the last two questions—their advice and ideas for supporting students—sounded uncannily alike.

In other words, while Christian students face diverse problems at universities, the solutions are largely identical. They're applicable to equipping Christian young people all around the world. And as we'll see in chapter 14, these same solutions apply to helping Christians in other challenging contexts, not only to keep their biblical worldviews intact but also to live out those worldviews in ways which impact their surroundings.

So what are these solutions? They all boil down to building and maintaining the same spiritual, intellectual, and interpersonal foundations that I'd found invaluable at my university. You'll hear this from some of the students themselves in just a few minutes. But first, to show you how universally these foundations apply to equipping young people worldwide, I'd like to invite you on a cross-cultural journey, highlighting 12 of the most common challenges Christian students experience.[3]

The West: Canada, Oceania, and Europe

Our journey begins in the West, where the worldview battle we examined in chapter 2 has been raging for nearly two centuries. Remember, that battle began when ideas like human evolution and millions of years started displacing many Westerners' trust in Scripture. Western cultures, as a result, largely began turning to man's word as their authority instead of God's Word. While visiting universities in Canada, Oceania, and (nearly six months later) Europe, I could see firsthand how this cultural shift has created multiple challenges for church-raised students. Examples follow.

1. Intellectual attacks

Because culture has largely dismissed Scripture as unscientific, Western public education often seems to take many unbiblical ideas for granted as facts—or even to directly argue against scriptural teachings. I experienced this in evolutionary classes, where textbooks explicitly attacked belief in biblical creation. Yet because so many professors have been taught that the Bible is bristling with blunders, students in any academic field may encounter arguments against biblical teaching. As a Christian student in Holland shared,

"Textbooks explicitly attacked belief in biblical creation."

> To me, the most challenging thing is the general university culture. In my degree of Hebrew studies, the context is the Old Testament. There are no Christians among my teachers, and if they are, they're very liberal. They assume that everyone else is just as liberal and that no one takes the Bible literally anymore.[4]

2. Relative truth

Once a culture dismisses God's Word as its authority, truth becomes a Jell-O salad of personal opinions. Many students I spoke with in Western countries, therefore, remarked how the worldview norm at their campuses is pluralism—the idea that all "truth claims" are equally valid (except maybe for statements from Scripture). Cultural consensus says there's no absolute truth, no exclusively correct religion, and no one way to be right. So Christian students often encounter the sentiment, "You be you, but don't try to tell me how to be me."[5]

3. Moral disturbances

This attitude fuels the relative moral values characterizing many campus environments—values I saw reflected on countless university bulletin boards. Christian students whose programs, classes, or living situations leave them constantly exposed to (or expected to join in) immorality can begin feeling like Abraham's nephew, Lot, in Sodom and Gomorrah.[6] Jesus' disciple, Peter, described Lot as "greatly distressed by the sensual conduct of the wicked," adding, "as that righteous man lived among them day after day, he was tormenting his righteous soul over their lawless deeds he saw and heard."[7]

Certainly, Jesus' passion for shining God's grace among even the most scandalous sinners reveals the importance of being lights in dark places. (Without maintaining a close connection with our light source, however, we're more likely to become involved in the darkness ourselves. That's one reason why it's so vital to maintain the strong spiritual foundations we'll cover in chapter 6.) But the Bible doesn't say that lights have an easy mission. Instead, 1 Peter warns that Christians in dark places can expect peer pressure, ridicule, and abuse because those who pursue sin "are surprised when you do not join them in the same flood of debauchery, and they malign you."[8]

Living day after day as a Christian in such an environment can become wearing, as a fine arts student in Paris knows well. She explained,

> The main focus in my program was perversion, vulgarity, and all things sexual—it was very weird. Some people were very shocking and violent in their approach to art. I didn't really know how to be in this environment and not be affected by it. It was really hard spiritually to be in a place so dark and so far away from God. . . . Healthwise, the university was really anxiety-provoking because I would go into the school and never know what to expect. I decided, "I can't do this," and took a break.

4. Dark spirituality

When a culture untethers its sense of truth from God's Word, like the art student witnessed, people begin inventing not only their own morals but also their own spirituality. We saw in chapter 3 how secular cultures often gravitate toward mysticism, which lets people feel spiritual without relinquishing their evolutionary beliefs or admitting their accountability to the Creator. While exploring Western campuses, evidence I found of mystical influences included posters promoting Buddhist meditation, yoga, or other Eastern religious practices, as well as business cards for a Wiccan university chaplain. In Australia, I passed a palm reading booth on one campus and an invitation to meetings about discovering the "divine nature within" on another. Later in New Zealand, a university chaplain I met for lunch confided,

> We have many lecturers in anthropology that are practicing Wicca. They use their examples of paganism all the time in their lectures, but if a Christian student were to use an example from *their* faith, they'd be ridiculed.

5. Social hostility

The chaplain's words highlight another challenge I heard in different interviews: Western cultures—and especially universities—are growing downright cold toward Christianity. Given that many Westerners consider Scripture outdated, religion obsolete, and truth offensive, this isn't surprising. The New Testament expressly guarantees that believers can expect to face the world's hatred because we don't belong to it.[9] Our thinking rests on a different foundation than the world's does. So as a Canadian university chaplain observed, students may encounter "some hostility reserved specifically for Christianity."

"We don't belong."

This hostility tends to vary by faculty, with interviewees naming anthropology, geology, or social work as among the most difficult. Recalling my own experiences studying anthropology, I had to agree.

6. Political pushback

One popular type of backlash which students often hear against Christianity is the neo-Marxist[10] idea that Christians are a politicized band of power-hungry, patriarchal oppressors who love nothing more than victimizing innocent minorities. I'd encountered such messages as a student myself, whether listening to lectures or passing posters in hallways. I glimpsed similar messages in Australia, too, including an ad for a play about Christian evangelization being the "white man's" agenda. At the same campus, I also spotted a drawing of a human figure hanging from a cross-shaped gallows, captioned, "Love? No thanks."

I didn't know it yet, but the alleged connection between Christianity and negative political plans would keep reappearing in country after country. Because these types of objections to Christianity, however misguided, are so common, we'll take a closer look at how to respond to such arguments in chapter 10.

Journeying on to Asia

The Philippines

Considering the negativity toward Christianity I'd documented in Canada and Oceania early in my travels, you can imagine how high my eyebrows leapt when I arrived at a Filipino state university and noticed Bible verses plastering the halls. My surprise mounted as I joined local Christians sharing the gospel on campus, only to watch the first students encounter Christ as we shared the gospel.

"Evangelism is not this straightforward in Canada," I told my Filipino friends, "because most Canadians believe science discredits Scripture."

They replied, "We'd just ask, 'Who created science?'"

Students' openness to evangelism on Filipino campuses made sense once I'd read Ken Ham's book *Gospel Reset*, which contrasts the Jewish audience Peter addressed in Acts 2 with the Greek audience Paul encountered in Acts 17.[11] Because the Philippines are mostly Catholic, many Filipinos, like the Jews who responded to Peter's preaching, already accept that sinning against our Creator results in death. These concepts, founded in Genesis, pave the way for the rest of the gospel. So Filipino Christian students share their faith easily.

Japan and Thailand

In Japan and Thailand, however, the next countries I visited, Christian students face a far different situation. That's because these cultures, like the Greek culture Paul tried reaching in Acts 17, rest on a completely different worldview foundation than anything associated with God's Word. While Thailand is nearly 95% Buddhist, about 70% of Japan's population practices a combination of Buddhism and Shintoism.[12, 13] According to a retired diplomat I interviewed, in fact, only 0.2% of Japan's population attends church. Understandably, Japan can be a lonely place for Christian students.

"Japan can be a lonely place for Christian students."

Because Japanese and Thai Christians base their thinking on such a different foundation than their societies', and due to other cultural complexities, Christian students in these nations may encounter additional challenges.

7. Heightened expectations to conform

While Western cultures are typically individualistic, countries like Thailand and Japan are collectivistic. Individualistic cultures revolve around (you guessed it) individuals, valuing independence, personal identity, and the mantra, "It's all about me." Collectivistic cultures, however, revolve around (yep) collectives, valuing teamwork, clan identity, and the mantra, "It's all about the group."

If you grow up as a collectivist, you learn to define your identity by your community, family, and circle of close friends. You must protect that identity, please your in-group, and avoid disgracing them at all costs. So the shame of nonconformity places Christian students under extra pressure to follow cultural and familial expectations, even when those expectations go against a Christian worldview—like bowing to statues or becoming Buddhist monks.

8. Pressure to practice other religions

On that note, it's worth mentioning that Christian students in any nation may face expectations to conform to the religions of their surrounding culture. In the West, this often involves pressure to affirm the values and beliefs of evolutionary-based secular humanism. Meanwhile, in places like Thailand and Japan, the religious nature of cultural expectations can be even more overt.

A graduate in Japan, for instance, shared that for him, pressure to adopt his culture's religious practices began right from elementary school. When his teacher saw him praying as a Christian, she told him that the sight made her want to throw up. She also forbade him from "bringing his religious style into class" when he refrained from bowing to the—um—*deceased* during a Buddhist-style funeral for a classroom hamster.

Restricted Access Nations

All these types of hardships only intensify for Christian students in restricted access nations I visited, known for persecution against Christians. For example, besides the challenges of being non-conformists in a collectivist society, Christian students in a communist nation I entered also face the following opposition.

9. Government pressure

The political tension associated with "foreign religions" (like Christianity) means that after graduation, Christian students can't work in government jobs. But the laws against Christianity go even further.

"Here in this city," explained one student, "the law says that we can believe the gospel, but we can't preach it. But in other cities—no. You can't preach; you can't believe. If you do believe, you could be kicked out of your village. Some Christians just live in the mountains."

10. Censorship

These pressures, however, don't keep Christian students from sharing the gospel. One such time, bystanders called campus security to tell the Christian students to stop. Another time, the Christians had to pause their evangelism upon realizing that they were being followed around campus.

"It's quite dangerous to share your faith in the school," a physics student told me. "The law is that you can maintain your faith, but you cannot share your religion or invite people to it. If you do, and the teacher knows about it, you will get in trouble."

"What would happen?" I asked.

"They would call you to their office and tell you that Christians are not good—that Christians will take your brain. Then the school will make you sign a promise that you will stop sharing your faith."

11. Risk of expulsion

Every student, the physics undergrad continued, has a behavior score. Ways to lose points include missing class, littering on campus, or sharing your faith after being warned to stop.

"If you lose all your points, then what?" I asked.

"You have no right to continue studying at the university."

"So you might have to stop studying if you keep sharing the gospel?"

"Yes, if the teacher knows."

Despite these risks, the tenacity with which the group shares Christ's goodness on campus makes these students some of the most missional I've met.

Islamic Nations

Like in a communist nation, Christian students in the Islamic nations I visited aren't technically allowed to evangelize. Churches do operate, though not necessarily with the same freedom as in many other countries. The United Arab Emirates, for instance, legally allows churches only on controlled compounds, buildings where different congregations gather to worship in various languages between Thursday and Sunday. The congregations' diversity testifies to the country's multiculturalism, as nearly 90% of people living there were born in other countries.

Turkey, however, where I traveled next, is 99.8% Islamic.[14] I found only one Christian student there, a guy who studied nursing. While he knew almost no other Christians at his university, he also didn't hear negative comments about Christianity on campus. Islam is a monotheistic worldview, worshipping a single God, so it makes sense that Christians may face fewer hostile remarks about religion, fewer references to Genesis 1–11 and other biblical accounts being mythical, and possibly less peer pressure like Western Christian students often face. But Christian students in places like Turkey face another kind of challenge—one which may be familiar to Christians on university campuses anywhere.

12. Loneliness

A Turkish campus ministry leader I interviewed said that across six universities in Turkey, a nation of over 82 million people, he knew of only about 100 Christian students. So one of the main challenges for Turkish students involves the comparative lack of a Christian community on campus. Active campus ministry groups do exist in several Turkish cities, however, where this leader quietly serves.

"I found only one Christian student there."

"People don't expect that you will be a Christian as a Turkish person," he said. "When people learn that I'm a Christian from the most conservative place in Turkey, they're just shocked."

OVERCOMING THE CHALLENGES

Christian students encounter a wide variety of challenges around the world. But whether those challenges include intellectual attacks, relative truth, moral disturbance, dark spirituality, social hostility, political pushback, heightened expectations to conform, pressure to practice other religions, government pressure, censorship, risk of expulsion, or just plain loneliness, the same solutions—three types of personal foundations—can help any Christian student overcome all these problems. Here are just a few examples of the insights which Christians worldwide had to share about each foundation.

Spiritual Foundations

One reason why spiritual foundations, or a close personal walk with God fueled with prayer and Scripture study, are so vital is that students are in a spiritual battle. As a Bible school student from Greece observed,

> We need to teach students to spend time with God personally and pray often. Through prayer, we get filled with the Holy Spirit so that God gives us the wisdom, grace, and courage to speak more openly, and he reminds us of Bible verses to help us. And that's very important. Remember, Ephesians 6 says that we aren't struggling against flesh and blood but against spiritual powers.[16] So

students need to spend time with God, praying, worshipping, and being filled with his Spirit.

On the other side of the world, a former Australian professor affirmed how urgently students need spiritual foundations for surviving the spiritual battlefield on campus. When I asked what advice he'd give Christian students, he responded, "Read the Bible every day. Pray every day. Read books about how to pray and how to read the Bible. Without Scripture and prayer, you won't be effective in your university. You'll come under incredible opposition."

On the flip side, how will students withstand this opposition if they've grown up being filtered through faith-based programs focused on entertainment rather than discipleship? I heard more than one campus minister say how often they see church-raised students arrive at a university without really knowing what the Bible teaches or how to study Scripture or how to make God's Word the starting point for their thinking. As the young woman studying art in Paris replied when I asked how churches can support Christian students, "[Students need] a solid foundation on the Bible. Churches should really teach students what the gospel is. If students are not really sure what they believe in, any time a question comes up, they'll be less able to defend themselves."

Intellectual Foundations

Unfortunately, this is exactly what happens all too often among church-raised students—especially when those students haven't been equipped with strong intellectual foundations, including apologetics training and critical thinking skills. A Canadian university chaplain and former youth pastor told me how frequently he watches students grow up without knowing how to defend their faith, confiding:

> A very painful thing for me to watch is when people that I've walked alongside as a youth pastor and tried my best to prepare for life at university lose their faith. I find most often that it's because they were sheltered from very real ideas that others buy into as truth, like evolution. . . . When students get to a university, they meet this theory held as valid for so many, and they feel like they've been betrayed by their faith community. They reject their faith because it has no traction in the world that they're in now.[17]

Halfway around the world from this chaplain who is watching youth lose their faith because they lack intellectual foundations, a young adults' pastor in Dubai commented on the same situation:

> Not only are more and more young people questioning their faith but we are also not equipping them enough to stand firm when their faith is questioned. For example, many youth groups might

tell students, "Don't ask how God created in 6 days because that's not important." But the first question they get from a nonbeliever at campus is, "Really? You believe God created the world in 6 days?" They don't have a logical answer because they didn't get one in youth group.

"They're not rooted."

Even in a restricted access Asian nation, a campus ministry leader is seeing this scenario unfolding among many church-raised students. "They're not rooted," he summarized. "They believe in Jesus or have Christian parents but don't know how to answer the questions that come up."

Likewise, a Bible student in Greece commented, "Many people go to church and have youth group, but they don't have good discipleship to know what they believe—to be stable and rooted."

Greece, Asia, Dubai, and Canada—these places represent four different regions of the world where Christians are observing a discipleship crisis involving a lack of intellectual foundations among church-raised students. Isn't it easier to understand, now, why so many Christian students are leaving the church?

On a hopeful note, I've seen the other side, too. Students who do intentionally build intellectual foundations, study apologetics, and pursue answers for defending their faith know what a difference the effort makes—even in hostile classroom environments. As the Hebraic studies student I met in Holland urges other young people:

> When you do have questions, don't be afraid of them. Instead, start looking for answers. Accept that you have questions, and that's not necessarily a bad thing. Read solid Christians books, articles, and blogs to keep connected with your faith and keep learning more. Even just acknowledging your questions by talking about them with other Christian students helps, and you might find that someone else already has an answer. Going to church helps as well because, even if your specific question isn't answered there, you're still being encouraged, learning, and being built up in your faith.

Interpersonal Foundations

This student's advice brings us to the final type of foundation students need, which emerged as the top interview theme I uncovered in every culture: interpersonal foundations—a strong Christian support network. Specifically, campus Christians emphasized the need for connection with three types of community.

1. A solid local church

Echoing the advice I'd heard from so many other campus Christians worldwide, a Christian student in New Zealand recommends, "Attach yourself to a church immediately so that you can be strong in your faith and remain strong, because it's so easy to go along with the temptations that campus offers."

Unfortunately, multiple campus Christians I met explained that, all too often, students fail to connect with a local church after they move to a university. But as the former professor in Australia observed, "Not attending church is the biggest mistake students make."

2. A Christian peer group on campus

In addition to expressing the urgency of local church involvement, students around the world often remarked on the benefits of Christian student groups. In Thailand, for instance, a political science student said he'd advise other students, "Find a Christian group you're comfortable with and has the right teaching. And make Christian friends since Christians are the minority here."

Because most Christian students worldwide embrace a different worldview than their cultures', Christians virtually anywhere can experience loneliness from being the minority. Combating this challenge is one of the main advantages students mentioned regarding campus ministries. For instance, when I asked an Australian engineering student what had helped her faith stay strong, she replied, "Definitely getting involved with the Christian clubs. You can feel very, very lonely very quickly if you can't seek out a group and know, 'This is where all the Christians are. This is where I'm going to find that support on campus.'"

Finding support from like-minded peers can be especially important for Christian students in hostile environments, like the arts student in Paris faced. As she would advise other students,

> Have Christian friends around you. Don't do it alone. Make sure that you have enough influence from the church as well as from the school. You need to be fed by people who can influence you, encourage you, edify you, and validate you, agreeing with you that what you're having to study is unbiblical.

3. Older adult mentors

This student's advice to find "people who can influence you" hints at one of the top themes from 360° in 180: Christian young people need meaningful connections with godly adult mentors. According to multiple Christians I met, a mentor is anyone available to pray with a student, listen to them, encourage their faith, help them find answers to their questions, and model what following Christ looks like. In the words of a Greek student who nearly lost her faith at her secular university,

> I'd recommend that students find a mentor in church who is older: someone more mature; someone who can give advice; someone who students can speak openly to without having taboos or feeling really bad about discussing or confessing sins. Students need to talk about the things that matter to them without keeping those questions inside and overanalyzing them alone.

Far away in Thailand, another student echoed,

> Spiritual mentors at church help the young people through all their questions and do personal Bible studies with them. I think that is the most efficient way for youth to keep their faith and grow in Christ. I've seen so many people drift away because no one took care of them; no one spent time with them; no one was praying with them.

As an example of someone who didn't drift away from Christianity thanks to the support of older mentors, the Japanese graduate who'd encountered the faith-compromising hamster funeral shared:

> There were a lot of times I just wanted to quit being a Christian, to fall into the shape of the world and say, "He's not my God." How many times I thought that would be easier! But while I didn't have many peers at my church, the elders there were really supportive. They had been Christians since WWII and they knew how hard it was to follow Christ, but they also told me how blessed they were and what God did for them. They loved to tell the story of Elijah on Mount Carmel, standing for God among the Baal worshipers. Without that story and without those elders, I might have lost faith during my younger years.

"Proof that God is faithful"

Like this graduate could tell you, being a mentor doesn't require having a long list of degrees and qualifications. A mentor can simply be anyone with a story of God's faithfulness to share. As a student minister in Holland explained, "Whether they're a homemaker or a CEO, everyone has a perspective that students don't have. And that's the main thing students crave. The best thing that can happen to a Christian student is being mentored by someone who is proof that God is faithful."

By encouraging students' personal walk with God and helping them grapple with difficult questions, mentors contribute to students' spiritual, intellectual, and interpersonal foundations all at the same time. That's what makes mentorship so powerful.

Ultimately, my 360° in 180 backpacking mission showed that all around the world, the challenges Christian students face are as diverse as the cultures themselves. Yet the solutions to those challenges, which revolve around strong spiritual, intellectual, and interpersonal foundations, look similar in every country. Now let's strategize specific ways you can start building and maintaining each type of foundation to not only survive the battlefields of secular education but also to come out stronger.

Endnotes

1. If you remember from chapter 3, over 60 nations' science education foundations have signed this declaration that "scientific evidence has never contradicted" ideas that include human evolution or millions of years. ("Inter-Academy Panel [IAP] Statement on the Teaching of Evolution," Inter-Academy Panel, 2006, http://www.interacademies.org/13901/IAP-Statement-on-the-Teaching-of-Evolution.)
2. This list certainly isn't exhaustive. For instance, Christian students in many countries may also face physical violence for their faith, but I didn't happen to interview anyone experiencing such challenges.
3. *Note:* Some quotes from student interviews relayed in this book have been adjusted for readability or clarity without changing the speakers' intended meanings.
4. For an introduction to responding to relativism, see the following article and its linked resources: Patricia Engler, "False Teach Lie #3: Truth Is up to You," Answers in Genesis, December 2, 2020, https://answersingenesis.org/blogs/patricia-engler/2020/12/02/false-teaching-lie3-truth-up-to-you.
5. Genesis 18:17–19:29
6. 2 Peter 2:7–8
7. 1 Peter 4:4
8. E.g., John 15:18–21; 1 Peter 4:12–16; 2 Timothy 3:12; 1 John 3:13
9. Neo-Marxism is a form of thinking associated with communism, which heavily influenced Western public education beginning from the twentieth century onward. (Lothar Peter, *Marx on Campus: A Short History of the Marburg School* [Boston: Brill, 2019]. See also Jerry Bergman, "The Darwinian Foundation of Communism," *Journal of Creation* 15, no. 1 [2001]: 89–95, https://answersingenesis.org/charles-darwin/racism/the-darwinian-foundation-of-communism.)
10. Ken Ham, *Gospel Reset: Salvation Made Relevant* (Green Forest: Master Books, 2018).
11. Country statistics retrieved January 2021 from the Central Intelligence Agency World Factbook, https://www.cia.gov/library/publications/resources/the-world-factbook.
12. For more on these religions, see Bodie Hodge and Roger Patterson, *World Religions and Cults, Volume 2: Moralistic, Mythical, and Mysticism Religions* (Green Forest: Master Books, 2016).
13. Country statistics retrieved January 2021 from the Central Intelligence Agency World Factbook, https://www.cia.gov/library/publications/resources/the-world-factbook.
14. Ephesians 6:12 (paraphrase)
15. Of note, the chaplain also expressed that he personally doesn't "have a problem at all with evolution" and teaches evolution to youth. However, for information on the biblical and theological pitfalls of suggesting that God created humans and all living things through evolution, check out chapter 2 or https://answersingenesis.org/theistic-evolution.

Part 2

BOOT CAMP

Developing spiritual, intellectual, and interpersonal foundations

SPIRITUAL FOUNDATIONS

6

A close, personal walk with God

"Tell us about another cool Christian, Tangent!"

Tangent.

I'd earned the nickname early at this summer camp where I occasionally counseled between semesters at the university. The title had something to do with my "tendency to go on conversational tangents," although I'm not sure how accurate this description is. (But speaking of needing accuracy, did you know that some fish species hunt by spitting at insects? Wait, what were we talking about?)

"Okay," I began, surveying the wide-eyed little faces poking out from several sleeping bags. *I love telling these campers stories that inspired my faith as a teenager.* "About a hundred years ago, there lived a lady named Gladys Aylward who wanted more than *anything* to tell people in China about Jesus. On her way, a storm left Gladys stranded near a Russian war front where officials seized her passport.

'I'm a missionary!' Gladys told them.

'Oh, a machinist!'

'No, a *missionary*!'

'Yes, a machinist!'

(Around me, the sleeping bags quivered with giggles.)

"Gladys realized that unless God rescued her, she'd be kidnapped into machinist work at a communist factory," I continued. "But that evening, a girl in a black dress walked past Gladys, whispering, 'Don't say a word and follow me!' When Gladys followed, the girl warned, 'You are in grave danger. But at midnight, you will hear a knock on your door. Go with the man—it's your only hope of escape.'"

As I described how Gladys evaded kidnapping, shared the gospel in China, stopped a prison riot, helped end the practice of foot-binding,[1] and single-handedly led 100 orphans safely through an active war zone, I felt it again—that sense of amazement at how God works through those who trust him.

While my brother and I were growing up, my mom often read us missionary accounts like this, which I continued devouring as a teenager. Hearing how everyday humans executed extraordinary exploits for God, finding him faithful even in the darkest trials, made me want to know God that way, too. Speaking from personal experience, I'd suggest that just like apologetics affirms our faith by demonstrating intellectually why the Bible is true, other Christians' stories can activate our faith by showing what happens when people live out the Bible's truth personally. Such stories inspired me to pray more, study Scripture, and make my faith real as a teenager—in other words, to build stronger spiritual foundations.

WHAT ARE SPIRITUAL FOUNDATIONS ANYWAY?

I've mentioned before that strong spiritual foundations, a must-have for surviving a secular university as a Christian, involve building and maintaining a close, personal walk with Christ. But what does that even mean?

Essentially, spiritual foundations are all about your individual relationship with God. This relationship begins in earnest when you first encounter Jesus. By way of analogy, what would happen if you asked someone to be your personal friend but then rarely talked to them, listened to them, or even acted like you knew them? That wouldn't be much of a relationship, would it? Later, if you began spending most of your time with people who didn't want anything to do with that friend, how likely would you be to stray from the relationship that you had originally said you wanted?

"Falling in love"

This is basically what happens to many students' relationships with God at a secular university if they haven't built strong spiritual foundations. No Christian student can *keep* a relationship with God without *having* their own relationship with him in the first place. So what does it take to have a close relationship with God?

Well, how would you develop and maintain any relationship? Through consistent communication. Spending time in Scripture lets you receive communication *from* God, while prayer and worship are ways you can communicate *to* God. The more you know God, the more you'll want to communicate with him. The more you communicate with him, the more you'll get to know him. It's a beautiful cycle, which some call falling in love.[2]

Let's look at how to cultivate this spiritual relationship. We'll explore practical ways to begin building stronger spiritual foundations now, anticipate possible counterattacks, and strategize how to maintain these foundations throughout secular education. To start, let's see what the Bible (not to mention scientific research) says about the benefits of building strong spiritual foundations while you're young.

What Scripture Says

If anyone from biblical times could talk about spiritual foundation-building as a young person, it'd be David—you know, the little guy who slaughtered a giant, became a king, and wrote most of Psalms. His close relationship with God since youngsterhood (because that should be a word) shines clearly through passages like Psalm 71:5–6: "For you, O Lord, are my hope, my trust, O LORD, from my youth. Upon you I have leaned from before my birth; you are he who took me from my mother's womb. My praise is continually of you."[3]

Later in Psalms, David offers some of the most relevant spiritual foundation-building advice geared specifically toward young people: "How can a young man keep his way pure? By guarding it according to your word. With my whole heart I seek you; let me not wander from your commandments! I have stored up your word in my heart, that I might not sin against you."

David's son, Solomon, also understood the urgency of actively pursuing wisdom from God as a young person, telling his own little nipper, "My son, be attentive to my words; incline your ear to my sayings. Let them not escape from your sight; keep them within your heart. For they are life to those who find them, and healing to all their flesh."[4]

Fast forward to the New Testament, and you'll spot similar active wording in Paul's foundation-building advice for his own spiritual son Timothy:

> Have nothing to do with irreverent, silly myths. Rather train yourself for godliness; for while bodily training is of some value, godliness is of value in every way, as it holds promise for the present life and also for the life to come. . . . Let no one despise you for your youth, but set the believers an example in speech, in conduct, in love, in faith, in purity.[5]

In Paul's next letter to Timothy, the importance of developing solid foundations in God's Word *from childhood* appears again:

> But as for you, continue in what you have learned and have firmly believed, knowing from whom you learned it and how from childhood you have been acquainted with the sacred writings, which are able to make you wise for salvation through faith in Christ Jesus. All Scripture is breathed out by God and profitable for teaching, for reproof, for correction, and for training in righteousness, that the man of God may be complete, equipped for every good work.[6]

Did you notice what all these passages have in common? For one thing, they indicate that spiritual foundation-building takes intentional effort. That's clear from all the action words like *seek*, *store*, *pay attention*, *incline*, *keep*, *train*, and *continue*. But look back at these passages, and you'll see they also show that the work required to build strong spiritual foundations is more than worth it.

What Research Says

Not surprisingly, scientific research backs what Scripture says about the benefits of building strong spiritual foundations early. Let's look at a couple of examples: the National Survey of Youth and Religion from 2009 and Barna research from 2019.

The National Study of Youth and Religion

After surveying over 2,400 American youth once at ages 13–17 and again at ages 18–23, researchers with The National Study of Youth and Religion (NSYR) found four key commonalities among religious teens who kept their faith into young adulthood:

1. They prayed frequently.
2. Their parents were strongly committed to the religion.
3. Their faith was important to them in their everyday life.
4. They read Scripture frequently.[7]

Really, most of these factors boil down to maintaining a close daily walk with God. And while the teens who scored lowest in these four areas only had a 0.4% chance of later being among the most spiritually committed adults, the teens who scored highest had an 85% chance.[8]

Although these four points aren't a magic formula for staying faithful to Christ in college, this study does show the importance of building solid spiritual foundations early and the incredible role that Christian families and mentors play in helping youth develop these foundations. It also shows that a lot of the onus is on young people to take responsibility for their own relationship with God in everyday life.

Barna Study: Faith for Exiles

Backing up both the NYSR findings and my 360° in 180 interviews is another major study, which Barna researchers documented in their book *Faith for Exiles*.[9] The study revealed that by 2019, only 10% of church-raised American young adults appeared to embrace a thriving biblical worldview.[10]

What practices set apart these faithful few, whom the researchers dubbed *resilient disciples*?[11] The researchers identified five traits that resilient disciples tend to display:

1. They base their identities on a close, personal relationship with Jesus, fueled by prayer, Scripture reading, and worship. (Sounds a lot like having strong spiritual foundations!)

2. They exercise "cultural discernment": beginning with a firm basis in biblical authority,[12] they flex their biblical critical thinking muscles to walk wisely in an ungodly world. (Sounds suspiciously like having intellectual foundations!)
3. They engage in close relationships with other Christians, including godly adult mentors. (Sounds like having interpersonal foundations!)
4. Their churches and mentors disciple them to pursue their God-given callings and embrace work as ministry.
5. They live as countercultural Christ followers, embracing the church's mission to love others and make disciples.

I'd suggest those last two traits are outcomes of having strong spiritual and interpersonal foundations grounded in a commitment to biblical authority, as we'll see again in chapter 14. For now, it's clear that however we slice these research findings, studies affirm that a close, daily walk with God is absolutely key for Christian youth to keep a vibrant faith into adulthood.

"Keep a vibrant faith."

This kind of Christian walk involves not only reading God's words but also applying them to every part of life. As Jesus said in Matthew 7:24–25, "Everyone who hears these words of mine and puts them into practice is like a wise man who built his house on the rock. The rain came down, the streams rose, and the winds blew and beat against that house; yet it did not fall, because it had its foundation on the rock."

SEVEN WAYS TO BUILD STRONGER SPIRITUAL FOUNDATIONS

What are some practical ways to build rock-solid spiritual foundations? To answer, I'm going to share seven stories with applications for spiritual disciplines and discipleship. (Just so we're clear, the fact that I'm about to discuss spiritual disciplines doesn't mean I'm some mushy, halo-wearing saint or that I never fail to exercise these disciplines myself the way I know is necessary. But these *are* truths which I've found both personally important and biblically essential.)

There's a lot more to these seven subjects than we'll have time to cover. Entire books exist on each, which I'd encourage you to dig into yourself. But these stories will help you get started.

Story 1: Country Music SOS—*Prayer*

It normally takes more than two chords of country wedding music to get me crying, but I had a good excuse. Wouldn't pulling six-day work weeks coleading a busy greenhouse department make *anyone* overtired? And when you're overtired while expecting an emotional event (in this case a friend's wedding) and mushy music starts playing—well, a couple of tears make sense. But when I tried decreasing the music volume on my mom's phone, telling her, "I'm just under a lot of work pressure—I can see why CEOs die early,"[13] things went slightly berserk.

See, I didn't realize my mom had an app which sends an SOS message, two pictures, and five seconds of audio to an emergency contact if you tap the power button three times while facing impending death (or while trying to quiet country music). So my dad was understandably perplexed when he, in the middle of work, received a text from my mom reading, "SOS, I NEED HELP," together with two pictures of our kitchen and a recording of me saying, "I can see why CEOs die early!"

At least the incident reminded me that my dad will respond whenever I'm apparently in trouble. But if I only talked to him while in danger or while facing country music, we wouldn't have much of a relationship. I know he'll help me *because* of our relationship, but that relationship doesn't subsist on emergency texts. It's an ongoing, daily thing.

"Emergency texts"

Prayer works the same way. Sure, we call on God when we need help or want to say thanks for something, the way I might call my dad. But the sort of prayer that fuels a strong relationship with our heavenly Father runs deeper than that. It, too, is an ongoing, daily thing.

Scripture repeatedly reflects the nature of prayer as continuous contact with God, urging us to pray without ceasing (1 Thessalonians 5:17), pray at all times in the Spirit (Ephesians 6:18), pray constantly (Romans 12:12), and continue steadfastly in prayer (Colossians 4:2). Such prayer includes thanksgiving (Philippians 4:6), rejoicing (1 Thessalonians 5:16), and praise (Hebrews 13:15), besides making requests.

Because we belong to Christ, everything we face in life we give to him (1 Peter 5:7), and everything we do, we do for him (Colossians 3:23). So we can take our moment-to-moment thoughts about whatever we're facing, feeling, or doing and turn them toward God in continuous prayer.[14]

Along with offering these ongoing "micro-prayers," it's important to set aside some specific daily prayer time—beginning with even just a few minutes a day. The story that encouraged me to take prayer times more seriously as a teenager came from the persecuted church in China, where a family known as the Kwangs lived. Whether escaping execution, assisting underground believers, or introducing would-be arrestors to Christ, the Kwangs watched God work in incredible ways. When a visitor asked about the secret to such an amazing relationship with God, the Kwangs replied, "One has to sacrifice to follow the Lord this way."

"You mean that one has to be persecuted before having this kind of faith?" the visitor asked.

"No," they answered, "the sacrifice is prayer."[15]

Prayer, like any worthwhile relationship, requires a sacrifice of time and effort. Paul spoke of laboring in prayer,[16] while Jesus illustrated the need for persistency in prayer with a parable about a widow's relentless quest for justice.[17] Jesus also modeled persistent prayer himself, even pulling all-nighters to pray. But hard work pays off. Powerful and effective,[18] prayer is key not only to building strong spiritual foundations for university life but also to influencing our cultures for Christ.

Even if those cultures love tear-jerking country music.

Practical ideas for pepping up your prayer life:

- To help structure your designated prayer times, try posting prayers or prayer points near a specific place you like to pray or listing them in a notebook you can take with you anywhere.
- Try prayer journaling, where you tell God about your day and write him your thoughts.
- Start or join a prayer group. Praying with others can't replace your personal prayer times, but it can supply encouragement, support, and accountability.
- Post verses and quotes about the importance (and rewards) of prayer where you'll see them.
- Try turning thoughts, feelings, disappointments, joys, mental conversations, worries, or anything else you find on your mind into prayers. (This is also part of "taking every thought captive," as 2 Corinthians 10:5 mandates.)

Story 2: Staying in Tune—*Worship*

Standing on a European street, guitars in hand, we could only guess whether our songs were making much impact. What could a few English worship lyrics change in a nation where evangelicals represent only 0.2% of the population? Discouragement weighed heavily on our short-term mission team, which I'd joined one summer during college. Still, we returned to sing on the streets again the next morning, handing out invitations for the evening's worship service.

After the service, our team leader relayed what a woman from the audience had told him. "When I came to this service," she'd said,

"I didn't believe in any God. But as you all stepped onto the stage to worship, I realized he exists. I knew it from the looks on your faces."

Walls break down in the context of worship. They broke in Europe when a few travelers glorified God on the streets as they broke in Philippi when Paul and Silas praised God in jail.[19] When we worship, we look to our infinite God instead of our finite selves, we remind ourselves the truth of who God is and what he's done, and we declare this truth to the surrounding spiritual darkness. That's why after my first anthropology lecture at my university where I'd heard so many unbiblical—but persuasive—ideas presented as fact, I went outside and listened to worship music.

Like the Israelites who won a war through praise,[20] we, too, can follow God on the battlefields of secular universities armed with a mindset of worship. Worship is a lifestyle, part of rejoicing always, giving thanks in everything, and praying without ceasing.[21] It's an attitude overflowing from a life rooted in Christ so that everything we do—including sitting in classes—is done for God, in recognition that all our lives belong to him. It's what we, being created for God's glory,[22] are designed to do.

Worship keeps us in tune with our Creator.

Practical ideas to "amp up" your worship life:

- Create an instrumental worship playlist for doing schoolwork. The lack of lyrics removes a layer of distraction, letting your mind keep working while your spirit sings along.
- Try kicking off your daily prayer time with worship.
- Check yourself throughout the day: what song is in your head?
- Write out your favorite worship lyrics (psalms count, too) to post where you'll see them. Or if you're the creative type, try incorporating them into artwork.
- Take study breaks to sing or play an instrument—it's good for your brain anyway.

Story 3: Hilariously Hairy Hazards—*Biblical Literacy*

The music kept playing, but we all knew something was wrong. I was a teenager at the time, costumed as a first-century merchant in a gospel dramatization held at our city's largest theater. Waiting behind the curtain with the other cast members, I listened as the actors playing Jesus and Satan sang their way through the wilderness temptation scene.[23] At least, Satan was *supposed* to be singing. Why had he stopped?

“It is also written, ‘Do not test the Lord your God,’” Jesus’ voice answered to no one in particular.

Apparently, I thought, *the audience is witnessing a bizarrely one-sided temptation out there.*

And what were all those gagging noises?

Not until intermission did we learn what happened—how the actor playing Satan had become so animated, he’d somehow inhaled part of his own wig, gagged on a hairball, and run offstage to throw up! Of course, I’m deeply sympathetic. But I still fall over laughing whenever I think about it.

“And what were all those gagging noises?”

Once I’ve dried my tears of mirth and stood back up, I remember what the *real* temptation scene teaches. It’s hard to imagine a tougher spiritual battle than Satan confronting us face-to-face while we’re worn down and all alone. Yet that’s exactly what Jesus experienced. And how did Jesus parry Satan’s every blow? With the sword of the Spirit, which is the Word of God.

In the spiritual battlefield of secular university, where Christian students may also feel worn down and alone, the same weapon applies. *Students need to know the Scriptures.* We can’t make God’s Word the foundation for our thinking unless we’re aware of what the Bible says in the first place and how its teachings apply to every aspect of life. Only through a deep familiarity with God’s Word can we readily detect lies, deflect temptations, protect our hearts, correct our thoughts, connect more fully with God, and live the life we’re designed for—on earth and in eternity.

I can’t possibly overstate the importance of consistently filling ourselves up with God’s Word.

It’s *far* more vital than avoiding the hazards of hairballs.

Practical ideas for digging deeper into Scripture:

- Find a Bible reading plan that works for you—and stick with it.
- Make sure you’re not missing out on the Old Testament—even parts that Sunday schools rarely cover.
- If you haven’t read the whole Bible, set a goal to do so—*before* university, if possible!
- Join (or start) a solid Bible study group.
- Tap into the amazing Bible study tools out there, take advantage of the maps and memos in study Bibles (but remember they’re not the inspired words of God), or look up potentially confusing passages in online commentaries.
- Try listening to an audio Bible during your spare time or daily tasks, like commuting.

Story 4: To Sunday School, and Beyond!—*Scripture Memorization*

I'd had nightmares about something like this. Shaking in my sandals, I stood on the dirt floor of the shanty as my wide eyes faced the expectant ones of my audience.

I had nothing to tell them.

Sure, I'd jumped at the chance to spend a few months in Uganda after high school. Sure, I'd offered to "help with the kids" at church my first day there. But I hadn't realized that "helping" meant literally leading Sunday school.

"Preach about Moses!" one girl suggested.

Moses?

In a flash, it came back to me—a passage about Moses from Hebrews 11, which I had learned long ago through a program called Bible Quizzing. Seven years in quizzing had helped me study and memorize large portions of New Testament books alongside friends. I say this as an encouragement. Even young people can and do commit much truth from God's Word to memory. Certainly you can, too.

The benefits it reaps are enormous. Long after quizzing, I continued drawing on previously learned verses not only in moments like the "nightmare" scene in Africa, but also during the constant indoctrination by evolutionary (or otherwise unbiblical) messages in my university. Even now, I can rest assured that God will continue reminding me of scriptural truths for any other faith-challenging moment the future might bring. Even if that moment requires teaching Sunday school.

Practical ideas for memorizing more Scripture:

(PS—these tips also apply to studying exam notes in a university!)

- Read it! In Bible Quizzing, a friend of mine developed a helpful chapter memorization tool she called the five-verse method, where she'd read each verse five times, each paragraph five times, and the chapter five times, until she'd learned the whole thing.
- Listen to it! As a Bible quizzer, I enjoyed listening to New Testament audio dramatizations to memorize passages. Sometimes I'd edit the audio files to repeat each verse several times. Then I'd go for a walk and listen to them.
- Say it! One tactic I've found especially useful is to combine the powers of repeated reading, listening, *and* speaking by recording myself saying each verse several times.
- Sing it! Setting verses to music, whether a song you like or a tune you invent yourself, lets you remember them long-term.

Story 5: Better than the Beale Bundle—*Wisdom*

71, 194, 38, 1,701. These numbers are the first in a series of digits which one anonymous treasure hunter said ruined his life. The digits come from the Beale Papers, three ciphers which allegedly say where three tons' worth of gold, silver, and jewels are sequestered. "Before giving the papers to the public," Mr. Anonymous wrote in 1885, "I would give them a little advice, acquired by bitter experience. It is, to devote only such time as can be spared from your legitimate business to the task . . . [and] never, as I have done, sacrifice your own and your family's interests to what may prove an illusion."[24]

"*Anonymous treasure hunter*"

Not that everyone heeded this warning. Some still seek the Beale treasure today. Others argue it's a hoax. But what if it doesn't matter? What if the whole mystery is a moot point because all along there's lain in plain sight a treasure map to riches which makes the Beale fortune look like used dental floss?

According to Solomon, this is just the case: "Blessed is the one who finds wisdom, and the one who gets understanding, for the gain from her is better than gain from silver and her profit better than gold. She is more precious than jewels, and nothing you desire can compare with her."[25]

Time and again, Solomon likened wisdom to a treasure, bringing profits which may include—but far outweigh—material wealth.[26] This treasure is especially valuable for Christian students who need as much wisdom to navigate the dynamic challenges of secular university as the disciples needed when Jesus told them, "Behold, I am sending you out as sheep in the midst of wolves, so be wise as serpents and innocent as doves."[27]

How do we find this treasure? According to verses like Proverbs 2:3–6, Proverbs 9:10, and James 1:5, the three-pronged key to wisdom is to fear God, know God, and ask God for wisdom. Interestingly, Solomon also said that fearing God involves hating evil.[28] As we seek God in our search for wisdom, we begin to love what he loves and hate what he hates. Knowing him, after all, is the ultimate treasure.

Practical ideas for seeking wisdom:

- Read Proverbs. Conveniently, this Bible book includes 31 chapters—one for every day of the month.
- Learn from godly mentors. Anyone who's known God for years has likely stockpiled pearls of wisdom from him, and you can ask them for some (more on that in chapter 8).

- Read books by wise Christians who share what they've learned from years of life with Christ.
- Ask God for wisdom, read his Word expecting to find it, and write down what happens.

Story 6: The Corniest Tale—*Identity*

In the golden evening glow, I paused at the field's edge and sized up my opposition. Row upon row, they stood there, silently challenging me. But I would overcome them. They were just cornstalks, after all.

I glanced at the map of the corn maze my family was visiting then folded the paper. A map might compromise the fun. Besides, while I didn't have the sharpest sense of direction, I figured I should *certainly* be able to outwit a cornfield.

"Perfect"

The setting sun is behind me, I thought, entering the labyrinth, *so that's west. The maze exits to the south. So, using the sun, I can consistently orient myself toward the exit.*

Perfect.

Except for one detail.

The *setting sun* dropped behind the cornstalks, leaving me lost in the dark, alone with a million ears of corn. I think they were laughing at me.

"What took you so long?" asked my family when an older, wiser version of myself finally emerged from the maze. Apparently, my family had read the map.

Years later during 360° in 180, I heard Christians in New Zealand say how easily church-raised students can get lost, too—not in a cornfield, but in the battlefields of secular university.

"When youth are still at home, their parents, school, sports clubs, and friendships are constants in their life, part of their identity," said the Christians. "But when they move away to universities, all of that disappears. Then students can feel like they must reconstruct who they are and who they want to be."

Like I became lost when I based my position on a fading landmark (the sun), church-raised students may grow disoriented if they stake their identities in anything potentially transient, like friend groups, career goals, relationships, or anything else *on earth*. That's why Christian students need to enter universities with their identity grounded in the only true fixed point available—not the sun, but the Son.

By securely knowing who God is, and who we are in light of him, we can navigate secular classrooms and cultures with confidence, not just in *who* we are but in *whose* we are. If we know we're his, we know that we don't need to follow the crowd, compromise our biblical beliefs (including with evolutionary ideas), or join in questionable groups and activities in order to belong. This is just one more reason to know the map God gave us for navigating the labyrinth of life: his Word, the Bible.

Practical tips for godly identity formation:

- When you're studying Scripture, highlight or write down passages that reveal who you are in Christ.
- How do you think about who you are? Are you basing your identity in fading landmarks or in who Christ is, what he's done, and who he's created and called you to be?
- Watch the messages your mind plays about yourself, recalibrating them to Scripture, as necessary.

Story 7: Not About to Bow—*Boundaries*

Wait a second, thought the Christian student, watching as several idols were placed on the chapel communion table. *This is not okay!*

He'd known that while training to become a hospital chaplain, he would likely encounter unbiblical ideas. But being told to bow before literal idols? This seemed like something straight from the Old Testament!

While everyone else walked forward to bow, the student took two steps *back*. Naturally, his response didn't sit well with some of the others present.

"You think you're better than us?" they accused the student. "You don't want to be part of this group?"[29]

In reply, he explained that he could learn about others' religious practices by respectful observation rather than participation.

How do I know this story? Because it happened to my dad.

Before he began chaplaincy training, he wrote down the non-negotiables of his biblical beliefs—like the Bible's inerrancy, Christ's divinity, and the fact that Jesus is the *only* way to God—on a paper contract for my mom and him to sign. If he started drifting from the non-negotiables, she was to talk to him, and, if he didn't listen, talk to his dad or denominational district office.

Like Daniel, who "purposed in his heart" that he would not compromise his beliefs in Babylon by eating the king's food, my dad set clear personal boundaries *before* beginning training. Christians I met in restricted access nations, where other religions permeate every facet of culture, also emphasized the importance of setting clear, biblically based boundaries guiding what they'll participate in. For Christian students expected to comply with unbiblical teachings, attitudes, or actions at secular universities, the same principle applies. If you draw clear lines beforehand, knowing *why* you've drawn them (based on Scripture—and often common sense), you'll be far better prepared to resist pressure to bow to your culture's idols.

Practical ideas for setting boundaries:

- Start thinking about various pressures or temptations you'll likely face at a university. Study what Scripture says about each and consider how to think and act biblically in response.
- Study how the Bible speaks to different controversial topics in culture so you can graciously respond from *Scripture* rather than from secondhand convictions you've passively absorbed from church or family.
- Like my dad did by writing a contract, consider the non-negotiables of your biblical worldview, ask someone to respond if they notice you compromising on those beliefs, and formulate a plan for handling questions and doubts (more on this in chapter 9).
- Bring a parent or mentor, and optionally, peer(s), into your boundary setting and accountability plan so you know you're not standing alone.

MAINTAINING YOUR FOUNDATIONS

Now that we've thought about ways to *prepare* strong spiritual foundations through prayer, worship, Bible study, Scripture memorization, identity formation, wisdom seeking, and boundary setting, let's strategize how to *maintain* those foundations during secular university. Even well-built structures crumble if neglected, and spiritual foundations are no different. How will you guard your relationship with God when armies of assignments, legions of lectures, and troupes of unbiblical teachings fight for your time—and for your heart? Here are a few suggestions.

Beware the Little Things

A verse in Song of Solomon, which considers human romance as a reflection of Christ and the church, says, "Catch us the foxes, the little foxes that spoil the vines."[30] Granted, pest control might not seem especially romantic. The point is that just like unchecked foxes can destroy an entire harvest, *little things* often pose the greatest threats to healthy relationships—including our relationship with God. A little act of love neglected, a little thought unchecked, a little careless word unleashed, a little boundary over-stepped . . . sooner or later, little compromises add up.

"*Little compromises add up.*"

And Satan knows it. If you're a strong Christian, do you think he'll likely tempt you to quit prayer, Bible study, and Christian fellowship entirely, or commit a devastating sin at once? That's not how a smooth con artist works. Often, major cons require a series of miniscule steps. Online romance scammers, for instance, have robbed people's life savings by posing as a lover before asking for a little money at a time, always providing justification for the victim to comply with each request.

In the same way, Satan may try robbing you of your spiritual foundations by suggesting you pray less, skip worship more, or merely skim your Bible, always with justification—like that exam coming up. But remember, in the words of well-known devotional writer Oswald Chambers, "You no more need a holiday from spiritual concentration than your heart needs a holiday from beating."[31] Christ is your life. So battling each temptation with the sword of the Spirit, fight for your relationship with him by staying faithful and pure in the little things.

Steward Your God-Given Time

The fact that academic responsibilities may seem like justification for neglecting your spiritual foundations raises the time management question. How can you pour the necessary time into schoolwork without neglecting spiritual growth?

One way is to ask God for wisdom when considering your priorities. Remember, your priorities aren't necessarily the things you say are important—they're the things you *actually invest* most of your time and energy into. What priorities, like spiritual health, academics, relationships, and physical health (including eating healthily, sleeping, and exercising) have the most long-term value, and what "priorities" (like reality TV reruns) might you need to reconsider?

Another way to succeed academically without neglecting your spiritual foundations is to approach education as worship. God created you for specific purposes, and the education which he's given you opportunity to pursue is equipping you to fulfill his callings. With this mindset, every hour you invest in your education can be an hour offered to God. You can bring him every detail of your academic life, asking him to guide you through all of it.

"you have the time."

Even while serving Christ through academics, you'll still need time set aside for being with him. Just ask Mary and Martha. You know the story from Luke 10—how Martha prepared dinner to (literally) serve Jesus while Mary sat at his feet. Martha seemed to think Mary a slacker, yet Jesus said Mary chose the right way to spend her time. And she was rewarded for it.

Like how the Israelites never lacked when they tithed their money back to God,[32] what if when we tithe our time to Jesus, the resulting wisdom, strength, and insight he provides helps us spend the rest of our time even better, so we don't lack for a minute? As a pastor I once heard in university said, "You have the time to do everything God wants you to."

Individualize Your Action Plan

Ultimately, taking responsibility to use your time wisely, cultivate your relationship with God, and make your faith your own is up to you. Because God wires us uniquely as individuals, the specifics of how we form habits for staying close to God will look different for each of us. So based on what you know about yourself, you can chart an individual action plan for staying spiritually strong throughout college by asking yourself a few questions:

- Knowing you, what are some intentional practices you can do to grow in the different spiritual foundation-building areas we talked about? (For instance, being the outdoorsy type, I liked taking my Bible and ukulele outside to seek God on a foothill or beach before class.)
- What do you see as potentially coming between you and your maintenance of these practices? What can you do to overcome or prevent these problems?
- How can you include other Christians in your spiritual development, for prayer, encouragement, and accountability?[33]

In the end, by intentionally cultivating a close, moment-to-moment walk with God—the kind of lifestyle which faith heroes like Gladys Aylward exercised—you'll not only be strengthening your spiritual foundations for college, but also living the life God created you for: a life of relationship with him.

How can you defend that relationship intellectually when others ask about—or argue against—the hope you have in Christ (1 Peter 3:15)?

Let's find out.

Endnotes

1. At that time in China, normal-size feet were considered ugly on women. So most girls' feet were forcibly scrunched up and bound to prevent growth, making walking difficult for life.
2. Jesus loved us first, while we were yet sinners (Romans 5:8).
3. Psalm 119:9–11
4. Proverbs 4:20–22
5. 1 Timothy 4:7, 8, 12
6. 2 Timothy 3:14–17
7. Christian Smith and Patricia Snell, *Souls in Transition: The Religious and Spiritual Lives of Emerging Adults*, ebook ed. (New York: Oxford University Press, 2009), 220, accessed on Google Books.
8. Ibid.
9. David Kinnaman and Mark Matlock with Aly Hawkins, *Faith for Exiles: 5 Ways for a New Generation to Follow Jesus in Digital Babylon*, ebook ed. (Grand Rapids: Baker Books, 2019), accessed on Hoopla.
10. The other 9 in 10 church-raised young adults had stopped identifying as Christians (22%), had stopped regularly attending church (30%), or still went to church but did not apparently embrace or live out core biblical beliefs (38%). (Ibid., 47)
11. Defined as "Christ followers who (1) attend church at least monthly and engage with their church more than just attending worship services; (2) trust firmly in the authority of the Bible; (3) are committed to Jesus personally and affirm he was crucified and raised from the dead to conquer sin and death; and (4) express desire to transform the broader society as an outcome of their faith" (Ibid., 47). Resilient disciples also had to affirm at least one "exile statement," such as "God is more at work outside the church than inside, and I want to be a part of that" (Ibid., 44), which may have nuanced who ended up in the resilient disciple category.
12. Summarizing the point that a defining hallmark of resilient disciples is their stance on biblical authority, the authors concluded, "In short, the lived reality of resilients is that the Bible is authoritative and central to their faith" (Ibid., 128).
13. Please don't panic if you know a CEO. I'd recently learned from my psychology classes that stressful jobs tend to take a toll on physical health over time—that's all.
14. Interestingly, "conversational intimacy" with Jesus is a hallmark habit of resilient disciples, according to the Faith for Exiles study. ("Only 10% of Christian Twentysomethings Have Resilient Faith," Barna Research Group, September 24, 2019, https://www.barna.com/research/of-the-four-exile-groups-only-10-are-resilient-disciples.)
15. Paraphrased from Brother David, Dan Wooding, and Sarah Bruce, *God's Smuggler to China* (Wheaton: Tyndale House Publishers, 1981), 218.
16. Colossians 4:12
17. Luke 18:1–8
18. James 5:16

19. Acts 16:25–31

20. 2 Chronicles 20:1–22

21. 1 Thessalonians 5:16–18

22. Isaiah 43:7

23. Matthew 4:1–11

24. Anonymous (James B. Ward), *The Beale Papers, Containing Authentic Statements Regarding the Treasure Buried in 1819 and 1821 Near Bufords, in Bedford County, Virginia, and Which Has Never Been Recovered* (Lynchburg, Virginia: Virginian Book and Job Print, 1885), 12–13.

25. Proverbs 3:13–15

26. E.g., Proverbs 8:10, 16:16

27. Matthew 10:16

28. Proverbs 8:13

29. These are examples of straw man fallacies, which we'll talk about in chapter 12.

30. Song of Solomon 2:15

31. Oswald Chambers, "April 15: The Relapse of Spiritual Concentration," in *My Utmost for His Highest: Selections for the Year* (New York: Dodd, Mead & Co, 1937), 106.

32. E.g., Malachi 3:10

33. More on this in chapter 8

INTELLECTUAL FOUNDATIONS

7

Apologetics knowledge and critical thinking skills

"Some people dismiss Darwin's ideas as 'just a theory,'" your professor states, quoting from this week's assigned textbook chapter. "However, as we have seen, the *pattern* of evolution—the observation that life has evolved over time—has been documented directly and is supported by a vast amount of evidence."[1]

"Choose your own adventure."

As the lecture continues, you listen to example after example of this "evidence," each case backed by a professionally illustrated diagram.[2] You can think of answers to some of the evolutionary arguments, but others you've never heard before. A couple of times, your textbook has even responded to arguments you'd previously heard *against* evolution! All the intelligent, authoritative professors and textbooks you've encountered clearly take evolutionary origins for granted. And looking around the lecture hall, you suspect all your classmates do, too.

Here's where you get to choose your own adventure. Do you . . .

Option A

Panic. Obviously, your church and parents didn't know the whole story when they taught you about creation and the Bible. The people you've encountered at the university understand what they're talking about. Now that you've been enlightened with higher education, you realize that you'll have to rethink what you believe—about a lot of things.[3]

Option B

Remember the truth. You may not have all the answers, but your prior learning, research, and life experience have fortified your confidence that God's Word is completely trustworthy. While studying how to defend your biblical worldview, you've seen over and over that Scripture always stands up to scrutiny. You realize new questions will arise, but you know how to think about faith-challenging information and where to seek scripturally and scientifically sound answers. As you do, you find that your biblical perspective isn't becoming compromised—it's growing stronger.

UNDERSTANDING INTELLECTUAL FOUNDATIONS

As you might have guessed, students are far better equipped to choose Option B if they have strong intellectual foundations. You've read before that intellectual foundations involve apologetics training and critical thinking skills for defending your biblical worldview. But what does all that mean—responding to skeptics' questions by getting defensive about your beliefs or apologizing for being a Christian?

Hardly.

Let's unpack what intellectual foundations truly means, strategize ways to strengthen them, and begin foundation-building by investigating evolutionary concepts to understand *before* university. For starters, we'd better take a closer look at what apologetics and critical thinking really are and why they matter.

Apologetics

The best way to understand the word *apologetics* is to travel back in time and get arrested in ancient Greece. Go ahead and do that, and you'll notice that at your trial, the prosecution will explain all the charges against you in a formal speech called a *katagoria* (κατηγορία). When the *katagoria* ends, you can answer the prosecution, refute their charges, and justify your position by delivering a defense speech, or *apologia* (ἀπολογία).

Apologia is the word Peter used when he wrote, "But in your hearts honor Christ the Lord as holy, always being prepared to make a defense [*apologia*] to anyone who asks you for a reason for the hope that is in you; yet do it with gentleness and respect."[4] Being prepared to make this defense is what *apologetics*, the field of study named after the word *apologia*, is all about.

As the examination of why biblical Christianity makes rational sense, apologetics equips us with reasoned, respectful answers about how we know the Bible is true. There are endless ways to study why the Bible is true, so apologetics covers questions about many subjects. Topics may include the following:

- **The Bible Itself**
  Where did the Bible come from? How can we know its manuscripts are trustworthy? Does Scripture contain contradictions?
- **The Bible and Human History**
  What does history show us about biblical prophecies? Do other historical sources mention events recorded in Scripture? Does archaeology affirm the Bible?

- **The Bible and Science**
  Did God really create the world in six days? Has science disproven Genesis? What about dinosaurs, ape-men, or carbon dating? Does observational science confirm the Bible?
- **Christianity and Other Worldviews**
  How do we know the Bible is true compared to other "religious books"? Does Christianity borrow from other religions? How can we defend and proclaim the gospel to friends who believe other worldviews?
- **The Nature of God**
  How do we know God exists? If we have a loving, all-powerful Creator, why is the world full of death and suffering?
- **Jesus**
  Did Jesus really claim to be God's Son? How do we know he was telling the truth? Did he really live, die, and rise again?

Because the Bible is true, we can be confident that answers exist to these and other questions,[5] recognizing that the real world around us confirms what Scripture teaches. Reality fully attests to God's truth, in fact, that Paul said in Romans 1:19–20:

> For what can be known about God is plain to [sinful humans], because God has shown it to them. For his invisible attributes, namely, his eternal power and divine nature, have been clearly perceived, ever since the creation of the world, in the things that have been made. So they are without excuse.

That phrase, *without excuse*, is the Greek word *anapologetos*, meaning "without defense." You might say being *anapologetos* is the opposite of having an *apologia*. This means that only people who embrace God's revealed truth can fully have apologetics on their side.

Why Apologetics Matters

Time for a pop quiz: what's the point of apologetics training?

A. To win arguments
B. To be confident in your biblical beliefs
C. To answer specific worldview questions that you have, as they arise
D. To prove how smart you are by using lots of Latin or Greek words, like *anapologetos*
E. To graciously defend the gospel to others, like Paul did (e.g., Acts 17:1–3, 22–31)
F. To disciple other Christians to better understand and defend their faith
G. B, C, E, and F
H. All of the above

Hopefully, you went with *G*. Apologetics is *not* about smacking people in the face with your brain. It's about answering questions which you or others have in truth and love so that everyone can "grow in the grace and knowledge of our Lord and Savior Jesus Christ."[6]

Critical Thinking

While apologetics can arm you with answers to specific worldview questions, secular classrooms and culture will almost certainly confront you with messages you've never encountered before. That's where critical thinking skills come into play.

Critical thinking is one of those phrases that's not super clear, because when we use the word *critical* in everyday life, it's often in a negative context—like being critical of others or being in critical condition. But what does critical *thinking* mean? Criticizing everyone we think about? Thinking quickly in critical situations? Or maybe critical thinking is just a synonym which textbooks use for "extra work."

While growing up, that's basically how I viewed critical thinking. I'd see it referenced in places like textbook exercises, which suggested that students "think critically" about different concepts but didn't often explain *how* to do so. So I began to suspect that critical thinking was just a vague phrase educators like using to make up assignments. But then I read another textbook that explained what critical thinking is really about: evaluating messages to see whether they're worth believing.[7]

"Sensing psychological manipulation"

I suddenly saw critical thinking transform from a scrap of junk jargon into an indispensable mental toolkit. The tools inside include skills like spotting faulty logic, sensing psychological manipulation, and sorting facts from opinions, interpretations, or assumptions. These tools let us avoid being taken in by bad arguments, manipulative advertisements, and false teachers. Since God's Word is the ultimate truth, such tools also prove themselves invaluable for combating the lies in messages that contradict Scripture.

In a world which often opposes the Bible's teachings, I started realizing that biblical critical thinking skills can come in handy for almost any situation. Whether online, in classrooms, or through the media, we're bombarded by persuasive (but often unbiblical) messages that try to alter our thinking, sway our beliefs, and direct our decision making.

Some of these messages may be at least partially true or promote useful ideas. But others, not so much. Critical thinking tools help us discern which are which. And after testing these tools over four years at a secular university, I'd rate them a must-have for any Christian in secular classrooms and culture.

Wait, isn't critical thinking a *secular* toolkit?

Some Christians might be concerned because critical thinking is a concept praised by secular humanists. Humanism is an atheistic worldview, relying on human reasoning alone as man's ultimate authority for truth. Humanists (and even many Christians) may contrast rational thinking with faith, mistakenly defining *faith as belief without evidence*.

Typically beginning with the assumption, "If you can't measure it, then it doesn't exist," secular humanists may try to incorrectly redefine *rational as excluding any mention of God*. The word *rational* means having reason or being reasonable.[9] So critical thinking is rational, in the technical (though not atheistic) sense of the word. But through a quick switcheroo of the definition for rational, some people claim that critical thinking is a bulwark of humanism. This doesn't mean critical thinking is secular; it just means the definition of rational has been manipulated. As a pamphlet from the American Humanist Association states:

> Since humanism is a rational philosophy, it is dependent on a methodology that successfully addresses questions and problems related to the natural world. Critical thinking provides that methodology and includes skills, attitudes and dispositions that a person can learn and practice. In fact, science itself can be thought of as a subset of critical thinking.[10]

Ironically, however, secular worldviews cannot provide a consistent foundation for the concepts critical thinking depends upon, like truth, logic, and reasoning. No human can know everything,[11] and human reasoning is fallible even by humanists' standards—especially since humanists believe the mind is a by-product of evolution (and ultimately a cosmic accident). And how do we know whether any thoughts resulting from a cosmic accident are trustworthy? Those thoughts would be accidents, too. Besides, truth, logic, and reason themselves can't be measured. So they technically wouldn't exist within a consistent humanistic worldview anyway.[12]

In contrast, a biblical worldview states that humans are made in the image of a logical God. Our Creator knows everything, is the source of absolutes, created an orderly universe, reveals truth through his Word, and designed us with faculties for learning, knowing, and reasoning. Unlike humanism, then, a biblical worldview provides a consistent philosophical basis for the use and existence of knowledge, logic, and critical thinking. And since the Bible is the revelation from God, who cannot lie, it will always stand up to scrutiny. So Christians have no reason to avoid critical thinking—and every reason to embrace it.

The Garden Analogy

Here's another way to look at critical thinking skills. At the house where I grew up, our backyard had a small garden surrounded by rocks. Tall, weedy grass would grow around the rocks, out of reach of the lawn mower. My job was to snip back the weeds with a massive pair of garden pruners. Sometimes, their blades would run into the rocks as I worked. But would the rocks get severed along with the grass? No way—they were too solid.

Similarly, critical thinking skills are like garden tools for destroying the weeds of lies, irrationality, and flawed logic in our thinking. God's Word, meanwhile, is rock solid. No matter how determinedly anyone might try hacking against biblical teachings with a critical thinking tool, God's truth will ultimately remain unscathed.

Furthermore, just like critical thinking is only possible because a biblical worldview provides a basis for logic, a gardener can only stand up to hack against the garden stones because deep underground, a foundation of bedrock is upholding everything. Grounded on the bedrock of God's Word, Christians have every right to apply their critical thinking tools against any weedy lies obscuring the rock-solid truths of biblical teachings.

We'll spend part 3 of this book unpacking practical tactics, tips, and tools for thinking critically about any unbiblical message. For now, the point to keep in mind is that critical thinking and apologetics work together to help you answer questions about your beliefs, strengthen your faith, share the gospel, exercise discernment, and make good decisions—potentially saving yourself a heap of heartache. Altogether, intellectual foundations can help you not only keep your faith in secular classrooms and cultures but also live a wiser life.

PRACTICAL FOUNDATION-BUILDING STRATEGIES

So how can you start building stronger intellectual foundations? The main way is to dive into the many biblically and scientifically sound apologetics and critical thinking resources available today. These include books, videos, articles, magazines, seminars, conferences, camps, and curricula that teach you not only how to answer apologetics questions but also how to reason about worldview topics yourself. Plunging into this ocean of information can seem overwhelming, so here are a few do's and don'ts to help you maximize your intellectual foundation-building efforts:

DO . . . take advantage of free resources!

Tons of solid apologetics articles, videos, podcasts, and even entire ebooks are available online for free, which (speaking from experience) is truly great news for starving students. As a student myself, I particularly loved large, trustworthy apologetics websites where I could quickly find articles responding to questions from my evolutionary classes. Even if I didn't have time to read a long scholarly paper, just seeing that a well-reasoned answer existed helped.

DO . . . make intellectual foundation-building part of your routine.

The mountain of solid apologetics materials out there might seem too daunting to climb for long, but remember, the way to conquer a mountain is one step at a time. Work a little intellectual foundation-building into your everyday routine, and you'll be gaining ground before you can say *anapologetos*. Even if you take a few minutes to learn about one apologetics topic every workday, you will have armed yourself with at least 160 apologetics answers after just one school year.

(Hint: listening to apologetics videos and podcasts while doing other activities, like cooking or commuting, lets you strengthen your intellectual foundations even when leading a time-crunched life. Find what works for you!)

DO . . . take time to learn the basics.

As you decide which apologetics topics to study, I'd encourage you to learn answers to some of the most common objections to Christianity you're likely to find in secular cultures and classrooms, no matter what academic field you study. Just a few of these include:

- If a loving, all-powerful God created everything, why is there so much death and suffering?[14]
- Haven't Christians done a lot of bad things throughout history?[15]
- Isn't the church full of hypocrites?[16]
- What does the Bible really say about gender and sexuality?[17]
- Hasn't science disproved the Bible?[18]
- Doesn't everyone know the earth is millions of years old?[19]
- What about evolution?[20]

DO . . . think ahead to your university classes.

Along with learning these basics, it's also wise to think about apologetics topics relevant to subjects you hope to study in the future. If you're planning to study zoology, for instance, you'll likely want to learn biblical ways to interpret supposed evidence for evolutionary relationships between animals. Or, if you hope to study psychology, you may want to think about how to answer claims that "religious beliefs" evolved due to the way our minds work.[21]

DON'T . . . hinge your faith on a single apologetics argument.

Researching all these topics will almost certainly strengthen your faith, reminding you just how true God's Word really is. But it's key to remember that while apologetics arguments can *confirm* your faith, your faith itself does not rest in any one argument or apologist. It rests in God and his Word.

I'm mentioning this because many of your non-Christian professors, classmates, and textbooks have likely heard arguments supporting the Bible or contradicting evolution, just like you have. If they offer a *counterargument* you've never heard before, you may feel like panicking if you've placed too much stock in that one argument. (This is especially true because not all "apologetics arguments" may be equally watertight to begin with—more on this in a moment.) However, tons of observations from different streams of reality, including science, history, philosophy, other Christians' stories, and your own personal experience affirm that God's Word is true. So your trust in God must not stand or fall on a single line of human reasoning.

DO . . . hone those critical thinking skills.

On that note, just because a counter response may exist to an apologetics argument, that doesn't mean the response is logically valid or scientifically strong. This is one reason why it's so important to have critical thinking skills, which help you evaluate counterarguments on the fly. Learning how to think like an apologist yourself is vital for answering new faith-challenging messages that come up in your classes. After all, there's no way you can memorize answers to every question you might encounter at a university—or in culture at large. Critical thinking will also help you keep from promoting faulty arguments yourself.

DON'T . . . use bad arguments to support your worldview.[22]

This brings up an important point: not all the pro-Bible arguments you hear may be logically sound—or even biblical. Of course, the fact that people can try using bad arguments to defend the Bible's teachings does not make the Bible any less true. God's Word is true no matter how humans reason about it, because truth is inherent to God's nature.[23]

Nevertheless, bad arguments *can* affect Christians' credibility in the eyes of others, who might not know about all the extremely sound reasons for trusting in Scripture. Bad arguments, when refuted, can also shake Christians' faith if they've banked their beliefs on that one flawed argument rather than God's infallible Word. Altogether, these are even more reasons to think critically and biblically about messages we encounter—even from apparently Christian sources.

DO . . . be careful who you're learning from.

That last point highlights the importance of making sure your apologetics sources are biblically sound and logically trustworthy. Even many Christians who truly believe in Jesus and offer brilliant apologetics insights may promote compromised doctrines, especially about Genesis. This *doesn't* necessarily mean we *shouldn't* learn from their many uncompromised teachings. (How's that for a triple negative?) It just means we must always be vigilant to esteem God's Word as our authority over any human reasoning which contradicts Scripture—even when those reasoning humans happen to be fellow believers.

DO . . . learn about other worldviews.

As chapter 2 mentioned, the only two worldviews any person can choose from boil down to believing God's Word or man's word. The religion of man's word manifests itself in endless forms, encompassing unbiblical belief systems around the world. By learning about other worldviews from a Christian perspective, you're less likely to be blindsided by new ideas when you hit campus. Plus, understanding different worldviews helps you anticipate barriers others may face when coming to Christ, letting you better communicate the gospel.

DO . . . be wise when learning from skeptics.

Speaking of other worldviews, while it's possible—and in many cases important—to strengthen our intellectual foundations by learning and responding to skeptics' arguments, skeptics clearly shouldn't be our sole information sources. When I was a teenager, I remember hearing an apologetics speaker warn, "As you start researching all these worldview topics, make sure you're not just spending all your time on atheistic websites. Even if you know their arguments can't possibly be true, you can get so turned around by them."

The speaker's point was that you become like who you listen to and who you spend the most time with. Now, I'm all for knowing what skeptics are saying, as understanding others' perspectives can let us better share and defend our faith. I even took four years at a university to learn evolutionary arguments from secular sources. But I went into those classes already having strong intellectual foundations and mentors who could offer a biblical perspective on the issues I was learning. Beforehand, when I was only beginning to build those foundations, I would instead learn about secular arguments by researching biblical *responses* to skeptics—for instance, through reading Christian reviews of atheistic books.

DO . . . find a biblically grounded mentor.

The reality that we become like those we hang out with reiterates the importance of having a mentor. As you begin arming yourself with answers about different apologetics topics, a biblically grounded mentor can talk through these issues with you, point you to additional resources, and help answer further questions. (Bonus points if you find a mentor with experience in the academic field you hope to study!) My own mentor, Dr. Margaret Helder, helped me prepare for college this way during my teen years and continued supporting my intellectual foundation development throughout college.

LET THE FOUNDATION-BUILDING BEGIN!

Now that we've covered the basics of what intellectual foundations are and how to build them, it's time to start developing those foundations in preparation for evolutionary education. To do that, we'll look at some key concepts every student needs to know *before* beginning evolutionary classes, including the basics of how natural selection and mutations work. Entire books (and lifetimes) have been dedicated to examining these topics in far more depth than we can delve into here. I'd highly encourage you to explore these subjects further,[24] especially if you plan to study life sciences. Meanwhile, this introduction will lay the groundwork for thinking critically about evolution, which we'll practice in chapter 11.

To start, let's recap a couple of important distinctions to keep in mind when thinking about evolution: the differences between two types of science and between two types of change.

Two Types of Science

The first distinction to nail down is the difference between observational and historical science discussed in chapter 2. By way of a quick recap, observational science involves making measurements in the present, using the scientific method to describe what we're seeing in the world around us now. This type of science deals with *facts*. Historical science, on the other hand, involves interpreting facts from the present to draw conclusions about the past. This type of science deals with *assumptions*. For example, while the size, mass, and description of a fossil would be facts from observational science, the assumption that the fossil formed 70 million years ago would be an *interpretation* from historical science.

Some evolutionists will tell you there's no real difference between observational and historical science. However, even prominent twentieth-century evolutionist Ernst Mayr (and many others[25]) recognized that not only is the distinction between observational and historical science real, but evolutionary origins ideas fall under *historical* science. In Mayr's words, "Darwin introduced historicity into science. Evolutionary biology, in contrast with physics and chemistry, is a historical science—the evolutionist attempts to explain events and processes that have already taken place."[26]

Of course, the fact that famous scientists have said something doesn't automatically make it true. But in this case, we can use common sense to check for ourselves. And common sense tells us that there *is* a difference between observable facts and historical assumptions. By keeping this difference in mind, you'll be able to sort fact from interpretation when studying each example of "evidence" for evolution.[27]

Two Types of Change

Along with the difference between observational and historical science, another key concept is the difference between two types of change labeled "evolution." The first involves genetic variation *within kinds* of living things God created, like the variation which yields different breeds of dogs. This kind of change is observational science and a staple of the biblical creation model.

The second type of change, however, involves one kind of creature supposedly transforming into a completely different creature—like land mammals evolving into whales. While we can document within-kind variation occurring in the present, we cannot observe between-kind transformation. So ideas about these supposed kinds of transformations fall under historical science. Yet textbooks call both types of change "evolution."[28]

Some textbooks will tell you there's no difference between these types of evolution. Given millions of years, they say, enough within-kind variation will eventually add up to one kind of animal changing into another. To see why this isn't really the case, we'll need to look closer at two alleged driving forces of evolution: natural selection and mutation.

Natural Selection

Head to the Arctic, and you'll meet (hopefully not too close) polar bears adapted for life in the ice fields. Skip a few latitudes south, and you'll find grizzlies suited for survival in warmer woodlands. Both species are from the family *Ursidae*, the bear kind.[29]

As with polar bears and grizzlies, we tend to see specialized variants of animal or plant kinds thriving in specific environments. Such patterns often result from natural selection—you know, the process where individuals which are the best suited to a given environment survive to pass their genes along to offspring, while less-suited individuals die off or otherwise fail to effectively reproduce.

"Frozen pupsicle"

As a classic example, think of what would happen if dogs with long or short hair migrated to hot or cold environments. The long-haired dogs would thrive in subarctic climates but shrivel into roasted "hot dogs" in a sizzling desert. Short-haired dogs, however, would "relish" the desert, but become frozen *pupsicles* in the subarctic. So natural selection would weed out genes for long hair in hot environments and for short hair in cold environments. The preexisting genetic variation God designed in living things—like the potential for long *and* short hair—therefore acts as a survival mechanism, letting creatures adapt to our fallen world's constantly changing environments.

In the case of canines, years of natural and artificial selection have produced hundreds of dog varieties, ranging from wily wolves to yippy yorkies. Yet natural selection will never change dogs into other kinds of creatures, like whales, because *natural selection cannot create new genetic information*. It can only select from genetic information that's already present, resulting in a net loss of genetic variation. That's why you can lose genetic variety from wolves by breeding them for certain traits until you end up with yorkies, but after you've selected all that variety away to make purebred yorkies, you can't breed those yorkies to come up with wolves again.

Mutation

So where does new genetic variation come from? Supposedly from mutations. Remember, mutations are mistakes in DNA, the molecules which encode genetic instructions for building and maintaining living things. Unlike in the movies, where mutations can morph average citizens into superheroes, real mutations don't *create* functional new genetic information—they destroy information that's already present. This is especially true because a single DNA fragment can contain multiple layers of information. As one geneticist, Dr. John Sanford, explained,

> Most DNA sequences are polyfunctional and so must also be poly-constrained. This means that DNA sequences have meaning

> on several different levels (polyfunctional) and each level of meaning limits possible future changes (poly-constrained). For example, imagine a sentence which has a very specific message in its normal form but with an equally coherent message when read backwards. Now let's suppose that it also has a third message when reading every other letter, and a fourth message when a simple encryption program is used to translate it. Such a message would be polyfunctional and poly-constrained. We know that misspellings in a normal sentence will not normally improve the message, but at least this would be possible. However, a poly-constrained message is fascinating, in that it cannot be improved. It can *only* degenerate. . . . Any misspellings which might possibly improve the normal sentence will be disruptive to the other layers of information.[30]

Because so many mutations cause more harm than good, natural selection isn't necessarily able to weed out the harmful mutations fast enough or specifically enough. This causes the gene pool to grow more and more degenerate—a dilemma known as genetic entropy.[31] Typical evolution, then, isn't so much "onward and upward" as "backward and downward," as mutations cause a net loss of functional genetic information.[32]

Ultimately, mutations and natural selection can remove genetic information to produce variation within kinds of living creatures. But they can't produce the new functional information required to change one kind of creature into another. That's why we can measure within-kind changes through observational science, but between-kind changes will only ever be assumptions from historical science.

MISCONCEPTIONS ABOUT EVOLUTION

Understanding processes like natural selection and mutation is important because teachers and textbooks often comment on how many misconceptions students have about evolution.[33] Steering clear of these misconceptions yourself helps you maintain credibility, avoid surprises, and defend your worldview from an informed perspective. Here are a few questions you can use to test yourself for misconceptions about evolutionists' beliefs.

True or False

Evolutionists believe that evolution happens because living things want or need to evolve a certain way.

False

Unlike biblical creationists, who affirm that God knowingly designed living things' components for specific purposes such as vision, swimming, or flight, evolutionists do not believe evolution is an intentional process. It's a natural one, and natural processes don't have foresight. That's why in my biology classes, we were taught to never interpret natural things as existing because they were *supposed* to exist. Eyes were not *meant* to detect light; light-sensitive structures simply gave organisms a survival advantage. Wings were not *meant* for flying, but their hypothetical precursors eventually lent themselves to flight. Secular evolutionists believe objects in nature can have *function* but not *purpose*.

True or False

Evolutionists believe that evolution always produces improvements.

False

In its broadest sense, *evolution* simply means "change over time." The basic unit of change is supposed to be the process of a mutation becoming established in a gene pool. This process produces within-kind variation and can be measured using observational science, so it is not evolution in a historical sense.

Such a change can happen by *nonrandom* processes like natural selection, which specifically acts for or against the mutation's physical results. However, a mutation which is apparently helpful in one environment may not be helpful in another environment. For example, a mutation for dark fur could help a mouse camouflage in a dark-sand desert but make the same mouse more visible to predators in a light-sand desert.[34]

Sometimes, however, mutations also become established by *random* processes. For instance, if a hurricane washed all but two lizards off an island, and both happened to have a mutation for a rare disease, all future lizards on the island would have the disease, too. This could be considered evolution (in the sense of within-kind variation), but the result wouldn't be an improvement for the lizards.

True or False

Evolutionists believe that the pattern of life's evolution looks like a tree, not a line.

True[35]

Some illustrations (especially in older books) may show life's supposed evolution as a parade of increasingly complex creatures, from mollusks to mankind. These images can make the idea of evolution seem linear—as if each group of creatures changed directly into another, more advanced group, leaving none of the "less evolved" life-forms behind. But really, the presumed pattern of Darwinian evolution looks more like a tree, with ancestral life-forms branching out into many kinds of descendants. The "early" or "ancestral" forms may go extinct, evolve into other lineages, or remain relatively unchanged for (supposedly) millions of years. So evolutionists don't propose that humans evolved *from* chimps; they believe both humans and chimps evolved from an extinct common ancestor.

THE NEXT STEPS

With a clear understanding of evolutionary concepts, you'll be well set to build your intellectual foundations further, learn more about creation-evolution apologetics, and think critically in evolutionary classes. We haven't even scratched the surface of the information available to help you do this. But the resources listed in appendix A will get you started, while the foundation-building hints, tips, and tricks we covered in this chapter will point you in the right direction to keep going. You'll also find many hands-on, practical foundation-building tools in part 3 of this book, where I'll share the top critical thinking techniques that helped me through four years of university. But first, we have one final type of interpersonal foundation to look at—the one which I heard students around the world talk about more than anything else.

Endnotes

1. This quote comes from my own first-year biology textbook: Jane Reece et. al., *Campbell Biology*, Canadian ed. (Don Mills: Pearson Canada, 2014), 499.
2. More about *how* to think through common examples of "evidence" for evolution in chapter 11
3. Rethinking beliefs doesn't necessarily mean abandoning faith. Many church-raised students may simply try to incorporate evolutionary (or otherwise unbiblical) ideas into their Christian worldview or avoid thinking about evolutionary origins' true implications for Scripture. However, for more on why evolution is not compatible with a consistent biblical worldview, see chapter 2 or https://answersingenesis.org/theistic-evolution.
4. 1 Peter 3:15
5. Countless, fantastic apologetics resources can help you answer questions like these, including resources listed in appendix A. You can also find answers to these and other questions at AnswersInGenesis.org.
6. 2 Peter 3:18

7. While not from the textbook which introduced me to critical thinking, this is the most helpful definition of critical thinking I've found, based on Chris MacDonald and Lewis Vaughn, *The Power of Critical Thinking*, 4th Canadian ed. (Don Mills: Oxford University Press, 2016).
8. This quote, which summarizes the atheistic belief of materialism, comes from the following TED talk, which a professor played in one of my university classes: Brene Brown, "The Power of Vulnerability," filmed June 2010, 20:04, TED video, https://www.ted.com/talks/brene_brown_the_power_of_vulnerability/transcript?language=en#t-126460. (To quickly show how the quoted statement is self-defeating, we could respond, "Can we measure the belief that if we can't measure something, then it doesn't exist?" In answer, we might be able to measure the extent to which someone *embraces* this belief, but we can't measure the belief itself because it is an immaterial abstraction which cannot exist in a strictly material universe.)
9. "Rational," Merriam-Webster.com Dictionary, Merriam-Webster, accessed June 7, 2021, https://www.merriam-webster.com/dictionary/rational.
10. "Humanism and Critical Thinking," American Humanist Association, 2016, http://americanhumanist.org/wp-content/uploads/2016/11/05_brochure.pdf.
11. As a result, when we inductively construct what we *think* we know from the information our senses give us, we cannot absolutely know whether our senses are reliable—or even real. Relying on our senses to inform us about whether our senses can reliably inform us is arbitrarily circular. (See chapter 12 and the resources in the note below for more information.)
12. For more on these and other inconsistencies of atheistic worldviews, see Jason Lisle, *The Ultimate Proof of Creation: Resolving the Origins Debate* (Green Forest: Master Books, 2009), or see Patricia Engler, "Six Principles Skeptics Borrow from the Bible," Answers in Genesis, February 17, 2021, https://answersingenesis.org/blogs/patricia-engler/2021/02/17/6-principles-skeptics-borrow-bible.
13. The appendix includes a list of such resources to help get you started.
14. E.g., Terry Mortenson, "The Problem of Death," Answers in Genesis, September 1, 2017, https://answersingenesis.org/suffering/dilemma-death, or Ken Ham, *How Could a Loving God . . .? Powerful Answers on Suffering* (Green Forest: Master Books 2007).
15. More on this in chapter 10
16. More on this in chapter 10
17. E.g., see the articles at https://answersingenesis.org/family.
18. E.g., see Ken Ham and Terry Mortenson, "Science or the Bible?" Answers in Genesis, June 14, 2007, https://answersingenesis.org/what-is-science/science-or-the-bible.
19. E.g., see the articles at https://answersingenesis.org/theory-of-evolution/millions-of-years.
20. E.g., see the articles at https://answersingenesis.org/evolution.
21. E.g., see Patricia Engler, "Is Belief in God a Psychological Fluke?" Answers in Genesis, August 26, 2020, https://answersingenesis.org/blogs/patricia-engler/2020/08/26/belief-god-psychological-fluke.
22. For a list of such arguments to avoid, see https://answersingenesis.org/creationism/arguments-to-avoid.
23. E.g., Numbers 23:19; John 14:6
24. Appendix A can help you get started.
25. See Troy Lacey, "First Usage of Origins vs. Operational Science: Did Young-Earth Creationists Invent the Term Origin Science to Discredit Evolution?" Answers in Genesis, February 1, 2018, https://answersingenesis.org/what-is-science/first-usage-origins-vs-operational-science.
26. Ernst Mayr, "Darwin's Influence on Modern Thought," Scientific American, November 24, 2009, https://www.scientificamerican.com/article/darwins-influence-on-modern-thought1.

27. More tips and examples on how to sort fact from interpretation in chapter 9.

28. This is how evolutionists claim "evolution" (in the first sense) has been observed, as supposed support for evolution in the second sense. E.g., Richard Dawkins famously said, "Evolution has been observed. It's just that it hasn't been observed while it's happening." ("Battle over evolution," Bill Moyers interviews Richard Dawkins, Now, December 3, 2004, PBS network, https://www.pbs.org/now/transcript/transcript349_full.html.)

29. A good clue that species are from the same created "kind" is if they can produce offspring together. In fact, polar bear-grizzly hybrids—aka "pizzly bears"—do exist, even in the wild. However, not all variations within every created kind can reproduce today, due to genetic mutations and other factors. For more on created kinds, see Georgia Purdom, "One of a Kind?" Answers in Genesis, July 1, 2019, https://answersingenesis.org/creation-science/baraminology/one-kind.

30. John Sanford, *Genetic Entropy & the Mystery of the Genome*, 3rd ed. (Waterloo: FMS Publications, 2005), 131.

31. John Sanford, 2005.

32. In my molecular evolution classes, some mutations were said to produce a "gain of function," where a mutation to a regulatory protein causes a gene to always be switched "on." This isn't so much a *gain* of function, however, as a *loss* of control. And again, the destruction of the regulatory protein reflects a net loss of functional genetic information.

33. Remember, although supposedly a driving process behind evolution, natural selection is *not* the same as evolution, as it does not generate the new genetic variation required to produce novel kinds of living things.

34. E.g., Michael Nachman, Hopi Hoekstra, and Susan D'Agostino, "The Genetic Basis of Adaptive Melanism in Pocket Mice," *Proceedings of the National Academy of Sciences* 100, no. 9 (2003): 5,268–5,273.

35. While Darwin's evolutionary tree is the model my textbooks taught, some evolutionists, such as Dr. Craig Venter, lead inventor of a synthetic bacterial genome, now recognize that observational science does not support the idea that all life-forms branched out from a single common ancestor. For instance, not all living organisms share the same genetic code. (See Craig Venter et. al., "The Great Debate—What Is Life?" panel discussion, February 12, 2011, www.thesciencenetwork.org.)

INTERPERSONAL FOUNDATIONS

8

A Christian support network

"Now is not the time to panic," I told myself, looking down. Beyond my own bare feet and the band of cliff they clung to, I saw only sharp boulders submerged in seawater some 12–15 feet below. *Oh dear. How did I end up here?*

The day started innocuously enough—just two university friends going camping before another fall semester began. Both of us preferred *experiencing* adventures to *planning* them, so we simply loaded our backpacks, hopped a ferry to a small island, and started hiking in search of a campsite.

For some time, we trekked along a beach flanked by a steep hillside. Ahead, I could see a rocky cliff projecting into the sea, blocking our path. *Now what?*

"Doesn't look like we can climb here," I commented, eyeing the steep boulders and slick, dry grass. "Do you think we can wade around that cliff to reach the beach again?"

"Let's try," my friend agreed, leading the way until we stood nearly waist-deep in saltwater. Venturing further, I realized, would mean soaking our backpacks. That's when I noticed my friend stepping up to edge her way along the submerged portion of the rock face. I followed, feeling for underwater footholds until no more remained. We couldn't move forward; we couldn't step down without soaking our gear; and edging backward seemed impossible, too. So we started climbing.

"How did I end up here?"

"I'll go first," my friend commented when we hit an especially steep patch. I nodded, slid one foot into a higher cleft, and pulled myself up to watch as she somehow passed the danger zone only by grace and friction. Then, trying to ignore the cliff's height, I searched for my own next handhold or foothold.

There were none.

But my troubles didn't end there. I could already feel tremors seizing my calf, the muscle supporting almost my entire weight plus my backpack.

"Um . . . I can't hold on much longer."

"Don't you have rope in your pack?"

Right—the paracord! Good thing I'd "happened" to stash it in the only compartment I could access without removing my backpack. Still standing on one trembling foot, I braced one hand against the cliff and maneuvered the other backward to locate the paracord.

"Got it!"

Tying one end into my belt, I weighted the other end with a stick my friend tossed down. A couple failed attempts and one dramatic lasso twirl later, I managed to send her the weighted end. She anchored herself deeper into the cliff, and together, we used the cord to work our way upward. At last, we reached the top, rock-scratched, rope-burned, covered in burrs—and thanking God for getting us to solid ground!

STUDENTS' NEED FOR CHRISTIAN CONNECTIONS

Just like I needed paracord connected to a friend who had a firm hold on the cliff, Christian students need connections with other believers who have a strong grip on the Rock, Jesus. That's where interpersonal foundations come in. A support network of like-minded believers can help Christian students stay grounded in Scripture during secular university, the way the paracord helped me stay grounded on the cliff.

As chapter 5 mentioned, interpersonal foundations emerged as the top theme Christian students worldwide raised when I asked what advice they'd give other students or how churches can support students better. Specifically, students identified the importance of staying connected with three types of Christian communities: campus ministries, local churches, and godly adult mentors.

Talking about the value of these communities is one thing. But *knowing* how to find meaningful connections, become involved in solid communities, and build strong interpersonal foundations at a university is something else. Let's look closer at the three types of communities which Christian students worldwide say are so essential and explore practical tactics, tips, and strategies for making the most out of each.

CAMPUS MINISTRIES

Often, when I asked campus Christians what their advice would be to a first-year student, the first thing they said was, "Join a solid Christian student group on campus!" Thinking back to my own time in a university, I have to agree how valuable campus ministries can be. I've seen and experienced the way meeting regularly with other Christian students for Bible studies, prayer, or just plain fun can pack multiple benefits. Here are a few of them.

Encouragement

By getting involved with a biblical campus ministry, students will ideally plug into the ongoing mutual encouragement that Hebrews 10:24–25 describes: "And let us consider how to stir up one another to love and good works, not neglecting to meet together, as is the habit of some, but encouraging one another, and all the more as you see the Day drawing near."

Prayer Support

Personally, I found one of the most valuable aspects of my campus ministry involvement was the chance to regularly join other Christians in prayer. If secular campus is a spiritual battlefield, then prayer is one of the most effective weapons we have for the war.[1] And as vitally as we need individual prayer times, group prayer is significant on a whole other level.

Accountability

Regularly meeting other Christians for prayer and encouragement can help keep you accountable in your spiritual walk. If you're regularly invested in a Christian group that gets to know you well, they may be the first to notice and respond if you begin drifting off course.

Outreach

Other highlights from my campus ministry involvement included opportunities to serve with other believers. Every week, for example, Christian students would set up a table on campus to offer prayer for passersby. And every year, each of the campus ministry's small groups organized its own community service project. By promoting outreach and evangelism, campus ministries can help students embrace their time at a university as an opportunity to serve others.

Foundation-Building

Ideally, campus ministry activities will foster spiritual and intellectual foundation-building for everyone involved. As students pray together, worship, study Scripture, discuss tough questions, seek biblical answers, and encourage one other spiritually, they're adding layers to each others' personal foundations *and* experiencing the lifestyle of fellowship to which Christians are called.[2]

Recharging

Even for introverts (speaking from experience here), sharing life with other Christians can refresh the spirit, mind, and emotions like nothing else. God hardwired humans for relationship, and research has documented the importance of supportive friendships for protecting students' mental health.[3] Staying buried in the books might be tempting for time-crunched students. But taking breaks to meet Christian friends can boost students' mental and spiritual well-being for combating the brainwashing conditions on campus.[4]

Solidarity

Campus can be a lonely world. When you're in a crowded lecture hall, hearing a professor dismiss biblical creation like it's a nearly eradicated disease that *real scientists* washed their hands of years ago, it's easy to wonder if you're the only person left who believes the Bible. But, like students worldwide have discovered, one of the best things about Christian community is the ongoing reminder that you are *not alone in your convictions*.

What to Look for in a Campus Ministry

As fantastic as campus ministries can be, not every student I've met has had positive experiences with them. Maybe the groups are cliquish, the teaching is shallow, or most of the members don't seem to live like they truly follow Jesus. Campus communities consist of people. People are human, and humans make mistakes. And yet the Bible does say that bad company corrupts good character.[5] Scripture warns us not to hang out with those who call themselves Christians but live contrary to God's commandments.[6] Multiple New Testament writers also urge believers to beware of false teachers—even ones among the church.[7] Ultimately, joining a group with mainly professing (but not practicing) Christians or compromised teaching will not only fail to strengthen your personal foundations—it will likely weaken them.

Given these complications, how can you discern whether joining a certain campus community will be helpful or harmful? One key is to remember Jesus' words in Matthew 7:15–17: "Beware of false prophets, who come to you in sheep's clothing but inwardly are ravenous wolves. You will recognize them by their fruits. Are grapes gathered from thornbushes, or figs from thistles? So, every healthy tree bears good fruit, but the diseased tree bears bad fruit."

These verses imply that you can immediately spot a good campus ministry because every fellowship night, the leader will serve a preponderance of grapes and figs.

I'm kidding.

Jesus doesn't specify exactly what "good fruit" means. But one explanation I find helpful is that the tree represents a teacher's doctrines, and the practical outworking of those doctrines in people's lives—like individuals' actions, decisions, and lifestyles—are the fruits. So, in one commentator's words, we can identify a "good tree" by "the measure in which, in the long-run, it promotes purity, peace, and holiness."[9]

Of course, the ultimate standard for discerning good or bad is God's Word. So worship styles, church traditions, and minor denominational differences aside, the most important element to look for in a campus ministry is whether the leaders' teachings and lifestyles align with the Bible. Being able to exercise biblical discernment this way is just one more reason why it's so vital for students to be deeply familiar with God's Word.

Ways to Gauge Potential Compromise

While a pattern of biblical doctrine and conduct is the key standard when seeking Christian community, you won't find a *perfect* campus ministry any sooner than you'll find a *perfect* church. There may always be aspects of the group which aren't fully your style, but that doesn't necessarily mean the ministry is compromised. A few questions to ask for discerning compromise levels include the following:

- **Are there doctrinal issues within the leadership?**
  Not every *member* of the group may espouse fully biblical doctrines, especially because so many church-raised students aren't necessarily familiar with God's Word in the first place. For instance, research reported in the book *Gospel Reset* found that 65% of churched millennials believe that being good is enough to get to heaven.[10] If an unbiblical doctrine like this is coming from the *leadership,* that's a problem. But for fellow students who might not yet understand the Bible deeply, you may simply need to exercise grace, pointing them to God's Word in love.

  On that note, you may find that one of the most common areas of doctrinal compromise will be groups' views on Genesis 1–11. If the leadership is actively advising students to reinterpret key doctrines from Genesis, you *may* want to think, pray, and seek biblical counsel about discussing these issues with them or potentially finding an alternative support network.[11]

- **How is spending time in this circle likely to impact my spiritual health?**
  Several students I've spoken with said they didn't end up joining a campus ministry because the members didn't live like they really knew Christ. They didn't look, sound, or act any differently from the world. We become like those whom we spend time with, so if most of a group's members (and especially leaders) aren't living like Jesus, then becoming integrated with them will

probably do your spirit more harm than good. The point here isn't about being self-righteous; it's about obeying Jesus, protecting your heart, and guarding your relationship with God.

- **Will my involvement with this group likely lead me to compromise?**
  Back in chapter 6, we saw the importance of setting biblically based boundaries to help prevent compromise in belief or action. But I can tell you, those boundaries will feel way easier to overstep if we see the professing Christians around us overstepping them, too. For example, I remember a Bible school student telling me, "Most people don't start swearing until they get to Bible school. When you hear other Christians swearing all the time, you start to think, *maybe it's not such a bad word after all!*"

  Granted, swearing may seem pretty minor. But Ephesians 4:29 does command, "Let no corrupting talk come out of your mouths, but only such as is good for building up, as fits the occasion, that it may give grace to those who hear." And little compromises add up. That doesn't mean you shouldn't extend grace to friends who may swear (or make similar compromises). But it does mean you need to closely guard your heart and rethink your level of group involvement if you notice your own biblical boundaries slipping.

What If *All* the Groups Are Compromised?

If, despite all these considerations, you don't find a biblical ministry group on your campus, you may need to seek alternative support networks. For instance, even if you find that a group leader's teachings are too compromised for you to join their Bible studies, maybe there's just one solid Christian student you've met through the group with whom you could connect in other settings. Maybe there's another campus close enough that you could join one of their groups' Bible studies. Or maybe you can connect with like-minded students through a local church. Even if you don't end up being able to build consistent Christian friendships on campus (I didn't my first two years), you can still maintain strong interpersonal foundations through other connections, including church, family, and mentors.

What If the Groups Are Cliquish?

While most students I interviewed relayed glowing reports of their time in campus ministries, a few shared that their attempts to join Christian student clubs felt something like this:

> A few days into your first semester at university, you enter the study lounge where the poster said the Christian students

would be meeting. Already, a few tight clusters of students have stationed themselves around the lounge. As you scan the room for a likely huddle to join, one guy saunters over to introduce himself as the leader. He asks you what you're studying and invites you to have a seat then calls the group in for worship and a brief message. Afterward, you introduce yourself to the student next to you and ask what she studies. She answers but quickly turns her back to hear the latest update about who's dating who. The other students have coagulated into their little clots again, and you wonder if trying to break through will be worth it.

Notably, a cliquish culture may not be the healthiest community to join. But based on insights I've heard from students and leaders, here are a few ideas for ways to work around cliquishness:

- Get involved early. Research Christian clubs ahead of time, contact the leaders before their groups' kickoffs, and show up for the first meeting—hopefully before too many cliques get established.
- Find someone who's not in the group and go together. (Though please don't start your own clique that way!)
- Volunteer to serve within the group. Seek out opportunities to help with anything that needs doing.
- Most of all, become the solution. Be welcoming to others, invite newcomers, and actively avoid growing cliquish yourself.

Ideally, healthy communities emerge when both the established group and the new students are proactive, outward focused, and involved with each other. This happens most effectively when two conditions are met. First, the established group intentionally creates a welcoming culture—a standard both set and modeled by the leadership. Second, newcomers actively invest themselves in the group as contributors rather than just consumers. Then, when both sides are concerned about sharing love rather than sponging attention, the body of Christ on campus can move to advance God's kingdom with unity, purpose, and vitality.

LOCAL CHURCH

As valuable as campus ministries can be, peer relationships alone aren't enough to build the rock-solid interpersonal foundations. The strongest Christian support networks consist of diverse relationships across the wider church. After all, the body of Christ is just that: a body. It's not simply a collection of 18–23-year-olds from one college. It's an interwoven unity of disciples representing diverse ages, occupations, and backgrounds. As I heard a student minister in Holland express,

> Christian student unions are amazing, but students cannot thrive only on unions—just groups of same-age people. Unions are fantastic because they draw students together who have the student experience in common, but those students don't necessarily become part of a wider body. They don't see people the age of their parents or little cousins. They need to be part of the whole body and bride of Christ.

Since New Testament times, the church is the primary institution God established outside the family for corporate worship, prayer, training in Scripture, encouragement, spiritual growth, community outreach, relationship building, and discipleship. So it's no wonder students worldwide express how crucial consistent church involvement is! As the Christian former professor I mentioned in chapter 5 exhorted, "Students must not give up on attending church and serving in that church. Not attending church is the biggest mistake students make."

Despite these observations, I also heard multiple student ministry leaders raise concerns about how easily students can give up church involvement (if not necessarily their faith) after reaching university. Students may be especially prone to this if they move away from home without connecting to a new church before the academic onslaught strikes. In fact, a major study uncovered that Christian students who don't find a new church within the first month of leaving home are far less likely to attend church during university at all.[12]

"Before the academic onslaught strikes"

However, this research also revealed that students who have someone from their home church connect them with a new church in the university city are *three times more likely* to attend church during university. That's why campus Christians I met in New Zealand urged home churches to help students transition to university churches. They also advised prospective students to start church hunting well *before* the semester begins.

That's what I did as a student, scoping out local churches before moving to college and then, later, before transferring to university. In both cases, I ultimately ended up attending *different* churches than I had originally expected. But I still never had to go a week without being surrounded by other believers. And both times, God ended up leading me to the church he knew would be best for developing the relationships he had in mind for me.

A student in Australia shared a similar story:

> Before I went to university, I really prayed for a church. Just two weeks after, I was ushered to a local church just a walk away from

the community. From there, I was introduced to opportunities which let me not only just socialize but also grow spiritually. So, I'd tell students to pray for a church and then get involved there, even if you're not sure how you fit into the church's age groups. The Lord will lead you to the right person or group.

What to Look for in a Church

If you're preparing to move away for a university, what kind of church should you start seeking? Just like with campus ministries, no church will be *perfect*—the main thing is to find a church with *biblical teaching*. I've heard plenty of students and campus ministry leaders express how vital it is for students to join a church that shares, studies, and stands on God's Word. But I've never heard a *single person* say that Christian students will be best equipped to keep their faith at a university if they attend a church with exciting music, a youthful congregation, and a flashy worship band.[13]

Ironically, these elements are what many churches seem to think will keep young people from leaving. But if students aren't finding real community, biblical answers, and solid discipleship to know what Scripture teaches and why it's true, gimmicks alone don't give young people a reason to stay. They don't equip students with the spiritual, intellectual, and interpersonal foundations necessary for surviving the battlefield of secular classrooms and cultures.

I had the chance to sample these realities as a student. One church I tried attending (which did have biblical teaching, by the way) was renowned for its heart-pumping young adult service. Throngs of students would pack the auditorium for a performance to rival any concert in town. But unless you came with people you knew, signed up for a newcomers' class, or joined a small group, it wasn't easy to build meaningful relationships there—or even to meet people.

"Interpersonal foundations"

But then I found another Bible-believing church just a short walk from my house. It didn't have a flashy band or fog machine, and only one or two other young women my age attended. But the seniors in my pew welcomed me like family. They expressed genuine interest in me. They regularly prayed for my exams. I'm still in touch with some of them today.

I continued attending the other church's young adult service some evenings as an outing with friends. But it was the second church that became my home.

What If You Don't Have Time for Church?

Trick question. You *do* have time because for your faith to thrive on the battlefields of secular classrooms and cultures, maintaining your spiritual health must rank among your highest priorities. And by definition, you always have time for your highest priorities.[14] During my busiest semester with five classes and three labs, church was one of the only study breaks I could afford. But without that consistent contact with God's people, I simply wouldn't have thrived.

I've quoted the retired Australian professor before, and I'll quote him again: "Not attending church is the biggest mistake students make." This doesn't mean you need to decorate the front pew every time someone unlocks the church door. But staying regularly connected to the wider body of Christ is vital for strengthening your faith, building relationships with other believers, and remembering that you're not alone.

Ideas for Building Connections in Church

What are some practical tips for getting involved, making connections, and forming relationships in church? Here are a few ideas:

- Don't rush away immediately after the service, even though you might have a mountain of homework to tackle. Stick around for at least a few minutes to visit.
- If it's a larger church, join a small group—especially if you're not part of a campus ministry's Bible study.
- Try meeting at least one new person every week for as long as you can.
- Sign up to participate or volunteer in special events, including community outreaches, game nights, or church dinners. Events like these allow you to make connections and serve without having to commit to recurring activities you may not have time to be consistently involved in as a student.
- Accept invitations for coffee or lunch (especially from sweet older people with no possible ulterior motives, like dating you). Accepting free food is the number one rule in the Official Code of Conduct for Starving Students. (Okay, I just made that up.) Better yet, extend the coffee invitations yourself.
- Use your God-given gifts to serve where you can, whether by joining an established ministry or offering your strengths in a brand-new way. For instance, the arts student I spoke with in Paris gave her church original paintings to decorate their foyer.

OLDER ADULT MENTORS

One of the most valuable aspects of local church involvement is meeting godly, older adults. While I hadn't expected to uncover this result from 360° in 180, connections with older mentors emerged as a top theme that campus Christians emphasized across cultures.[15] But what is a mentor anyway? Someone who sits under a tree and utters cryptic riddles to a huddle of toga-wearing wisdom seekers?

Fortunately, no. A mentor is simply anyone willing to personally share valuable experience, knowledge, and insights which can benefit someone else—especially someone younger. As a result, mentors can strengthen students' spiritual and intellectual foundations, even while being keystones of their interpersonal foundations. What does this process typically look like? Here are a few examples of what mentors may do:

- Intentionally guide students to grow stronger in their walk with God.
- Coach students in a certain career field to excel as professionals and Christ followers.
- Be available to talk with and listen to students.
- Be a role model, setting a pattern and example for students to follow.
- Help students find biblical answers to tough questions about life, faith, or career-related issues.
- Share personal stories of experiencing God's faithfulness.
- Share insights gleaned from years of walking with God.
- Pray with and for students.
- Teach students the Bible.

As a student, I had the privilege of befriending someone who excels in many of these areas. He's a retired pastor, teacher, and missionary in his eighties, radiating a love for university students which outshines even his enthusiasm for telling stories. Attending the Bible study he led for our campus ministry became one of the highlights of my time at the university.

If you had knocked on his door on a Tuesday evening, you would have found a group of us students clustered around his table, enjoying his wife's homemade soup. Later, we'd have headed to the living room together to read the Bible, discuss the gospel, and listen to his incredible stories of walking with God. If you had walked into the university chapel earlier the same day, you'd have found him there among the students gathered for weekly prayer. And if you'd returned to campus on Thursday, you would have found him strolling the grounds with one or two students, praying together for the university. He told me in a video interview,

> The Christians need to have a voice on campus, and the greatest thing we can do for them as laypeople is to be praying for them, and encouraging them, and mentoring them. There are many young students who would love to have a godly man or woman come alongside with us in a prayer walk, or whether it is simply to show interest in them as a church.

Between this leader and Dr. Helder, I've personally seen how spending time with mentors can build all three types of foundations that students need at the same time.

What to Look for in a Mentor

The more you spend time with your mentors, the more you begin to resemble them. That's why it's so crucial to choose your mentors carefully. As with finding a campus ministry and local church, the top trait to seek in a mentor is someone who believes, teaches, and lives according to the Bible. Ideally, you'll also find at least one godly mentor who has experience in your chosen field. However, people outside your field can be invaluable mentors, as well. As a campus minister in Holland explained,

> Whether they're a homemaker or a CEO, everyone has a perspective that students don't have. And that's the main thing students crave. The best thing that can happen to a Christian student, in terms of mentorship, is not [just] to be mentored by the "role" that they want to play in the future—a super successful lawyer, for example. It's being mentored by someone who is proof that God is faithful.

Types of Mentors

As this campus minister hinted, not all mentorship relationships look the same. Mentoring can be as formal as a weekly meeting to discuss spiritual goals or as informal as a chat in the church foyer on Sunday. Looking back at my own student experiences, I can identify at least three types of mentors:

1. The Sage

The sage is the person who might first come to mind when you think of a mentor—that wise or experienced human who knows more about God (and perhaps your career field) than you could learn in years. Sages are the individuals you might approach to begin more formal mentoring relationships. They're the people you meet for regular discipleship, discussion, or Q&A. They're your personal trainers in the gym of spiritual development or your trail guides on the mountain pathway called life. You get the idea.

2. **The Ally**

   Allies are the many mentors in your life who might not even realize they're your mentors. They're the seniors in the pew across the aisle—the ones who greet you with a hug every Sunday, offer you rides to church, or invite you for lunch. Over the seasons, they've learned that they're not perfect, but God is faithful. And they have stories about his faithfulness to share. Like another set of parents or grandparents, they ask about your exams, listen when you need to debrief about university, and let you know they're praying for you throughout the week. Never underestimate the value of an ally!

3. **The Responder**

   If you had to summarize responders in one word, it would be *available*. You might not see them very often. In fact, they may live a few time zones away. But even though you don't connect with them regularly, you know you can call them anytime. You're free to share your questions, concerns, or prayer requests with them, knowing they'll do their best to offer encouragement, advice, and support.

These mentorship categories aren't necessarily separate. Some mentoring relationships may include elements of all three. But whatever the specifics, the strongest interpersonal foundations will ideally incorporate each of these three mentor types. For instance, even if you can't arrange regular meetings with a sage, you could still maintain a strong support network through consistent contact with allies and sage-like responders.

In my case, Dr. Helder took on a sage-responder role, for while I couldn't meet her in person regularly due to our different locations, I knew that she'd welcome any questions I might email her and could meet in person whenever I came to town. Meanwhile, I surrounded myself with allies and made contacts with geographically closer responders.

Ideas for Finding Mentors

What are some practical tips for forging mentorship connections? Here are a few ideas.

Ways young people can find mentors

- Seek people you want to be like (including trusted Christians in your field of study) and ask them if they'd be willing to meet.
- Intentionally take (or make) opportunities to interact with older adults in your church, especially if they seem to have a close relationship with God. Ways to connect might include

participating in church events, taking time to visit after the service, and meeting for dinner or coffee—even though you could always be studying more.

- Find ways to serve (or serve alongside) older adults, for instance, by helping with community outreach initiatives or volunteering at your church.
- Be open to asking older Christians to pray for you. For example, if an ally asks how your classes are going, you can say, "Great, but I have an exam on Tuesday I'd appreciate prayer for!"
- Remember: books and media act like mentors, too. Especially through biographies and autobiographies, you can be mentored by some of history's most amazing men and women of God. (But on the flip side, watch out for negative influences from other forms of media which may also be discipling you.)

Ways older Christians (or more experienced Christian students) can become mentors

- Invite "starving students" over for lunch, ask what's going on in their lives, and lend a listening ear.
- Share your testimony, including stories of God's faithfulness in everyday life.
- Look for ways to serve (or serve alongside) younger people in your church or community. For example, at a campus ministry I visited in Australia, seniors from a local church would bring a homemade dinner to the students every week and stay for Bible study.
- Talk to campus ministry leaders or university chaplains about ways you can get involved with the students. Resist discouragement if this requires persistence and creativity because you're an essential member of Christ's body with something valuable to offer.[16]
- Look for young people who want to do something with their lives that you have done. Let them know you'd be available to talk with them about it, answer any questions, or mentor them on the job.
- Ask younger people how you can pray for them—and let them know you're doing so. Follow up with them later, find out how they're doing, and check if there's anything else you can be keeping in prayer.
- Show that you're available to answer questions, listen, and debrief with students.
- Try taking a prayer walk around a university campus, praying for the students, staff, campus ministers, and any needs you see. Maybe you can even find students to join you.

Ways churches and campus ministries can foster mentorship connections

- Provide service and leadership opportunities for young people to use their God-given gifts, passions, and ideas. Have older Christians available to support the youths' efforts.
- Approach trusted older adults about getting involved with youth or student ministries. For instance, older Christians could host Bible studies, become mentors, participate in a Q&A night, join students for outreach and prayer initiatives, or help with special events.
- Host monthly men's or women's events specifically designed to foster intergenerational relationships.
- Run mentorship initiatives to connect church members with students in their occupational or academic fields. For instance, a pastor in Dubai explained how a church he attended ran a program where business leaders from the congregation met weekly with senior-year students to equip them in matters of career and faith.

MOVING FORWARD

Older mentors, a local church, and campus ministries comprise a three-stranded support system that can help you stay anchored to the rock of God's Word during college. And like Ecclesiastes 4:12 (NIV) says, a cord of three strands is not easily broken. However, as my cliff-hanging adventure reminded me, our friends, churches, and mentors will only help keep us from slipping if *they* have a sure grasp on the rock themselves. That's why it's so important that no matter who our main Christian support network contains, God's Word is the foundation for their teaching, thinking, and actions.

At this point, you're well on your way in preparing yourself to thrive as a Christ follower in secular classrooms and culture. You are armed with strategies to build strong spiritual, intellectual, and interpersonal foundations—and to maintain those foundations throughout college. Now it's time to learn practical tactics for navigating the trenches of real-world classrooms.

Endnotes

1. Ephesians 6:12; James 5:16
2. E.g., Hebrews 10:24–25; Colossians 3:16; 1 John 1:7
3. Jennifer Hefner and Daniel Eisenberg, "Social Support and Mental Health Among College Students," *American Journal of Orthopsychiatry* 79, no. 4 (2009): 491–499.
4. More on this in chapter 13
5. 1 Corinthians 15:33
6. E.g., 1 Corinthians 5:11
7. E.g., 2 Peter 2:1; Acts 20:29.
8. "Matthew 7," Jamieson-Fausset-Brown Bible Commentary, accessed January 5, 2021, https://biblehub.com/commentaries/jfb/matthew/7.htm.
9. "Matthew 7," Ellicott's Commentary for English Readers, accessed January 5, 2021, https://biblehub.com/commentaries/ellicott/matthew/7.htm.
10. Ken Ham, *Gospel Reset: Salvation Made Relevant* (Green Forest: Master Books, 2018).
11. For caveats and further insights, see Paul Scharf, "Should I Leave My Church over Creation?" Answers in Genesis, January 1, 2015, https://answersingenesis.org/culture/should-i-leave-my-church-over-creation.
12. Rick Hiemstra, Lorianne Dueck, and Matthew Blackaby, "Renegotiating Faith: The Delay in Young Adult Identity Formation and What It Means for the Church in Canada," Faith Today Publications, 2018, accessed January 5, 2021, https://p2c.com/renegotiating-faith.
13. The only time I remember hearing anyone mention music was a graduate student in the UK, who said that the church she attended as an undergrad had "a student ministry that met every Tuesday, with free food, really good teaching, and worship."
14. More on time management for maintaining spiritual health at university back in chapter 6
15. Multiple major studies back the importance of mentorship for helping youth develop a lasting, thriving biblical worldview, including the National Survey of Youth and Religion and *Faith for Exiles* research cited in chapter 6, along with the *Renegotiating Faith* study cited earlier in this chapter (reference 12).
16. See 1 Corinthians 12.

Part 3

IN THE TRENCHES

Practical strategies for surviving a secular university

CRITICAL THINKING 101

9

The 3 Rules and 7 Checks of Critical Thinking

The moment has arrived. After years of diligent training, study, and preparation, you are finally setting foot onto the spiritual battlefield of a university. This is it. This is what you've been waiting for! Ready or not, you have arrived on the front lines, armed with the sword of the Spirit,[1] a ridiculously heavy backpack, and a pair of glistening garden pruners.

Wait, garden pruners?

Oh yeah.

In case you missed that spiel in chapter 7 (I know, it was a while ago), I mentioned that critical thinking tools are like intellectual garden pruners for tackling the weeds of lies, irrationality, and flawed logic that crop up in our minds—and in the messages we encounter daily. Even when those messages contradict the Bible's teaching, they can sometimes sound incredibly persuasive. And they're not only a hazard of secular classrooms. Take, for instance, the following scenarios:

Scenario 1

A parade of cat videos and political memes tumbles across your social media feed when a headline screams for you to stop scrolling: "New Discovery Casts Light on the Origins of Life." Unaware that you're holding your breath, you click on the link to read, "Scientists have unveiled yet another layer of evidence proving that life's important building blocks could have evolved naturally."[2]

Scenario 2

"From the time religious beliefs evolved," an accented voice narrates as images of battles, conquests, and inquisitions fill the television screen, "the pages of religious history have been written in blood—blood which fundamentalists have shed in the names of their mystical deities." You change the channel but cannot erase the images from your mind. If "religious" people have committed such crimes, what does that say about their beliefs?[3]

Scenario 3

You're sitting in a friend's church contemplating the design on the pastor's tie when his words jostle you to attention: "This so-called miracle, like the others which Jesus performed, certainly had a natural explanation—because Jesus was a natural person. Hebrews 2:17

says he was like us in every way,[4] although legends later grew around his name, borrowing from pagan folktales after his death."[5]

Whether online, in classes, or anywhere else, messages that challenge a biblical worldview are bound to confront us in everyday life. Sometimes these untruths stalk on silent paws, cloaked in woolly sounding doctrines. Other times, they leap snarling into our path and threaten to seize our faith by the throat. Either way, the world is their territory—and they're only going to multiply. As the Apostle Paul warned Timothy, "evil people and impostors will go on from bad to worse, deceiving and being deceived."[6] Paul added, however,

> But as for you, continue in what you have learned and have firmly believed, knowing from whom you learned it and how from childhood you have been acquainted with the sacred writings, which are able to make you wise for salvation through faith in Christ Jesus. . . . The time is coming when people will not endure sound teaching, but having itching ears they will accumulate for themselves teachers to suit their own passions, and will turn away from listening to the truth and wander off into myths.

In this world of deception, how can you equip yourself to "continue in what you have learned and have firmly believed"? Fortunately, a few practical, accessible tools can help you walk through any information that challenges your worldview, process each component, and handle remaining questions—all without draining too much valuable study time. Having tested these tools during four years of secular university, I know how useful they are. They all come down to three rules of critical thinking: don't panic, break it down, and follow up.

Let's unpack each of these rules, focusing especially on Rule #2, where we'll walk through 7 Checks of Critical Thinking, which you can use to break down messages. Based on the top critical thinking tools I found invaluable in a university, these 3 Rules and 7 Checks are designed to help you think like an apologist, process any faith-challenging message, and arrive at a biblical, logical conclusion yourself.

RULE #1: DON'T PANIC

When you encounter a persuasive—but unbiblical—message, the first thing to do is . . . stay calm. This might sound obvious. But when you're listening to a professor present an argument against Christianity you've never heard before while all of your classmates are nodding and taking notes, then (if you're anything like me) you might notice your heart beating a little faster. You might find your pencil hesitating over your notebook. And you might begin to wonder, *what if I'm wrong about my biblical beliefs*?

This is when it's time to take a deep breath and remind yourself what you know. You know God's Word is true. You have an unbelievable amount of evidence confirming that, including facts from science, history, eyewitness testimony, and your own personal experience of walking with God. Since you know God's Word is true, you know anything which contradicts his Word must be a lie. And on some level, all lies have to fall apart. Like Romans 3:4 says, "Let God be true though every one were a liar."

Because the Bible is true, it can handle any question you throw at it. It will always stand up to scrutiny. So when you hear information that seems to threaten your biblical beliefs, relax. This is no time to let your heart go running out the door screaming that everything it knows must be wrong. Instead, wrestle down your heart and tell it to chill. Give it a paper bag to breathe into for awhile. New information might shift your perspective, but it can never overturn God's Word.

"Here are a couple of tips."

When you first encounter an unbiblical message in class, you may need to wait for a moment of free time before you can break the message down with biblical critical thinking. Here are a couple of tips for warding off anxiety in the meantime.

Use Quotation Marks

As you're taking notes in class, put quotation marks around information which might contradict a biblical worldview. Doing so frees you psychologically from feeling as though you're writing down a definite fact because you're just noting what somebody said.

Even the religious rulers in Jesus' day recognized the power of quotation marks. When Pilate wrote the sign for Jesus' cross, it read, "This is the King of the Jews." But John 19:21 records that the chief priests, who did not want to affirm Jesus' kingship as fact, told Pilate, "Do not write, 'The King of the Jews,' but rather, 'This man said, I am King of the Jews.'"

Those wee little marks make a world of difference. If you're like me, you might become tired of sprinkling your notes with quotations after four years. But I'd encourage you not to stop.

Write Down Your Questions Immediately

Another pertinent practice for panic prevention is proactively penning potentially problematic points for postponed perusal purposes. In other words, when you hear a faith-challenging message in class, flip to the back of your notebook and write down your questions so you can follow up on them later.

Having that physical record of your questions lets you seek answers from apologetics databases or biblical mentors when you have the chance. Otherwise, you may begin to sense a weight of vague uncertainties amassing against your worldview without being able to remember, identify, and deal with specific concerns. (And that would pose a perplexing problem.)

RULE #2: BREAK IT DOWN

Now that you've coached your heart to stop racing, it's time to rationally assess the "facts." The most effective system I've found for doing so involves filtering the "facts" through a series of mental checkpoints called the 7 Checks of Critical Thinking.

Check 1: Check Scripture

Imagine someone handed you some money that looked a little off. What's the first step you would take to determine if the currency were counterfeit? You'd compare it to real money.

You can always detect a lie by comparing it to the truth. And God's Word, like the real currency, is our measuring stick for truth. After all, God is the only one who's always been there, knows everything, and cannot lie. God also confirms the truth of his Word in countless ways, from the intricacies of creation to the fulfillments of prophecies to the way we can see promises from the Bible playing out in our personal lives. So the first step to identify a lie is comparing claims against what Scripture says.

We'll be far better equipped to do this, of course, if we're familiar with God's Word in the first place. That's one reason why it's so critical to build strong spiritual foundations, consistently study Scripture, and have godly mentors who can help us process information through the lens of Scripture. Then we can be like the Bereans in Acts 17:11, who examined the Scriptures every day to see if others' claims were true.

Along the way, we can expect to face counterattacks from a certain someone who asked Eve in the garden of Eden, "Did God actually say you shouldn't eat that fruit?"[6] Even today, Satan loves trying to make us second-guess God's Word, asking, "Did God actually say that he created everything in six days, or that there was really a global flood, or that Jesus is really the only way to God?" Yes, God did say so. And we're called to make his Word the foundation for our thinking in every area.

Basing our thinking on God's Word involves checking everything we hear, believe, and tell ourselves against Scripture. You know that verse which talks about taking every thought captive to obey Christ?[9] I once heard a young woman explain this passage by asking, "What does it mean to take a thought captive? It means you hold that thought at spearpoint and interrogate it, asking, 'Why are you here? What are you doing in my mind? What does Scripture say about you?'"

I like to share this illustration when speaking to students, reminding other young people that comparing our thoughts against Scripture can save us so much trouble. It helps us guard our minds against falling into unhealthy thinking patterns, and it helps us guard our hearts—potentially saving years of regret.

Check 2: Check the Challenge

Sometimes as you compare a new message against Scripture, you realize that the message doesn't directly challenge your *faith* so much as your *ideas* about your faith. Maybe the message confronts your opinions about church traditions, worship styles, or some other nondoctrinal issue—like the question of how many magi visited Jesus. We don't know how many magi made the trip—the Bible doesn't say. It's a side issue. That's very different from a foundational doctrine of Christianity, like the reality that Jesus came to earth as God in human flesh.

"A negotiable side issue?"

Take another issue—the existence of Adam. If humans descended from apelike ancestors, as my textbooks insisted, then a real man named Adam would never have existed as the first person. Instead, a population of apelike creatures would have slowly evolved into the first group of humans. Is Adam's existence a negotiable side issue or a foundational doctrine?

Like we saw in chapter 2, the short answer is that Adam's *existence is a foundational doctrine*.[10] The gospel's significance hinges on the reality of the historical Adam described in Genesis. There had to be a real Adam made in God's image as the first human, who committed real sin, leading to real physical and spiritual death for all humanity. This explains why Jesus died a physical death to offer life to descendants of the first Adam who put their faith in the last Adam (1 Corinthians 15:45).

You can use Critical Thinking Check #2: Check the Challenge to arrive at this answer yourself. The key lies in asking a few honest questions which help separate negotiable side issues from foundational doctrines.

Does this message conflict with a clear teaching from specific verses in Scripture?

To discern whether messages contradict biblical teachings, we must be deeply familiar with God's Word—an essential part of having strong spiritual foundations. The more we study the Bible, the better equipped we'll become to recognize unbiblical messages. In this case, the Bible does clearly teach the existence of a real Adam, not only in Genesis or genealogies but also in New Testament passages like Romans 5 and 1 Corinthians 15 that link Adam's sin to Jesus' death.

Does this message conflict with the big picture of what the Bible teaches?

Often, false teachers may misinterpret Bible verses, take them out of context, or twist them to suit human ideas. (PS—injecting human ideas into Scripture is known as *eisegesis*, a concept we'll examine closer in chapter 12.) Again, it *does* matter for the big picture of Scripture whether Adam existed. From the entrance of sin in Genesis to the laws of Moses to the prophecies of a Messiah who would pay the penalty for sin to the death and resurrection of Jesus to the new heaven and earth described in Revelation, the metanarrative of Scripture ties back to the actions of a historical Adam.[11]

Does this message conflict with the way the majority of Christians interpreted the Bible for hundreds of years?

Ideas which don't come from Scripture have sneaked into many Christians' beliefs throughout history, requiring reformations to call believers back to the foundation of biblical authority. We can safely assume, however, that most of the genuine believers preceding us (especially in the early centuries after Christ) were passionate to "teach what accords with sound doctrine."[12] It's a *major* red flag if someone else comes along offering a completely novel spin on Scripture.

Paul warned about such spin-offs, telling the early church in Galatia, "Even if we or an angel from heaven should preach to you a gospel contrary to the one we preached to you, let him be accursed."[13] And, like you can learn more about in other resources,[1] historical Christianity has long acknowledged the existence of a real Adam, right from New Testament voices, including Paul,[14] Luke,[15] and Jesus himself.[16]

Check 3: Check the Source

The next Check of Critical Thinking is to consider your information source. Who is telling you this message? To better understand what kind of source you're dealing with, it's helpful to think about their credibility, worldview, and possible motives, along with how the source collected and reported any relevant information.

Source Credibility

Sometimes, valid information can come from less-than-credible sources, and invalid information can come from credible sources. Still, a source's credibility, or trustworthiness, often lends you solid insight into how seriously you can take their message.

The most credible *human* source is an expert in a relevant field. So a message about microbiology will be far more trustworthy coming from a professional microbiologist than from someone who's an expert in another field, like chemistry, or from a random person on the internet. Trying to back up a statement solely by citing a nonexpert (like a random internet user) is a type of fallacy, or flawed logic, called *appeal to false authority*.

A related fallacy is simply called *appeal to authority*, which involves saying a message is true just because an expert said so, without supplying other supporting evidence. For example, someone relying on an appeal to authority might argue, "Dinosaurs evolved into birds because my paleontology professor said so." A paleontology professor might know a ton about dinosaurs. But even experts can make mistakes, believe wrong information, and are biased by their starting worldview assumptions.

Source Worldview

On that note, the next question to ask is whether your source is starting from the worldview foundation of man's word or God's Word. The worldviews people begin with help determine the assumptions they use and the conclusions they reach—and experts are no exception. While experts are often fantastic sources for knowledge about certain facts, remember that many experts may be interpreting those facts through the lens of a false worldview. Knowing the source's worldview will therefore come in handy for separating facts from assumptions later in the critical thinking process.

Source Motives

The third point to consider is whether the source might have other motives for communicating the message.[17] People say and do things for various reasons, not all of which may be obvious. News reporters, for instance, must write in a way that appeases their readers and advertisers. Financial and political motives may influence which stories get published, what facts are included, and how information is worded.

Not even scientists are immune to the sway of ulterior motives. Popular culture may deify scientists as an infallible caste of robo-researchers unhampered by emotions, biases, subjectivity, or other plagues of the plebeians. But the reality is that all scientists are human. They have reputations to build, grant money to source, and careers to secure. Given these factors, a report published by the Royal Society of Open Science observed:

> As recently described, three closely inter-related sub-systems (science advancement, reputational rewards and financial returns) collectively form an overall scientific publishing system that has become heavily flawed. It encourages scientists to distort and exaggerate their results in striving for new grants, promotions and distinctions; and encourages publishers to cherry-pick work, hype results and distort refereeing in the competition for high status and correspondingly high profits from publication charges. Both authors and publishers are incentivized to game the system to their mutual advantage. In the extreme, the perverse incentives generated result in authors fabricating data, predatory journals hunting for papers and fake journals being created that seek only the authors' fees for article processing.[18]

Not all researchers will (hopefully) allow these factors to undermine the pursuit of accurate information. But knowing that ulterior motives do influence the scientific community can remind us that man's word is fallible. God's Word, therefore, remains the only completely reliable information source.

Information Collection

Sometimes, part of checking the source involves thinking not only about who is sharing information but also how they collected the information. For instance, once when I was writing an article about evolutionary beliefs in Britain, I nearly shared that only 3% of English science teachers believe that God created humans and did not use evolution. But then I realized that the study which uncovered that statistic only looked at 55 teachers in four schools, out of tens of thousands of science teachers across the UK. The study still uncovered some interesting information, but its sample size (the number of teachers the study looked at) was too small for me to safely write that 3% of all British science teachers accept creation.

"a hefty proportion"

In the same way, a report from 2017 suggested that a hefty proportion of natural selection studies don't necessarily consider large enough sample sizes to draw accurate conclusions.[19] Like we saw in chapter 7, natural selection can't produce the types of changes required to transform one kind of living thing into another anyway.

The point is that sometimes researchers make mistakes. Studies normally go through a review process designed to catch as many mistakes as possible. But like the 2017 report showed, even widely accepted research practices don't always yield accurate results.

Similarly, a study's conclusions may become outdated if new research comes along which overturns or reinterprets the original study. This is especially true for fields like biology, where new discoveries constantly update the scientific knowledge base. It can be worth checking how long ago a study was published and whether other researchers have since reconsidered its findings.[20]

Information Reporting

Have you noticed that often the popular press and social media circulate information without explaining how that data was collected?[21] In these cases, you may find it worthwhile to go back to the original research to see where the information came from and if it's being reported accurately. What can you learn about the *original* source's credibility, worldview, motives, and information collection?

Looking into a message's origins not only keeps you from falling for potentially unreliable information sources[22] but also helps prevent the spread of misinformation.

Check 4: Check the Definitions

Once you've checked a message's source, the next step is to think about how that source might be defining any key words in the message. After all, we can't fully understand, discuss, or respond to a message unless we're clear about exactly what its words mean. Clarifying definitions can help us resolve conflicts, detangle controversies, and prevent confusion in our everyday communication.

For example, one day at a greenhouse where I worked as a student, an elderly gentleman walked over to ask me about the "time."

"It's quarter to three, sir!" I responded.

"No, no. *Time*."

"Yes, sir. It's quarter to three."

"T-H-Y-M-E."

"Oh. We have thyme plants right this way, sir."

Time and *thyme* are different words, but sometimes even the same word can have multiple meanings which require clarification. One word may carry different connotations, communicate different ideas in different contexts, or mean different things to different people. Words like *science* and *evolution* are prime examples,[23] highlighting why it's so important to understand the difference between the two types of science and two types of "evolutionary" change discussed in chapter 7.

For instance, when my textbooks offered examples of scientists observing "evolution," it was almost always evolution in the sense of variation within the original kinds of living things God created—like finches. In my biology classes, we talked about how mutations and natural selection can let finches with long beaks give rise to finches with short beaks. That's cool, but it's not an example of evolution in the sense of change *between* kinds of living things, like dinosaurs evolving into finches.

Textbooks and other mainstream sources, however, often call these types of changes equal. They argue, "We can see finches evolving into finches; therefore, we know dinosaurs evolved into finches." But did you catch what happened there? The meaning of evolution switched. If you notice a word's meaning subtly switching during a discussion, you've detected a type of logical fallacy called *equivocation*, or *bait-and-switch*.

Another common bait-and-switch target is the word *science*. My evolution textbook, for instance, blurred the lines between observational and historical science by calling evolutionary origins "as much a scientific fact as the atomic constitution of matter or the revolution of Earth around the Sun."[24]

The earth's revolution is something we can measure with observational science. Even prominent evolutionists, however, have pointed out that assumptions about evolution involve historical science.[25] So beware of equivocation, and always take "thyme" to define your terms.

Check 5: Check for Propaganda

Once you've clarified important definitions, you can start separating the facts in a message from other elements which may *sound* persuasive but aren't based on truth or valid reasoning. The first way to filter facts from nonfacts is to check for propaganda.

Propaganda is a manipulative type of communication that tries to persuade by appealing to something other than logic. Take, for example, the following real-world messages:

- "Religion is humanity's most lethal weapon, and the most dangerous people are people of faith."
- "This is the twenty-first century. No one follows the Bible's teachings anymore."
- "Teaching children that the Scriptures are true is nothing less than child abuse."

- "No true scientist questions evolutionary human origins."
- "Intelligent design is a whacked-out tea party movement."

Sound familiar? These are messages I've personally encountered in my readings, classes, and conversations—and they all make arguments based on something irrelevant to truth. Instead, they persuade through channels, including emotion, eloquence, positive or negative associations, name-calling, and powerful psychological phenomena, like humans' need for acceptance.

Often, propaganda-based arguments rely on types of faulty logic known as *fallacies of irrelevant premises*. What do these fallacies have in common? They use anything but sound reasoning to distract from whether something is true.

We'll look at classic examples of these fallacies, explore the science behind *why* they're persuasive, and identify an easy hack for answering propaganda-based arguments in chapter 10. For now, it's enough to hint that all you need to do to outsmart propaganda is ask, "Why does this message sound persuasive? Does it appeal to logic or to something else, like emotion or appearance? Are those things relevant to whether the message is true?"

Check 6: Check the Interpretations

Asking yourself why something sounds true helps you filter out a host of compelling—but irrelevant—appeals from propaganda, leaving you with "just the facts." Even "facts," however, are not always what they seem.

For example, imagine you're walking through a museum when suddenly you come face-to-face with an ape-woman (okay, a colorful *illustration* of an ape-woman, along with a few fragments of an apelike skeleton). The entire display is presented as truth. But which elements are really *facts* and which are *interpretations* of facts?

"Untangle genuine facts."

One of the easiest ways to untangle genuine facts from a web of interpretations is to remember the difference between observational and historical science. When you encounter a faith-challenging message, ask, "Which parts of the message involve facts we can observe in the present and which are assumptions about the past?"

In the case of the museum display, you might say that the fossil fragments are the bare-bones facts. Any observations we can make about those bones in the present—like their lengths, masses, and radioisotope ratios—are the observational science. The evolutionary story and artistic rendering the museum created around those observations, however, is historical science.

Constructing stories about the past often requires using assumptions to fill in for gaps in the facts. Which assumptions researchers use will depend on which worldview "glasses" they're wearing. For instance, a researcher viewing apelike bone fragments through the glasses of man's word may assume the missing pieces of the skeleton included long arms like an ape's but hips for walking upright like a human.

These types of assumptions explain why now, standing before the skeleton's reconstruction, you see a bipedal ape-woman with humanlike eyes instead of a hairy knucklewalker with gorilla-like eyes. Yet those imaginary humanlike features may be presented as if they were facts set in stone, like the fossil fragments themselves.

Because assumptions and interpretations so often masquerade as facts, seeing through their disguises is a vital skill for navigating a university—not to mention life. We'll explore how to sharpen this skill using real textbook examples of "evidence for evolution" in chapter 11.

Check 7: Check the Logic

At this point in the critical thinking processes, you will have already caught most of the potential fallacies in a message by checking its source, checking words' definitions, checking for propaganda, and checking the interpretations of any facts. But other, more elusive lines of sketchy logic may still be lurking behind the facts. Critical Thinking Check #7 involves a final scan for faulty logic, including fallacies like circular reasoning, straw man arguments, faulty analogies, and other common logical errors we'll examine in chapter 12.

RULE #3: FOLLOW UP

Alright, time for a quick recap. When you encounter information that seems to challenge a biblical worldview, first—don't panic. Second, break the message down by checking Scripture, checking the challenge, checking the source, checking the definitions, checking for propaganda, checking the interpretations, and checking the logic. While this system will help you filter enormous volumes of persuasive untruths from everything you hear and read, you'll almost certainly still have some unresolved questions about your faith.

Congratulations. You are now free to panic.

I'm kidding.

There never is a valid reason for leaping off a Rock so true as Christ. So instead of panicking, remember Peter's response when Jesus asked his disciples if they wanted to walk away from him after his teachings became tough to accept: "Simon Peter answered him, 'Lord, to whom shall we go? You have the words of eternal life, and we have believed, and have come to know, that you are the Holy One of God.'"[26]

These words encouraged me repeatedly throughout university, reminding me that the weight of evidence for my faith far surpassed the uncertainty of my unresolved questions. As humans, we'll never understand everything. The key is to remember that God has the answer, to ask him for it, and to trust him that there is an answer, even if he never reveals it to us on this side of heaven. Unanswered questions can be a devious faith killer. But faith crises don't happen when Christians begin asking questions. They happen when we stop seeking answers.

"Devious faith killer"

Tips for Following Up

When seeking answers, you can consult three types of sources corresponding to the three types of personal foundations that let Christian students thrive at a university.

1. Apologetics Resources

Biblical apologetics resources correspond to the intellectual foundations students need for defending their biblical worldview. As a student, I found it incredibly helpful to type my questions into the search boxes of trusted apologetics websites like AnswersInGenesis.org, where I could quickly access answers from thousands of articles and videos freely available online. Even if I didn't have time to read a long article that instant, it helped me just to see that a thoughtful answer existed.

2. Biblical Mentors

The second source to consult when seeking answers are biblically grounded mentors, keystones of the interpersonal foundations students need. As a student, I wrote down a running list of questions written down to ask my mentor, Dr. Helder. When we had a chance to meet during Christmas or reading breaks, she'd go through my questions with me, share insights about each topic, and point me to resources where I could find even more information.

3. God and His Word

The final and most important source to consult when seeking answers is God himself. Maintaining a close, personal walk with God is central to the spiritual foundations that Christian students need. And personally, I found that I could use tough questions to *build* my spiritual foundations by taking those questions to God, using them as opportunities to pray, and trusting that God had the answers, even if I didn't.

Ultimately, by drawing me closer to God, driving me to learn more about apologetics, and showing me that Scripture always stands up to scrutiny, I've found that tough questions often *strengthened* my faith. And I'm not the only student who's discovered this. A Christian student in Holland told me,

> I'd advise students, when you do have questions, don't be afraid of them. Instead, start looking for answers. Accept that you have questions, and that's not necessarily a bad thing. Read solid Christian books, articles, and blogs to keep connected with your faith and to keep learning more.

She added,

> Before I started, I was really scared that university would change my faith. But there just came a point where I thought, "If God is real, and he is who the Bible says he is, it makes absolutely no difference what classes I'm going to take or what I'm going to learn. If God is real, nothing about him is going to change." I'm not scared to find out new information, because even if I might be shaken, that's not going to change who he is.

SHARPENING YOUR CRITICAL THINKING TOOLS

This student realized that, like we saw in chapter 7, the garden pruners of critical thinking will never scathe the rock-solid truth of God's Word. They do, however, prove themselves invaluable for hacking back weedy untruths that contradict sound doctrine.

"Rock-solid truth"

With the crash course we've just covered, you're well on your way to processing faith-challenging messages yourself using the 3 Rules and 7 Checks of Critical Thinking. There's a lot more to some of these checks, however, than we could unpack in this brief overview. So let's move on to the finer "points" of how to master these mental weed-whacking tools. For starters, we'll dive into the science of persuasion to take a closer look at what propaganda is, how it works, and how to outsmart it.

Endnotes

1. Ephesians 6:17
2. For information on why life cannot come from nonlife, see https://answersingenesis.org/origin-of-life or *Critical Thinking Scan*, Season 9, Episodes 2–3, available on Answers TV.
3. We'll see how to respond to this issue in chapter 10.
4. For tips on how to recognize false teaching that misinterprets Scripture, see chapter 12.
5. For a response to this claim, see Tim Chaffey, "Mistaken or Stolen Identity?" Answers in Genesis, March 8, 2013, https://answersingenesis.org/jesus-christ/resurrection/mistaken-or-stolen-identity.
6. 2 Timothy 3:13
7. 2 Timothy 3:14–15, 4:3–4
8. See Genesis 3:1.
9. 2 Corinthians 10:5
10. For more detailed answers, see Terry Mortenson, ed., *Searching for Adam: Genesis and the Truth About Man's Origins* (Green Forest: Master Books, 2016); William VanDoodewaard, *The Quest for the Historical Adam: Genesis, Hermeneutics, and Human Origins* (Grand Rapids: Reformation Heritage Books, 2015) or the articles at https://answersingenesis.org/adam-and-eve.
11. This doesn't mean that the big picture of Scripture is *about* Adam, but that Adam's disobedience established the need for the One whom Scripture is about: the last Adam (1 Corinthians 15:45), Jesus.
12. Titus 2:1
13. Galatians 6:8 (See also verse 9.)
14. E.g., Romans 5:12–21; 1 Corinthians 15:21–22, 45–49
15. Luke 3:38
16. E.g., in Matthew 19:4–6, Jesus talks about God's design for marriage "from the beginning of creation" by quoting from the Genesis account of the first man and woman.
17. Saying a message is false *because* its source has a personal motive for communicating it is a fallacy called appeal to motive. However, recognizing sources' motives can help us discern the lens through which they're interpreting facts.
18. Henning Hopf et. al., "Fake Science and the Knowledge Crisis: Ignorance Can Be Fatal," *Royal Society Open Science* 6, no. 5 (2019): 190161.
19. Mark Grabowski and Arthur Porto, "How Many More? Sample Size Determination in Studies of Morphological Integration and Evolvability," *Methods in Ecology and Evolution* 8, no. 5 (2017): 592–603.
20. One easy way to do this is to look for recent or citing articles in an online research database, as appendix E explains.
21. For numerous examples of how popular press headlines misrepresent research findings, see Harry Sanders, "Can We Trust Science Media?" Answers in Genesis, July 10, 2019, https://answersingenesis.org/science/can-we-trust-science-media.
22. Remember though, a message isn't true or false based *only* on who said it, as we'll see in chapter 10.
23. Even the word *Christianity* can mean different things to different people, so clarifying a biblical definition of what it means to be a Christian may prove valuable when discussing your beliefs.
24. Douglas Futuyama, *Evolution*, 3rd ed. (Sunderland: Sinauer Associates, 2013), 631–632.

25. E.g., Ernst Mayr, "Darwin's Influence on Modern Thought," Scientific American, November 24, 2009, https://www.scientificamerican.com/article/darwins-influence-on-modern-thought1/. See also Troy Lacey, "First Usage of Origins vs. Operational Science: Did Young-Earth Creationists Invent the Term Origin Science to Discredit Evolution?" Answers in Genesis, February 1, 2018, https://answersingenesis.org/what-is-science/first-usage-origins-vs-operational-science.

26. John 6:68–69

DODGING PSYCHOLOGICAL BULLETS

10

How to handle illogical persuasion

When you encounter the words *bacon and eggs*, what's one of the first thoughts that comes to mind?

If you answered *breakfast*, you might have a journalist named Edward Bernays to thank.

Born in 1891, Bernays was the close nephew of Sigmund Freud, the rather notorious psychologist whose unbiblical (and largely unscientific) conjectures drove people to think about how unconscious processes may affect human behavior. Bernays, fascinated by Freud's ideas, wondered if he could exploit others' unconscious processes to influence public behavior—and ultimately culture.

In World War I, the US Committee on Public Information hired Bernays to garner public war support. Meanwhile, the government used findings from psychology and sociology to develop new ways of shaping popular opinion about the war. These efforts produced an arsenal of highly effective propaganda techniques for manipulating public beliefs and behavior.

"Propaganda is a process."

Like we saw in chapter 9, propaganda is a type of communication that persuades by appealing to something besides logic. According to one psychologist's 1943 definition, "propaganda is a process which deliberately attempts through persuasion techniques to secure from the propagandee, before he can deliberate freely, the responses desired by the propagandist."[1] In other words, propaganda tries persuading people to form an opinion about something *before* they can think it through rationally.

Bernays noticed that wartime propaganda techniques included harnessing the influence of authority figures, generating clichés, and creating emotional appeals. Could these same techniques apply to manipulating people's behavior *after* the war? Bernays believed so. Rebranding propaganda with the term "public relations," he offered his powers of persuasion to the marketing world. And his methods largely succeeded.

Take breakfast, for instance. In the 1920s, the Beech-Nut Packing Company recruited Bernays to stoke consumers' appetite for bacon.

Bernays' research team discovered that most Americans preferred a light breakfast—coffee, orange juice, and perhaps toast. Recognizing the power of authority figures, Bernays recruited a doctor to ask over 4,500 other physicians whether they agreed that a heavier breakfast (say, bacon and eggs) provided more energy. Bernays publicized the results in newspapers, demand for bacon rose, and the campaign became a sizzling success.[2]

Unfortunately, not all of Bernays' campaigns were so benign. To increase tobacco consumption among women, for instance, Bernays linked smoking with women's rights by dubbing cigarettes "torches of freedom." In his influential book *Propaganda*, Bernays concluded, "Those who manipulate this unseen mechanism of society constitute an invisible government which is the true ruling power of our country. . . . We are governed, our minds are molded, our tastes formed, our ideas suggested, largely by men we have never heard of."[3]

"This shocked me."

Bernays recognized propaganda's potential to promote evil as well as good. In 1933, newspaper correspondent Karl von Weigand visited Bernays after meeting Hitler's propagandist, Joseph Goebbels, in Germany. Bernays recounted, "Goebbels, said Weigand, was using my book *Crystallizing Public Opinion* as a basis for his destructive campaign against the Jews of Germany. This shocked me, but I knew any human activity can be used for social purposes or misused for antisocial ones."[4]

PROPAGANDA AND EDUCATION

While much propaganda endorses fairly neutral products[5] (like breakfast foods), other propaganda promotes unbiblical messages that undermine the gospel and society—like the idea that humans are evolutionary by-products rather than persons created in God's image. Propaganda I've seen promoting this message includes textbook pictures that make apes look humanlike, museum displays that make humans look apelike, and classes where authoritative professors assert, "Intelligent design is a whacked-out tea-party movement," or, "There is not a single piece of evidence against evolution."

Schools are such strategic centers for disseminating propaganda that Bernays wrote, "The normal school should provide for the training of the educator to make him realize that his is a twofold job: education as a teacher and education as a propagandist."[6]

In today's propaganda-riddled classrooms and culture, Christians need biblical critical thinking skills more than breakfast needs bacon.[7] Let's dive into the art and science of honing those skills, beginning with a practical hack for answering almost any propaganda-based argument. We'll see how to quickly catch the fallacies in such arguments—including two of culture's top objections to Christianity. Last, we'll explore the psychology behind *why* propaganda works.

The Quickest Way to Override Propaganda

In chapter 9, I mentioned that propaganda-based arguments often involve a class of flawed logic called fallacies of irrelevant premises. There's a long list of these fallacies, but one critical thinking hack can help you catch any of them. All you have to do is ask one question: "Is this message true or false because . . . ?"

For instance, is a message true because many people seem to think so? Not necessarily. History and social psychology have shown that large groups of people can be—and often are—wrong together. This is a fallacy called *appeal to popularity*, or *ad populum*. The number of people who believe something is irrelevant to whether it's true.

Similarly, is a message true because someone smart, famous, wealthy, or beautiful said so? Is it false because someone unsophisticated, immoral, or hypocritical said so? Again, not necessarily. These arguments all use types of *genetic fallacies*, which claim a message is true or false based solely on its *source* rather than its *content*.

"Not necessarily"

Here's another example: is a message false because people can disagree about it? Different church denominations, for instance, have different ideas about certain biblical concepts like worship or baptism.[8] Does that affect the Bible's truth? No. Saying that a message is false because people can disagree about it is a fallacy called *inflation of conflict*.

What if a message is skillfully communicated? Some of my evolutionary professors spoke so eloquently that almost whatever they said sounded true. But I had to remind myself that a message isn't true because it's strikingly expressed.

How about this one: is a message false because people who believe it are ridiculed? Again, no. Attacking a message by attacking the messenger is called the *ad hominem* fallacy, which is Latin for "to the man."

You can find a summary of these and many other fallacies of irrelevant premises in Table 10.1 below.[9] But did you notice that you don't need to know the Latin names for all these fallacies to recognize they're not true? It's just like if you're weeding a garden, you don't need to know the Latin species names for all the weeds to recognize they're not flowers. Similarly, "weeding" countless fallacies from arguments just requires asking, "Is this true or false because . . . ?"

Table 10.1: Catching Common Fallacies of Irrelevant Premises

Question: Is this message . . .	Fallacy
False because people who believe it are ridiculed?	*Ad hominem*
True or false because it evokes strong emotions?	Appeal to emotion
True because there's no evidence for it? *(Or false because there's no evidence against it?)*	Appeal to ignorance
True because it's difficult to imagine it being false? *(Or false because it's difficult to imagine it being true?)*	Appeal to incredulity
True because it's natural? *(Or false because it's unnatural?)*	Appeal to nature
True because it's modern to think so?	Appeal to novelty
True because it might be true?	Appeal to possibility
True because it's probably true?	Appeal to probability
True because it's repeated often?	Appeal to repetition *(ad nauseum)*
True or false because many people think so?	Appeal to the people *(ad populum)*
True because it's been believed for a long time?	Appeal to tradition
False because people can use flawed arguments to defend it?	Argument from fallacy *(ad logicam)*
True because it's the middle ground between two other options?	Argument to moderation *(ad temperantiam)*
True or false only because of the kind of people who say so? True only because an expert says so? True because someone famous says so? True because someone smart says so? False because the source had a certain motive for saying so? True because someone wealthy says so? True because someone charming or beautiful says so? False because a hypocrite says so?	Genetic fallacy Appeal to authority Appeal to celebrity Appeal to intelligence Appeal to motive Appeal to wealth Argument by personal charm You too *(tu quoque)*
False because people can disagree about it?	Inflation of conflict
False because people may have a psychological explanation for believing it?	Psychogenic fallacy

This approach can come across as far more gracious anyway. After all, accusing people in Latin ("Bro, you're using an *ad populum* fallacy!") isn't always the gentlest tactic.[10] By respectfully bringing a matter back to the question of what truth is—and Whom truth comes from, we can communicate a biblical, logical response, expressing the truth in love.

PROPAGANDA AND OBJECTIONS TO CHRISTIANITY

Importantly, asking "Is a message true or false because . . . " can help you respond to two of the top objections to Christianity in secular classrooms and culture:

1. "There's just so much hypocrisy in the church!"
2. "People who call themselves Christians have committed wrong-doings throughout history—and they've even quoted the Bible to justify their actions."

The first objection implies that Christianity isn't worth believing because people who call themselves Christians can act hypocritically, saying one thing but doing another. According to the book *Already Gone*, which examined why many Christian-raised American youth are leaving the church, hypocrisy of church leaders was the third top reason ex-churchgoing young adults gave for vacating the pews.[11]

The second objection pinpoints specific cases of hypocrisy to imply that Christianity is meaningless—if not evil. Christian students I've spoken with across cultures have encountered these types of arguments in their classes. Because such objections are so common, let's take a minute to think about them.

For starters, it's important to recognize that these objections highlight genuine problems. Hypocrisy *does* exist among churchgoers. And tragically, some who identified as Christians *have* committed great wrongs. As Christ followers, we do not downplay these wrongs. But we do need to know how to give a gracious answer (1 Peter 3:15) to those who raise these objections to dismiss the truth of Scripture. These three points can help you get started.[12]

1. The fact that professing Christians can do wrong, misapply Scripture, or commit hypocrisy is irrelevant to whether the Bible is true.

Using the question "Is a message true or false because . . .", we can ask, "Is the Bible false because people who claim to believe it may act hypocritically or commit wrongdoings?" Stated this way, it's easier to see the answer is no. Truth is truth regardless of who believes it, what they've done, or how they twist the truth to rationalize their actions.

Remember, it's a genetic fallacy to claim a message is false based only on the kind of people who espouse it—including hypocrites. To illustrate, let's say I was casually wolfing down a sack of pure granulated sugar, pausing only to wave my spoon at a bystander and advise, "You should avoid consuming excessive sugar—it's hazardous to your health." That person could point out my hypocrisy, saying, "But Patricia . . . *you're* consuming excessive sugar!" Fair. My actions wouldn't be *reflecting* the truth of my statement. But does that mean my actions changed the truth of my statement? No. Excessive sugar consumption would remain unhealthy regardless of what I was doing.

"you're consuming excessive sugar!"

Discounting a message—including the Bible—because of someone's hypocrisy is a type of genetic fallacy called *tu quoque*, which means "you too." To be sure, this fallacy does not diminish the sadness or wrongness of hypocrisy within the church. It just means that hypocrisy is not a logically valid reason for dismissing the Bible's claims. Similarly, the fact that some professing Christians try using the Bible to excuse wrongdoings doesn't tell us whether the Bible is true—or even if Scripture supports those wrongdoings. To find that out, we need to examine the Bible itself, consider the whole message it teaches, and look at what happens when a biblical worldview is consistently lived out. After all, a worldview must be judged based on its consistent application—not its misapplication.

2. Jesus' teachings do not justify wrongdoing or hypocrisy.

For Christians, looking at our worldview's consistent application means looking at Jesus. He defined, summarized, and modeled God's moral standards better than anyone, saying, "Do to others what you would have others do to you,"[13] and "Love your neighbor as yourself."[14]

Examine the life and teachings of Jesus, and you'll find he was no hypocrite. In fact, Jesus detested hypocrisy. If you read Matthew 23, you'll notice that Jesus had some incredibly strong words for the hypocritical religious leaders of his day. People who object to professing Christians' hypocrisy are *affirming* the statements and stance of Jesus.

Ultimately, if people who call themselves Christians have done things that oppose Jesus' teachings, God's character, and the big picture of Scripture, you can be sure the ideas behind those actions did not come from the Bible. Instead, people were putting their ideas *into* the Bible (or simply rebelling against God's commands) because a holistic biblical worldview does not justify wrongdoings.

On the other hand, an atheistic, evolutionary worldview *can* consistently justify many wrongdoings, even though atheists may behave morally themselves. After all, if humans and their morals are nothing but evolutionary happenstance, why *shouldn't* we wrong others to advance our genes' evolutionary success? This type of reasoning has played—and still plays—a role in some of history's worst atrocities, as multiple researchers have documented.[15] So while Jesus' claims cannot consistently be used to justify wrongdoings, Darwin's claims can.

3. Moral judgments assume a moral lawgiver.

Let's take a step back and look at the moral assumptions required to criticize wrongdoings or hypocrisy in the first place. For instance, denouncing hypocrisy involves a moral judgment: hypocrisy is wrong. But for a moral judgment to mean anything, morals must exist. Before we can talk about whether Christians' deeds are right or wrong, we need a foundation for deciding what right and wrong are.

Naturalistic, evolutionary worldviews do not provide that consistent foundation for morality, as various scholars have explained.[16] Without absolute standards for defining right and wrong, we have no ultimate basis for objecting to someone's hypocrisy. We might say hypocrisy is wrong in *our opinion*, but maybe for someone else, hypocrisy is right. Who can absolutely say which of these conflicting opinions is the best?

A biblical worldview, however, *does* supply a consistent basis for morality. Our Creator's character is the source of moral standards, which he reveals to us through his Word, the Bible. So dismissing the Bible because some professing Christians disobey Jesus requires not only committing a logical fallacy but borrowing moral standards from the very book being dismissed: God's Word.[17] This is an example of how bringing back an argument to the question of what truth is—and Whom truth comes from—lets us not only filter out propaganda but point people to Jesus.

THE SCIENCE OF PERSUASION

Now that we've covered the basics of what propaganda is and how to catch it, let's delve into the science of how propaganda works. By understanding how persuasion happens in the brain, you'll be better equipped to recognize propaganda, avoid psychological manipulation, and make careful decisions.

Propaganda and Decision-Making

Whether choosing a university, buying a car, or deciding what to eat for breakfast, we face countless decisions throughout our lives. The number of ways we can make each decision skyrockets in materialistic cultures, where multiple brands compete for our attention. Just think of all the places you encounter advertisements: cereal boxes, bus stops, billboards, bulletins, store fronts, store interiors, food courts, crosswalks, vehicle decals—not to mention websites, movies, magazines, television, radio, online videos, and, of course, social media. How do our brains process all that information—and how do propagandists take advantage of the fact?

Decision-Making Channels

Many theories of persuasion look at two different channels the brain uses to make decisions.[18] Different researchers have given different names to these channels. But essentially, one channel involves careful, logical reasoning while the other involves automatic, intuitive processing. When thinking with the automatic channel, we base our decisions on cues which have little to do with logic—like how something looks or how it makes us feel.

As you might have guessed, propaganda exploits this automatic channel, persuading us to make snap decisions without relying on logic. How does propaganda achieve this? It taps into the brain's decision-making shortcuts, known as heuristics.

Heuristics (rhymes with *few mystics*) work like mental rules of thumb to save us time and brainpower when facing everyday decisions. For instance, we use the *follow the majority heuristic* when we copy other people's choices, obeying the rule of thumb which assumes the majority's decision is probably best. This heuristic may work in many cases (think one-way streets or dinners with multiple forks). Yet as history illustrates, public consensus is not always correct. So as useful as heuristics are, they can also mislead.

Thanks to their fallibility, heuristics may give rise to faulty thinking patterns called cognitive biases. The follow-the-majority heuristic, for instance, corresponds to a cognitive bias dubbed the *bandwagon effect*. This bias describes humans' tendency to follow the crowd, even if the crowd is going the wrong direction. Because we're socially wired creatures who want to follow each other, be accepted, and be liked, propagandists love harnessing bandwagon power, suggesting,

"Everyone else is doing something, so you should, too!" Instead of appealing to logic, this argument wields the *ad populum* fallacy.

Heuristics and cognitive biases help explain why bad logic can sound so persuasive: they enable propaganda and fallacies to hijack our automatic thinking processes, bypassing our logical reasoning.

COMMON PERSUASION FORCES

The follow-the-majority heuristic, bandwagon effect, and *ad populum* fallacy revolve around the psychological force of *conformity*—our desire to be like those around us. Because resisting conformity is such an essential skill for Christians in secular classrooms and cultures, let's look at some telling research on peer pressure before we move on to examine other top persuasion forces.

Conformity

Imagine you're a college student recruited to participate in a study about perception. You sit down at a table with several other young people, who you don't realize are actors in the study. At the front of the room, a researcher displays two cards with lines drawn on them.

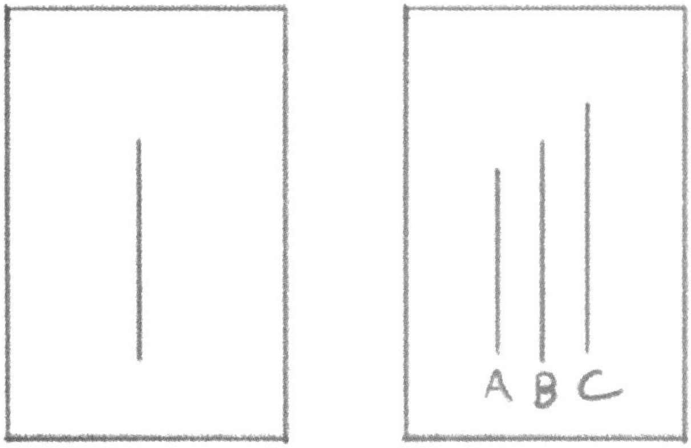

Your job is to report which line on the right appears the same length as the line on the left. Easy, right?

Everyone takes a turn saying the answer aloud. For the first couple of rounds, everything goes smoothly. In the third round, you can see that the correct answer is line B. But everyone else in the room answers, "Line C!" When your turn arrives, what do you say?

If you're like many of the students this study tested, you would say line C because everybody else did—even though your eyes assure you the answer is B. *Three out of four* students conformed to the majority's mistaken answer at least once during the experiments, and on average, students' answers aligned with those of the (faulty) majority one third of the time.[19] In the words of Solomon Asch, the psychologist who conducted this study in the 1950s, "That we have found the tendency to conformity in our society so strong that reasonably intelligent and well-meaning young people are willing to call white black is a matter of concern. It raises questions about our ways of education and about the values that guide our conduct."[20]

Fortunately, there's good news, too. Further experiments showed that if just one other person in the room also gave the right answer, conformity rates dropped dramatically.[21] In other words, we feel far less obligated to follow the crowd if we're not resisting peer pressure alone.

All these findings carry special relevance for Christians in secular classrooms and cultures, where—speaking from experience—we can easily feel isolated in our convictions. The power of consensus helps explain why beliefs like life's supposed evolution from nonliving chemicals go largely unquestioned, despite *opposing* what we know from observational science. Students simply tend to accept the mainstream ideas they're taught, like their professors did before them, and *their* professors before *them*. Other studies have also observed this effect, showing that students are far less likely to think critically about arguments that supposedly voice a majority opinion.[22]

On the bright side, the finding that a like-minded person's presence can neutralize peer pressure illustrates the value of knowing that even one other student believes the Bible. It also shows the power of *being* that one other student.[23]

Authority

Along with conformity, another potent persuasive force to be aware of is authority. Messages may sound true just because they come from authoritative-looking sources, like professors. As we saw at the beginning of this chapter, Bernays harnessed the power of authority by recruiting doctors to promote the "health benefits" of bacon. Today, you can spot the same tactic in advertisements that feature people with lab coats, clipboards, or intelligent-sounding accents.

These types of ads persuade us via the *authority heuristic*—the rule of thumb that experts usually know what they're talking about it, so it's reasonable to believe what they say. This shortcut comes in handy much of the time, but even experts are fallible. The authority heuristic spawns the *authority bias*, a cognitive bias describing our tendency to be influenced by authority figures regardless of their messages' content. However, believing a message *only* because an expert shared it is the *appeal to authority fallacy*.

The Science of Authority

In the 1960s, a psychologist named Stanley Milgram revealed how far authority's tidal-strength force can sweep people.[24] To see what his studies entailed, imagine arriving at a lab where you meet a well-dressed researcher and an unassuming, grandfatherly civilian. The researcher hands you a list of memory-testing questions to ask Mr. Unassuming, who is being strapped into an electric-shock generator. You're to deliver increasingly strong shocks every time he answers incorrectly. In reality, the shock device doesn't generate electricity and Mr. Unassuming is an actor. But you don't realize that.

"Mr. Unassuming is an actor."

If you're like most people, you'd probably feel uncomfortable being ordered to hurt another person. But according to Milgram, nearly two-thirds of participants in this study not only went ahead with it but proceeded all the way to delivering the final 450-volt shock at the researcher's demand.[25]

This study understandably raised ethical concerns, and some psychologists also question other parts of Milgram's methods. But later studies confirmed Milgram's results, revealing that well over half of people will act against their consciences because an authority figure says to.[26, 27]

Now, let's think about these findings in the context of classrooms and culture. My professors never asked me to shock anyone, but they did expect me to believe ideas I knew weren't right based on God's Word, like human evolution.[28] The fact that these messages came from authority figures made them seem true, even though a message's source does not logically affect its truth. Ultimately, the power of authority helps us understand why unbiblical messages can sound persuasive, reminding us that our highest authority is God and his Word.[29]

Repetition

Sometimes, messages aren't persuasive because of *who* shared them but because of *how* they're communicated. For instance, how many times have you heard a message like this:

> 65 million years ago, the dinosaurs which had ruled the world slowly became extinct or evolved into birds. Eventually, mammals took over the dinosaurs' kingdom.

I encountered such statements repeatedly as a kid, even while growing up in a Bible-believing family. Certainly, I knew Genesis reveals that God created humans and land animals (which would include dinosaurs) on day six of creation week. I read books which taught about dinosaurs from a biblical perspective. But other books, museums, and kids' television shows hammered the evolutionary "age of the dinosaurs" narrative into my mind. I didn't realize how effectively they'd indoctrinated me until one summer when I was counseling at a Christian camp.

The realization struck me in a tepee. There, another counselor and I had gathered a group of kids for Bible study. After the lesson, one of the campers mentioned mammals and dinosaurs living together.

"Dinosaurs were around long before mammals,"[30] I automatically "corrected."

"That's not biblical teaching," pointed out my co-counselor.

Oh yeah.

"That's true," I replied. *Where had THAT come from?*

I *knew* the information I'd just shared was false. I'd studied creation for years and hoped to become a Genesis apologist. Yet here I was *teaching evolution to kids during a Bible study that I was leading as a Christian camp counselor*. How had this happened?

The Science of Repetition

I didn't know it at the time, but I'd just fallen for a cognitive bias called the *illusionary truth effect*. This bias describes the way repeated messages tend to influence us, even when we know they're false.

The illusionary truth effect stems from two related mental shortcuts nicknamed the recognition heuristic and fluency heuristic. Our brains use the *recognition heuristic* to make snap judgments about something based on whether we recognize it, with more familiar objects typically seeming more likable and trustworthy. We rely on the *fluency heuristic*, meanwhile, to make snap judgments based on how quickly our brains can process the relevant information.

"yet however illogical"

Messages we've heard before are easier to process—and so are messages that simply "make sense." Messages that make sense are often true, so the brain automatically associates processing ease, or *fluency*, with truth. For instance, studies have found that people are more likely to rate messages as true when they're written in easy-to-read font colors, which the brain can quickly interpret.[31] Fluency also helps explain why I found professors' eloquent evolutionary storytelling compelling as a student: messages that are skillfully communicated often sound true simply because they're easy to understand.

While repetition makes lies easier for the brain to retrieve, repetition cannot make false information correct. (You can test this yourself by chanting "2 + 2 = 7" for several hours before a math exam.) Saying a message is true because it's repeated often is a fallacy called *appeal to repetition*, or *ad nauseum*. Yet however illogical, repetition remains an effective propaganda technique because illusionary truth effects are so powerful—especially when repeated messages stem from multiple sources (such as kids' books, television shows, and museums).

Notably, research reveals that young people may be especially susceptible to repetition's sway. One study, for instance, discovered that university students consistently rated repeated lies as more likely to be true, even when *knowing* the statements were false![32] Opposite of what researchers expected, young adults were more likely to rely on the fluency heuristic first, *above* prior knowledge, when evaluating messages.

But amazingly, a similar experiment with both students *and* seniors above age 65 found something else. While repetition trumped knowledge in young adults, seniors relied on their knowledge foremost, only using the fluency heuristic when they didn't already know if a message was true.[33] The researchers suggested that seniors rely on fluency less because older people have had more time to become familiar with what they know, making their knowledge easier to retrieve. That's just one more example of why Christian youth need connections with older mentors—not *despite* the fact that older adults may think differently than students but precisely *because* of it. This research also highlights why students need to regularly fill their minds with God's Word and retrieve Scripture's truth more readily for resisting repetitive lies.

Emotion

The final persuasive force we'll cover is a bit of an emotional subject. Take, for example, the following message:

"Rallying anger"

> With creationism today, we are witnessing a growth of modes of thought which, the better to impose religious dogma, are attacking the very core of the knowledge that we have built up little by little concerning nature, evolution, our origins and our place in the universe. There can be no doubt that this is a serious attack on human rights. There is a great risk of a serious confusion being introduced into our children's minds between what

> has to do with convictions, beliefs and ideals and what has to do with science, and of the advent of an "all things are equal" attitude, which may seem appealing and tolerant but is actually extremely harmful.[34]

This quote comes from the draft report of the Parliamentary Assembly of the Council of Europe's Resolution 1580, "The Dangers of Creationism in Education," which I mentioned in chapter 3. Did you notice all its emotionally charged phrases? *Impose, dogma, attacking, attack, rights, risk, serious, children, extremely harmful.* Each word seems selected to pack the greatest emotional punch, rallying anger, fear, and pity to persuade nations' leaders against letting any origins teaching besides evolution reach the next generation.

Speaking of reaching the next generation, even textbooks may wield emotionally evocative wording, examples, and images. My anthropology textbook showed a picture of three gorillas captioned:

> One quick glance at this female gorilla and two children at play attests to all that we share with our closest living relatives. We are equipped to read their body language, their facial expressions. Our bodies possess the same basic form. In them we can discern the joy of play and the ease across generations, perhaps recalling our own experiences just from looking at them.

Naturally, any image of furry, frolicking animals is bound to stoke some sentiment in a warmhearted human. Does that mean we evolved from those animals' ancestors? Nope. Like we'll see in the next chapter, similarities between different kinds of living things (including similarities which make us say *awww*) don't require an evolutionary explanation. Still, this image's emotional appeal enhanced its caption's persuasiveness.

A Biblical View of Emotions

Does the fact that unbiblical messages often rely on emotional appeals mean that emotion-based persuasion is always negative? Not necessarily. To understand emotions' proper place in our thinking, we can start by asking, "What's a biblical view of emotions?"

In answer, Genesis reveals that God created humans in his image as relational beings. Scripture indicates that God himself experiences emotions, including joy, grief, and righteous anger. So it makes sense that God hardwired us with emotional capacities. As a result, emotions help comprise the fabric of our humanness, being woven into our experiences, relationships, and communication. Even Jesus infused emotions into his teachings—for example, the remorse, delight, and anger portrayed in his parable of the prodigal son.

Emotions and Propaganda

In our fallen world, emotions like fear play protective roles in keeping us from danger. But emotions may also mislead us. Propaganda can easily manipulate our emotions, compelling us to believe wrong or illogical ideas. This is possible thanks to a mental shortcut called the *affect heuristic*, which the brain uses to base decisions on how something makes us feel rather than whether a decision is logical. Advertisements, for example, might show appealing images of junk food in hopes we'll buy the food to feel good while consuming it, despite recognizing our actions' potential health hazards.

Some advertisements appeal to fear, implying that buying a product will save us from negative outcomes. Either way, linking products to positive or negative emotions is a popular propaganda technique called *association*. For instance, have you noticed how often commercials play upbeat music while showing happy people enjoying a product? Marketers compose such commercials to help you associate their products with positive emotions. On the other hand, messages in culture may link biblical teaching to negative emotions—like the fear evoked by those threats of "a serious attack on human rights" and "risk of confusion being introduced to our children's minds."[36]

Not only do emotional appeals beget powerful propaganda, but certain emotions can also make us more susceptible to *other* propaganda techniques, like gain-framing or loss-framing. *Gain-framing* puts a positive spin on a message, while *loss-framing* gives messages a negative spin. Take the following logically identical statements:

1. New medication shows an 80% success rate!
2. New medication fails to help 1 in 5 patients.

As you might have guessed, statement A is gain-framed, while statement B is loss-framed. Research reveals we're more susceptible to gain-framed messages when we're experiencing positive emotions. When experiencing negative emotions, however, we find loss-framed messages more persuasive.[37]

"A message is true or false."

Along similar lines, multiple studies suggest we're more likely to make judgments without logic while experiencing positive emotions, like happiness, or emotions like anger, which involve a strong sense of feeling certain about something.[38] One study asked students to remember a time when they felt a particular emotion and then read a persuasive essay written by either a professor or another student.[39] Students who remembered feeling angry or content were more often persuaded by the professor's "expert opinion," suggesting these students had relied on an authority heuristic rather than thinking critically about the message's content.

While some emotions can help us make logical decisions—like not touching fire because we're afraid to burn, arguing that a message is true or false *only* because of how something makes us feel is the fallacy of *appeal to emotion*. For example, people may argue against the Bible by attacking the moral character of God, claiming that a loving God would not drown people in a global flood or condemn people to hell. These arguments may have strong emotional appeal. But they neglect the logical reality that God's justice demands judgment for wickedness, even while his mercy and love provide a way of salvation—like the ark and the cross.[40] These are just a few examples of how emotions can affect our thinking, but how we can respond by remembering the truth.

Table 10.2: Persuasion Forces Summary

Force	Heuristic	Cognitive Bias	Fallacy of Irrelevant Premise	Propaganda Example
Conformity	Follow the majority	Bandwagon effect	Appeal to the people (*ad populum*)	"Everybody knows evolution is a fact!"
Authority	Authority heuristic	Authority bias	Appeal to authority	"We can be certain that humans evolved from apelike ancestors because paleontology experts believe so."
Repetition	Fluency heuristic	Illusionary truth effect	Appeal to authority	"Books, movies, and museums all show dinosaurs living before mammals, so obviously that's what happened."
Emotion	Affect heuristic	(Multiple examples, such as gain-framing and loss-framing)	Appeal to emotion	"People who believe the Bible are a danger to society."

BULLET DODGED

There you have it—a crash course about how propaganda manipulates our minds, hijacking the mental shortcuts and cognitive biases our brains use to make decisions. Understanding these processes is important because, as research has shown, students who avoid cognitive biases tend to be stronger critical thinkers.[41] By knowing how our minds work and filling them with God's Word, we become better equipped to dodge psychological bullets on the battlefields of secular education—and resist gimmicks extolling the "health benefits" of bacon.

The critical thinking journey isn't over yet. Once you've filtered the irrelevant persuasion from a message, you'll likely be left staring at a mixture of facts and assumptions. How do you distill the *real* facts from interpretations about the facts? That's what we'll uncover next.

Endnotes

1. Edgar Henderson, "Toward a Definition of Propaganda," *The Journal of Social Psychology* 18, no. 1 (1943): 71–87.
2. You can watch Bernays telling the story of this campaign in the following video: *Edward L. Bernays Beech-Nut Packing Co.*, The Museum of Public Relations, September 12, 2014, 2:24, https://www.prmuseum.org/video-and-audio?rq=bernays%20bacon.
3. Edward Bernays, *Propaganda* (New York: Horace Liveright, 1928), 9.
4. Edward Bernays, *Biography of an Idea: Memoirs of Public Relations Council* (New York: Simon and Schuster, 1965), 652.
5. Of course, even neutral-seeming products may involve unethical manufacture and distribution practices or lead to other unintended consequences.
6. Bernays, 1928, 60.
7. I'm kidding, of course—but only about the bacon.
8. Usually, Christians discussing such topics support their views with Scripture, keeping God's Word as their authority. That's far different from disagreements about Genesis 1–11, which often involve using external human ideas to reinterpret Scripture. See https://answersingenesis.org/bible-questions/where-do-we-draw-the-line.
9. You can also find a "catalogue" of common fallacies discussed throughout this book in appendix B.
10. See 1 Peter 3:15.
11. Ken Ham and Britt Beemer, *Already Gone: Why Your Kids Will Quit Church and What You Can Do to Stop It* (Green Forest: Master Books, 2009).
12. You can arrive at these three points yourself using Critical Thinking Checks #1 (point 2), #5 (point 1), and #7 (point 3, see chapter 12).
13. Luke 6:31
14. Matthew 22:39
15. E.g., Dr. Jerry Bergman, *How Darwinism Corrodes Morality* (Kitchener: Sola Scriptura Ministries International, 2017).
16. For instance, the late Yale law professor Dr. Arthur Leff discussed the problems with trying to base morality apart from God in his secular essay "Unspeakable Ethics, Unnatural Law" (*Duke Law Journal* [1979]: 1,229). See also Dr. Georgia Purdom and Dr. Jason Lisle, "Morality and the Irrationality of an Evolutionary Worldview," Answers in Genesis, May 13, 2009, https://answersingenesis.org/morality/morality-and-the-irrationality-of-an-evolutionary-worldview. Further information

is available in *Critical Thinking Scan*, Season 12, and its associated resources on Answers TV.

17. This is a type of "stolen concept fallacy," which we'll examine in chapter 12.

18. Bertram Gawronski and Laura Creighton, "Dual Process Theories," *The Oxford Handbook of Social Cognition,* ed. Donald Carlston (New York: Oxford University Press, 2013), 282–312.

19. Solomon Asch, "Studies of Independence and Conformity: I. A Minority of One Against a Unanimous Majority," *Psychological Monographs: General and Applied* 70, no. 9 (1956): 1–70.

20. Solomon Asch, "Opinions and Social Pressure," *Scientific American* 193, no. 5 (1955): 31–35.

21. William Morris and Robert Miller, "The Effects of Consensus-Breaking and Consensus-Preempting Partners on Reduction of Conformity," *Journal of Experimental Social Psychology* 11, no. 3 (1975): 215–223.

22. E.g., Javier Horcajo, Richard Petty, and Pablo Briñol, "The Effects of Majority Versus Minority Source Status on Persuasion: A Self-Validation Analysis," *Journal of Personality and Social Psychology* 99, no. 3 (2010): 498.

23. Scriptures for resisting conformity: Romans 12:1; Galatians 1:10; 1 Peter 4:3–5.

24. Stanley Milgram, "Behavioral Study of Obedience," *The Journal of Abnormal and Social Psychology* 67, no. 4 (1963): 371.

25. Encouragingly, a follow-up experiment showed that when two other people, whom participants didn't realize were actors, refused to deliver shocks beyond a certain intensity, 90% of participants also refused to continue with the experiment. While not all replications of Milgram's experiments have also found this result (see reference 26 below), it illustrates the value of belonging to a network of like-minded Christians who can support one another in obeying God's Word rather than man's. (Stanley Milgram, "Some Conditions of Obedience and Disobedience to Authority," *Human Relations* 18, no. 1 [1965]: 57–76.)

26. Jerry Burger, "Replicating Milgram: Would People Still Obey Today?" *American Psychologist* 64, no. 1 (2009): 1.

27. Dariusz Doliński et. al., "Would You Deliver an Electric Shock in 2015? Obedience in the Experimental Paradigm Developed by Stanley Milgram in the 50 Years Following the Original Studies," *Social Psychological and Personality Science* 8, no. 8 (2017): 927–933.

28. There are clear differences between being a research subject ordered to hurt another person and being a student told that unbiblical messages are true. So this is not meant to be a perfect analogy but rather to illustrate the psychological power of authority and serve as a reminder that our Creator must be our ultimate authority in any case when the words of human authorities conflict with the Word of God. (See chapter 9 for more on weighing expert opinions in everyday situations.)

29. E.g., Romans 3:4; Acts 5:29.

30. While this is the story I'd heard repeated in the media, even modern evolutionists recognize that mammals, including squirrels, beavers, platypuses, and badger-like animals, lived alongside dinosaurs.

31. Christian Unkelbach, "Reversing the Truth Effect: Learning the Interpretation of Processing Fluency in Judgments of Truth," *Journal of Experimental Psychology: Learning, Memory, and Cognition* 33, no. 1 (2007): 219.

32. Lisa Fazio et. al., "Knowledge Does Not Protect Against Illusory Truth," *Journal of Experimental Psychology: General* 144, no. 5 (2015): 993.

33. Nadia Brashier et. al., "Competing Cues: Older Adults Rely on Knowledge in the Face of Fluency," *Psychology and Aging* 32, no. 4 (2017): 331.

34. Anne Brasseur, "The Dangers of Creationism in Education," Parliamentary Assembly of the Council of Europe, Committee on Culture, Science and Education,

September 17, 2007, https://assembly.coe.int/nw/xml/XRef/X2H-Xref-ViewHTML.asp?FileID=11751&lang=EN.

35. William Haviland et. al., *Anthropology: The Human Challenge*, 14th ed. (Belmont: Wadsworth, 2014), 52.

36. It's a common tactic of culture to say that teaching kids about creation stunts their intellectual growth and love for science. But like we saw in chapter 7, a biblical worldview provides the foundation for scientific reasoning in the first place.

37. Changmin Yan, James Dillard, and Fuyuan Shen, "The Effects of Mood, Message Framing, and Behavioral Advocacy on Persuasion," *Journal of Communication* 60, no. 2 (2010): 344–363.

38. Vladas Griskevicius, Michelle Shiota, and Samantha Neufeld, "Influence of Different Positive Emotions on Persuasion Processing: A Functional Evolutionary Approach," *Emotion* 10, no. 2 (2010): 190. (Applies evolutionary interpretations to observational science that positive emotions correlate with less reliance on logic.)

39. Tiedens, Larissa Z., and Susan Linton, "Judgment Under Emotional Certainty and Uncertainty: The Effects of Specific Emotions on Information Processing," *Journal of Personality and Social Psychology* 81, no. 6 (2001): 973.

40. See *Critical Thinking Scan*, Season 12, Episode 3, "Is the God of the Bible a Bully?" on Answers TV.

41. Richard West, Maggie Toplak, and Keith Stanovich, "Heuristics and Biases as Measures of Critical Thinking: Associations with Cognitive Ability and Thinking Dispositions," *Journal of Educational Psychology* 100, no. 4 (2008): 930.

ASSESSING INFORMATION

11

How to handle "facts"

Early one Sunday morning, as I slumbered tranquilly behind a closed door, the rest of my family awoke to a horrendous stench saturating our house. My parents ventured downstairs in a bleary quest to identify its source, only to find my brother one step ahead of them, examining our aged dog. It wasn't the dog.

Looking around the room, my family wracked their collective brains to come up with an explanation—anything—to resolve the odious conundrum.

"I think the fridge is broken," my mom proposed.

"*Au contraire, mon cheri,*" I envision my dad responding, although none of us spoke French. "It must be our neighbor, Norm, smoking game meat in his garage."

"No, no. No, no, no. It's probably just the fridge."

"But Norm's a hunter."

"Fridges can smell bad—"

"So do dead animals. I'll just knock on Norm's door and ask him to kindly stop roasting his deer."

"But it's 5:00 a.m. on a Sunday morning! Let's check the fridge first."

"O-o-okay."

Sure enough, my mom had guessed right—sparing Norm from awakening to the inexplicable sight of my pajama-clad dad requesting him to please cease curing venison in the garage.

The moral of the story, besides the importance of proper refrigeration, is that identical facts can lead to vastly different explanations. From the same pool of observations—a dastardly odor, a malfunction-prone appliance, and a hunter next door—my parents constructed unique stories using different starting assumptions. These assumptions led my parents to different interpretations of the same facts, which in turn led to different conclusions.

> *"Identical facts can lead to different explanations."*

Many of the explanations you'll encounter in life, especially in fields like science, archaeology, and forensics, work this way. Everyone has access to the same facts—the same fossils or fauna, measurements or murder weapons. But not everyone arrives at the same conclusion. The evolutionary conclusions you're taught in classrooms or online likely developed from people filtering select observations through the lens of man's word, creating a cocktail of facts, assumptions, and interpretations. But when you're handed this concoction in class, you'll be ordered to swallow it all like it's pure fact.

HOW TO SEPARATE FACT FROM INTERPRETATION

How can you identify genuine facts amid a kaleidoscope of interpretations? Let's look at several practical steps which fall under Critical Thinking Check #6: Check the Interpretations. Then we'll try applying these steps to separate facts from interpretations in common textbook examples of "evidence for evolution."

Step 1: Identify the Observational Science

The first step in separating fact from assumption is to (naturally enough) locate the facts. Like we saw in chapters 2 and 7, facts occupy the realm of observational science—the kind of research which measures, describes, and experiments on things in the present. To identify the facts from observational science, ask, "What are the measurements, observations, and raw data about which everyone can agree?"

Of course, even observational data can be faulty, thanks to issues like measurement uncertainties, experimenter errors, instrument glitches, biased surveys, small samples, or other methodological mishaps. You can also consider whether the observations themselves might have been misled.[1]

Step 2: Identify the Historical Science

Once you've identified the real facts of observational science, you know there's a strong possibility the other "facts" in a message involve interpretations from historical science.[2] Remember, historical science examines observable facts through a particular worldview lens (man's word or God's Word) to draw conclusions about the past. Those conclusions are not facts themselves but rather interpretations of facts based on researchers' starting assumptions. To pinpoint these interpretations, ask, "What explanation is being presented about the past?"

A quick way to spot historical science is to notice flag words like *could*, *might*, *probably*, *possibly*, and *may*. These words often appear in evolutionary contexts, signaling an assumption from historical science rather than a fact we can observe in the present. Yet textbooks and the media often use these words to suggest that something *did* happen because it *could have* happened.

My biology textbook, for instance, featured a diagram showing how eyes supposedly evolved from "simple" patches of light-sensitive cells into the complex visual organs we wear sunglasses over today. This idea has more holes than a porcupine's air mattress,[3] but the textbook didn't get into them. Instead, by illustrating how eyes *might* have evolved in certain steps (assuming those evolutionary changes are even possible), the textbook basically taught that eyes *did* evolve in certain steps.

> "A porcupine's air mattress"

Suggesting that evolution *did* happen because certain evolutionists have proposed that it *could* have happened (whether or not their ideas are true) is the fallacy of *appeal to possibility*. Using the critical thinking hack from chapter 10, you can spot this fallacy by asking, "Is a message true because it *might* be true?"

Step 3: Notice the Assumptions

Historical science typically relies on assumptions to fill in for gaps in the facts. Especially for evolutionary explanations, these assumptions often have their own issues given what we know from observational science. For example, any interpretation that one kind of animal evolved into another kind—say, dinosaurs evolving into birds—rests on two pillars of assumption:

- Evolution *can* change one kind of animal into another, forming the novel features unique to each kind. For instance, evolving birds from dinosaurs would require producing birds' feathers, wings, flight-navigation mechanisms, air-pocketed bones, specific knee structure, and unique respiratory system involving air sacs and lungs for highly efficient, one-way airflow.
- Earth is millions of years old to allow time for such evolution, if it were possible, to happen.

If only naturalistic explanations are considered acceptable (in other words, if nobody's allowed to mention the Creator), then a third assumption states that life must have arisen from nonlife to give evolution a starting point. You can learn much more about the problems with all these assumptions in other resources, including those listed in appendix A.

Step 4: Remember, There's Probably More to the Story Than You're Hearing[5]

Almost any class you can take at a university barely touches (let alone scratches) the surface of an entire academic field. Even if you devoted your entire life to studying that field, you'd only be learning a fraction of its information. Much of that information may be observational science. But one fact from observational science may yield numerous explanations from historical science. There simply isn't space in a single textbook section to tell the whole story. In other words, the information you're learning in class is not exhaustive. Likely, it's the most polished presentation of the secular side of the story, and there's another side you aren't hearing. The information you may be missing includes:

- Other secular researchers' explanations of the same facts from observational science.
- Biblical researchers' explanations of the same facts from observational science.
- Other facts from observational science which contradict the evolutionary interpretation(s) and lend themselves to a biblical explanation.

Step 5: Consider Alternative Explanations

To learn the other side of the story, ask, "Is there another way to look at the same facts and arrive at a different conclusion which makes at least as much sense?" You can go to solid apologetics websites, including AnswersInGenesis.org, to find out, ask a biblical creationist mentor, or research what other scientists have said about the same topics.[6] Incidentally, the habit of checking for alternative explanations will also help you spot *either-or fallacies*, a type of faulty logic which presents only two options when other possibilities exist.[7]

THINKING ABOUT PRIME "EVIDENCE FOR EVOLUTION"

Now that we've seen how to separate fact from interpretation, let's try applying these steps of Critical Thinking Check #6 to real textbook examples of "evidence for evolution."[8] (To prepare for Check #6 in some of these cases, we'll also need to run through any relevant steps from Checks #1–5.)

You can dive far deeper into all the following topics through the resources listed in appendix A. But this introduction will help you practice how to think through common evolutionary arguments in general.

Evidence for Evolution #1: Observable Natural Selection

Under the heading "Evolution is supported by an overwhelming amount of scientific evidence," my biology textbook listed "direct observation of evolutionary change" as the very first point.[9] To illustrate a classic example of such "evolutionary change," let me introduce you (from a distance, of course) to a microbe named *Staphylococcus aureus*. This jaunty germ may not be much to look at, but it's a star player in the true story[10] my textbook called "The Evolution of Drug-Resistant Bacteria."[11]

"The Evolution of Drug-Resistant Bacteria"

The story goes like this. Within two years of penicillin becoming a widespread drug, some harmful strains of *S. aureus* bacteria became penicillin-resistant. As my textbook put it, "These bacteria had an enzyme, penicillinase, that could destroy penicillin."[12] So doctors began prescribing other antibiotics, including methicillin, which inactivates a protein that the bacteria need to build their cell walls. Again, within two years, methicillin-resistant bacteria appeared. In the textbook's words, "some individuals were able to synthesize their cell walls using a different protein that was not affected by methicillin."[13]

So *does* the biography of *S. aureus* provide overwhelming evidence for evolution? Let's apply some Critical Thinking Checks to find out. First, Check Scripture. Genesis explains God created organisms to reproduce according to their kinds, and in this case, we're seeing *Staphylococcus* produce more *Staphylococcus*. That's not a problem from a biblical perspective.[14] However, the textbook's interpretation that drug-resistant bacteria show all life evolved from a single ancestor *does* challenge biblical doctrines, failing Critical Thinking Check #2: Check the Challenge.

Under Check #3: Check the Source, we can remember that the textbook is starting from the worldview of man's word using naturalistic, evolutionary assumptions.[15] This will affect how the book interprets observational science.

Moving on to Check #4: Check the Definitions, we should beware of how the textbook wields the word *evolution*. The book teaches that bacterial resistance supports "evolution" in the sense of change *between* kinds. However, the "evolution" we're observing is variation within *Staphylococcus*, thanks to mechanisms, including mutation and natural selection. Like we saw in chapter 7, these processes don't produce the types of changes required to evolve one kind of creature into another. This use of the word *evolution* could be considered a bait-and-switch fallacy.

With that groundwork laid, let's jump to Check #6: Check the Interpretations.[16] First, what's the observational science? Facts we can observe in the present include the observations that bacteria always reproduce according to their kinds and can become drug-resistant. The historical interpretation in my textbook states the processes behind drug resistance (like mutation and selection) were responsible for the evolution of all other life-forms. This *assumes* mutations can produce new genetic information, which we saw in chapter 7 isn't the case. So there's probably more to this story.

To learn the rest of the story, I had to dig deeper into the observational science of drug resistance. As it turns out, bacteria can become drug-resistant a number of ways—none of which involves creating completely new genetic information.[17] For instance, mutations can cause bacteria to *lose* control over how much protein they make from a certain gene, so they overproduce proteins that destroy or remove drugs. That's what my textbook didn't say about the penicillin-resistant bacteria: they already had the genetic information to make penicillinase; they just lost control over how much they produced.

> "I had to dig deeper."

Other times, mutations cause defects to proteins that normally let antibiotics enter or bind to bacteria. That's what happened with the methicillin-resistant strains my textbook mentioned. Methicillin normally binds to a protein the bacteria need to build their cell walls. But many resistant bacteria have a mutated version of this protein, which is so deformed that the antibiotic can't bind to it. Like any mutation, this isn't the *creation* of new genetic information so much as the *corruption* of existing information.[18]

Is this mutation beneficial for bacteria exposed to antibiotics? Sure, but it's not beneficial to the big-picture story of evolution. Even mutations that can provide a benefit under specific circumstances often come at a price, involving some loss of function or efficiency.[19] In this case, the deformed proteins can't fully accomplish their job to build the cell wall. They depend on unmutated proteins to help them.[20] Similarly, superbugs with resistance to multiple antibiotics have so many mutational defects that they can't outcompete normal bacteria under normal conditions.

If that wasn't enough, something else that's not often clear from textbooks is that multiple studies have identified drug resistance in ancient bacteria, as microbes produced antibiotics long before modern medicine. For instance, a study on antibiotic-resistant bacterial DNA in supposedly 30,000-year-old Canadian permafrost revealed what researchers called "conservation of gene sequence and synteny with modern resistance clusters in the clinic as well as protein function and structure."[21] In other words, the ancient bacteria looked and acted like modern antibiotic-resistant bacteria, right down to their DNA and proteins. Altogether, far from being textbook evidence for evolution, the observational science about bacterial resistance is consistent with a biblical worldview.

Evidence for Evolution #2: Similarities Between Organisms

How often have you encountered statements like these?

- Of course we're related to chimps—our DNA is over 90% identical!
- All vertebrates have a backbone because they descended from an ancestor with a backbone.
- The embryos of different vertebrates look alike, thanks to their shared evolutionary history.

Crack open almost any biology textbook, and you're bound to read that living things' genetic, physical, or developmental similarities are sure-fire evidence for evolution. The idea goes that different kinds of living things display similar traits because their shared ancestors handed those traits down the evolutionary family tree. It's sort of like how siblings resemble each other because they inherited similar traits from the same parents. Evolutionists dub such similarities *homologies* (rhymes with *apologies*).

As a classic example, cats, bats, whales, and humans all have similar forelimb skeletons, which textbooks call homologous. Many different types of living things share genes with similar DNA sequences. The embryos of different creatures also show certain developmental similarities. For instance, vertebrate tetrapod embryos have segmented bodies, tissue folds called pharyngeal clefts near the head, and limb buds which become arms and legs. Do such similarities mean different organisms evolved from the same ancestors?

"Homologies (rhymes with apologies)"

Let's try separating fact from assumption to find out. First, what's the observational science in homology arguments? The facts we can observe in the present are the similarities themselves, whether similar forelimbs, similar genes, or similar embryo segments. Next, what's the historical science? The story about the past states that once upon a time, there lived an evolutionary ancestor which passed along certain similarities to all its descendants. This *explanation* assumes that evolution *can* change one kind of creature into another, that the earth is old enough to allow time for this to happen, and that mechanisms like mutations can explain the differences between supposedly related organisms.

Could there be more to the homology story? Absolutely. A little deeper digging into the facts from observational science reveals the idea of homology has some serious difficulties.

For one thing, different types of similarities don't lend themselves to the same evolutionary conclusions. It's not unusual to come up with different evolutionary "family trees," depending which similarities you consider—for instance, whether you group organisms according to similar genes versus similar physical traits, similar noncoding DNA, or similar RNA.

Likewise, if you define similarity as "looking the same," you might lump lizards, frogs, and humans into one happy evolutionary family because their embryos' limb buds and body segments look similar. But if you define similarity as "developing the same way," your explanation runs into trouble because the forelimbs of lizards, frogs, and humans develop from different body segments.[22] If you define similar structures as "encoded by similar genes," you also run into trouble because different sets of genes can control the development of supposedly related structures, like body segments in fruit flies versus grasshoppers.[23]

"Fruit flies vs. grasshoppers."

Because similar-looking structures so often develop through different pathways or from different embryonic cells, one influential researcher suggested that "embryological origins are irrelevant for the developmental basis of homology."[24] This researcher proposed that networks of genes regulating development make for better gauges of shared ancestry. In 2019, however, other researchers argued that not even these gene networks are especially helpful for defining homology because, among other issues, different networks can produce similar-looking structures.[25]

Furthermore, many creatures which are *not* considered closely related also show strikingly similar features. Pill bugs and pill millipedes, for instance, look and even behave similarly but represent completely different subphyla. You and the squid nearest to you can't call yourselves close relatives. Yet both of you see through similar eyes. Deeming such similarities *analogous* instead of *homologous*, evolutionists must assume analogous features developed independently through a process called convergent evolution.

What's an alternative explanation for creatures' similarities? One reasonable interpretation is that living things show similarities not because they share the same ancestor but *because they share the same Creator*. This Creator, in turn, engineered certain design plans which work well in many different applications, serving similar functions under similar constraints. It's sort of like how many man-made vehicles have similar wheels because wheels are an excellent design applicable to everything from unicycles to spacecraft. But we wouldn't say spacecraft evolved from unicycles.

"They share the same Creator."

A designer can apply similar building blocks to different products, and the products don't have to be related. Design presents a much more straightforward explanation for the many cases where similar genes—like those for hemoglobin proteins—would otherwise have had to evolve separately multiple times.[26] Viewing similarities in terms of common design rather than common ancestry makes even more sense of the observational science.

Evidence for Evolution #3: Vestigial Structures

Random question, but can you wiggle your ears? I can, sort of. Ear-wiggling muscles are said to be one of the body's many "vestigial structures," evolutionary relics which served a purpose in our supposed ancestors but have no (or at least limited) function today. In my evolution textbook's words,

> The adaptions of organisms have long been, and still are, cited by creationists as evidence of the Creator's wise beneficence. But no such claim can be made for the features, displayed by almost every species, that served a function in the species' ancestors, but do so no longer. Cave-dwelling fishes and other animals display eyes in every stage of degeneration. Flightless beetles retain rudimentary wings. . . . In *The Descent of Man*, Darwin listed a dozen vestigial features in the human body, some of which occur only as uncommon varieties. They include the appendix, the [tailbone], rudimentary muscles that enable some people to move their ears or scalp, and the posterior molars, or wisdom teeth, that fail to erupt, or do so aberrantly, in many people.[27]

My textbooks also listed the reduced hind limbs in some fossil snakes, and bones called "vestigial hips" in some whales, as evidence for evolution. You can find specific answers to all these claims through other resources.[28] For now, let's look at how to think about vestigial structure arguments more generally.

From Check #1: Check Scripture, we know God created living things to reproduce according to their kinds. Biblically, we wouldn't interpret vestigial structures as leftovers from one kind of creature evolving into another. Genesis also teaches that God's creation was *very good*, so we wouldn't predict that living things originally featured completely useless design structures. However, Genesis also explains creation didn't *stay* very good because Adam sinned. This means we shouldn't be surprised to see loss or degeneration of structures within kinds of living things. Biblically, then, we'd expect that vestigial structures likely either represent a loss or degeneration of some good design feature—or are not vestigial at all but rather serve important functions.

With that in mind, let's try separating facts from interpretations. First, what's the observational science? We're observing structures like tailbones, appendixes, and wisdom teeth. What are the historical interpretations of these structures? The textbook's conclusion about the past states our evolutionary ancestors bequeathed these structures to us like so much outdated furniture.

We've already identified that an alternative, biblical explanation predicts vestigial structures represent useful designs or losses of function. And sure enough, when we look deeper into the observational science to see the other side of the story, we find that vestigial structures usually do fall into one of these two categories.

For example, cave fish losing functional eyes, beetles losing functional wings, or snakes potentially losing limbs[29] all involve genetic information losses within kinds of living things. But evolving all living things from single-cell ancestors would require the *addition* of much functional new genetic information.

> "Beetles losing functional wings"

How about other vestigial structures—do they perform important functions? You bet your wisdom teeth they do. For instance, the tailbone is a crucial attachment point for muscles that support internal organs. The appendix plays a role in the immune system as a reservoir for helpful bacteria. Even pelvic bones in whales serve important reproductive functions, as a study reported in the journal *Evolution* the year after my textbook edition was published.[30]

And what about wisdom teeth? Interestingly, wisdom teeth don't often cause problems in humans living on coarser diets, but modern processed food seems to have contributed to wisdom tooth issues since the 1800s.[31] Again, this illustrates degeneration of an originally good design.

Altogether, the observational science is consistent with a biblical interpretation and requires no evolutionary assumptions. And speaking of assumptions, what must happen for organs to be considered vestigial anyway? For evolutionary leftovers to exist, evolution would need to be true. Textbooks must assume evolution is true to argue that vestigial organs show evolution is true. This is an example of circular reasoning, which we'll unpack in chapter 12.

In the end, "vestigial structures" are not the clear-cut evidence for evolution that textbooks can make them appear. They're typically either useful designs or examples of genetic information losses within kinds of living things.

Evidence for Evolution #4: Biogeography

Precocious Child: Why are kangaroos in Australia?

Zookeeper: Because that's where they evolved. We can tell this from a branch of science called biogeography.

Precocious Child: Bio-geo-what?

Zookeeper: Biogeography.

Precocious Child: Oh, I get it. "Bio" refers to living things, so biogeography must be the study of where different organisms are located around the world. The reality that marsupials are primarily concentrated in Australia is a fact from observational science, but you're evidently interpreting that observation through an evolutionary lens.

Zookeeper: Um . . . what?

Like the zookeeper started to explain, evolution is culture's go-to explanation for living things' dispersal patterns. My textbook insisted:

> Suffice it to say that the distribution of many taxa [or categories of living things] makes no sense unless they have arisen from common ancestors. For example, many taxa, such as marsupials, are distributed across the southern continents, which is easily understood if they arose from common ancestors that were distributed across the single southern landmass that began to fragment in the Mesozoic.[32]

The idea is that once upon ~200 million years ago, a supercontinent called Pangea began breaking into several continents.[33] As those continents drifted apart, they carried the ancestors of modern organisms with them. The distribution of species we see today supposedly reflects their evolutionary histories. Let's apply some Critical Thinking Checks to this idea.

From Check #1: Check Scripture, we know the assumption that different kinds of animals evolved in different locations contradicts a clear biblical teaching. However, biblically, we *could* expect to see a great deal of variation *within* kinds, including different species separating out in response to their fallen planet's changing environments. Genesis also teaches that a global flood reset the world, which will be important to remember in a minute.

Meanwhile, let's continue with Check #6: Check the Interpretations. What's the observational science of biogeography arguments? As Precocious Child pointed out, we're observing the modern distributions of living (or fossil) organisms. We might even observe new species emerging in certain locations, but again, speciation within created kinds is quite consistent with a biblical worldview. And how about the historical science? The textbook's historical interpretation states that living things' distributions reflect their evolutionary histories.

How could we interpret the same observational science through an alternative, biblical lens? Biblically, we'd interpret the distribution of most fossils to represent the way animals were buried during the global flood. Living things' current distributions, meanwhile, would reflect the dispersion, migration, speciation, and (in some cases) later extinction of organisms which survived the flood.

Creationists suggest different models for how living things repopulated the world after the flood. For example, organisms could have migrated across land bridges that the post-flood ice age likely exposed, been transported by humans, or been carried by floating rafts of logs and vegetation ripped up by the flood. Even some evolutionists propose rafts to explain some organisms' biogeography;[34] one paper lists 15 cases where biogeography patterns that don't otherwise make sense can be explained by "oceanic dispersal."[35] And a creationist model examining how sea currents could have carried log rafts showed a better than 90% fit with animal distributions observed today.[36]

To uncover more of the biogeography story, we can ask, "What other facts from observational science support a biblical interpretation?" In this case, floating log rafts could help make sense of not only coal deposits but also marine organisms fossilized in tree amber.[37] Sea creatures and trees don't normally mix, but a global flood could explain that.

Biblically based models of how living things spread around the earth following the flood may continue to change as observational science unveils more facts. But God's Word does not change—including the truth of the Genesis flood, established by God's eyewitness testimony and collaborated by observational facts. And when it comes to biogeography, those facts do not supply clear-cut "evidence for evolution" quite like textbooks may indicate. Instead, they pose problems requiring other explanations—like oceanic dispersal—which *are* consistent with a biblical worldview.

"*Floating rafts of logs*"

Evidence for Evolution #5: Transitional Fossils

Have you been indoctrinated by evolutionary interpretations of famous fossils?

Take this quiz to find out!

(PS: If there's a fossil below you haven't heard of, feel free to look up its picture—but try your best guess first.)

What is *Tiktaalik*?

A. An evolutionary intermediate between reptiles and mammals
B. An evolutionary intermediate between aquatic creatures and land animals
C. A fossil of a lobe-finned fish
D. A game played on a hand-drawn grid

What is *Archeopteryx*?

A. An evolutionary intermediate between dinosaurs and birds
B. A fossil of an ancient, potentially flightless bird
C. An evolutionary intermediate between ungulates and whales
D. Probably a disease

What is Lucy?

A. A 78-million-year-old fossil sauropod, the second largest dinosaur on record
B. An evolutionary intermediate between apelike ancestors and humans
C. An evolutionary intermediate between a twentieth-century comic and sitcom
D. A fossil of an extinct ape

Calculate Your Score

Question 1	Question 2	Question 3
A = 5 points	A = 10 points	A = 5 points
B = 10 points	B = 1 point	B = 10 points
C = 1 point	C = 5 points	C = 0 points
D = 0 points	D = 0 points	D = 1 point

Total Score: _____

If you ended up with . . .

- **30 points:** You have been successfully indoctrinated with evolutionary teachings as they appear in textbooks. Please see chapter 2.
- **5–25 points:** You have been indoctrinated with at least some evolutionary teachings, even if you were mostly guessing the answers. Please see chapter 2.
- **3 points:** Congratulations—your evolutionary indoctrination seems to have been unsuccessful.
- **1–2 points:** You are likely a cheeky creationist.
- **0 points:** You did that on purpose.

Even if you scored low for indoctrination regarding these fossils, new "transitional fossil" claims which appear in classes or on the news may sound convincing. How can you think through any transitional fossil argument using the 7 Checks of Critical Thinking?

First, Check Scripture. Because Genesis indicates God designed creatures according to their kinds, biblically, we wouldn't interpret a fossil as being halfway between two kinds. Saying that fossils represent an evolutionary process of death and suffering leading up to humans also challenges clear teachings from Scripture, failing Check #2: Check the Challenge.

Jumping to Check #6, what is the observational science in any transitional fossil message? The facts are the fossils themselves and the rocks in which they were found. But when it comes to fossils, observational science doesn't always have much to go on. For instance, we can't directly observe function from fossils. We don't know exactly how creatures used some of their now-fossilized features. Coelacanth fossils, for example, have lobed fins that some evolutionists thought represented precursor limbs—until live coelacanths were observed using those fins for swimming.

"Missing pieces of incomplete fossils"

Observational science also can't tell us for certain what the missing pieces of incomplete fossils looked like. Ideas about how missing bones affected the animals' body plans, how all the soft tissue might have looked, and how everything worked together are all interpretations from historical science. Presenting these interpretations as reality in textbooks and museums is just propaganda—an attempt to make evolutionary stories seem persuasive by appealing to aesthetics rather than fact. Finally, remember the very label "transitional fossil" (and any story about the past that goes along with it) is an interpretation based on evolutionary assumptions, not a definite fact.

So what's an alternative explanation for intermediate-looking fossils? Biblically, we can predict that any transitional fossil claim probably involves one of three scenarios.

Scenario 1

The fossil represents a specimen from either one kind or another kind—not something in between. For example, observational science reveals that "ape-man" fossils are fully ape or fully human, even if movies and textbooks try to represent ancient humans as more apelike (or ancient apes as more humanlike) than the bones alone indicate. *Archaeopteryx*, the poster-bird for "feathered dinosaur evolution," was an interesting but unequivocal bird.[39] And *Tiktaalik*, the alleged ancestor of tetrapods, was simply a fish.[40]

Scenario 2

The fossil is made of bones from different specimens belonging to separate kinds. This is especially possible if the bones were found in different locations or in the case of forgeries. For instance, the infamous Piltdown Man skull was forged from human and orangutan bones.

Scenario 3

The fossil represents another, separate kind, with a mosaic of features resembling those of other organisms and reflecting creatures' shared Designer. Platypuses, for example, have characteristics spanning multiple animal groups.

With these three possibilities in mind, you can look closer at observational science to see if there's more to transitional fossil stories. A biblical explanation makes much more sense of the abrupt appearances of many living things (and their distinguishing features) in the fossil record. Furthermore, evolutionary dates for rocks surrounding fossils don't always support a straightforward evolutionary explanation. For example, *Tiktaalik* is considered younger than fossil footprints of a four-footed animal, which supposedly came *after Tiktaalik*.[41] Evolutionists could speculate that *Tiktaalik*'s ancestors were "transitional forms." But the point is, observational science doesn't necessarily match what straightforward evolutionary scenarios predict. That's why, although textbooks may still show linear diagrams of transitional fossil series, modern evolutionists usually believe intermediate forms follow branching patterns rather than linear sequences—including in the famous horse and whale fossil series.

Even for the most supposedly straightforward sequences, "transitional" features don't always develop as smoothly as textbooks suggest. My own biology textbook declared, "The fossil record shows that the unique features of mammalian jaws and teeth evolved gradually over time, in a series of steps," adding, "If all the known fossils in this sequence were arranged by shape and placed side by side, their features would blend smoothly from one group to the next."[42]

Actually, geologist John Woodmorappe *did* arrange those fossils by evolutionary date back in 2001, concluding, "One of the most striking findings uncovered by this analysis is that the *majority* of anatomical traits (the ones actually used by evolutionists in the construction of their cladograms) *do not* show a unidirectional progression towards the mammalian condition!"[43] (emphasis in original).

> "Striking findings"

Instead, many mammal-like traits disappeared and reappeared throughout the sequence, and large evolutionary gaps occurred in the few traits that did progress linearly. Crossing large gaps would require gaining functional new genetic information. Other useful questions include: What else would have had to happen for this fossilized creature to transform into another kind? And does observational science support such transformations as being possible?

FREEING FACT FROM FANCY

Whether viewing "transitional" fossils, animals' distributions, "vestigial structures," organisms' similarities, bacterial resistance, or any other phenomena, the same observational science may be claimed as evidence for an evolutionary or a biblical worldview.[44] The difference lies in which worldview lens we use to interpret that evidence. By beginning with a biblical worldview and applying a little critical thinking to any "evidence for evolution" claim, we can discover the observable facts fall far short of "proving" evolution. Rather, observational science often causes *problems* for evolution yet is consistent with biblical interpretations.

By now in the critical thinking process, you should have whittled away nearly every irrelevant or unestablished aspect of a message, leaving only the facts and relationships between them. Not all those relationships, however, are necessarily logical. Let's move on to unpack some of the most common remaining logical errors to watch out for in Critical Thinking Check #7: Check the Logic.

Endnotes

1. See Critical Thinking Check #3: Check the Source in chapter 9. You can also find tips for tracking down original research in appendix E.
2. Or other types of interpretations, assumptions, and conjectures about things we cannot directly observe
3. E.g., see Elizabeth Mitchell, "Does the Diversity of Eyes in Nature Support Evolution?" Answers in Genesis, January 28, 2016, https://answersingenesis.org/human-body/eyes/diversity-of-eyes-in-nature-evolution.
4. Textbooks may try defining science to exclude any mention of God. For why this definition is incorrect, see Jason Lisle, "Must Science Exclude the Supernatural?" Answers in Genesis, May 30, 2008, https://answersingenesis.org/what-is-science/must-science-exclude-the-supernatural.
5. The order of steps 4 and 5 may be interchangeable, as looking for alternative explanations often reveals parts of the story (facts from observational science) which you weren't initially taught.
6. See chapter 14 and appendix E for tips on how to do this.
7. More on that in chapter 12
8. Remember, both evolutionists and creationists have the same evidence—the same facts from observational science. They just interpret the evidence through different worldview lenses.
9. Jane Reece et. al., *Campbell Biology*, Canadian ed. (Don Mills: Pearson Canada, 2014), 493.
10. At least the observational facts of drug resistance are true. The "evolution" connection is less so, depending how you define *evolution*, as we'll see momentarily.
11. Ibid.
12. Ibid., 494.
13. Ibid., 494.
14. We might ask how some of these bacteria began causing disease after sin entered the world since Genesis says creation was originally very good; see Alen Gillen, *The Genesis of Germs: The Origin of Diseases and the Coming Plagues* (Green Forest: Master Books, 2007), or Alen Gillen, "The Genesis of Methicillin-Resistant *Staphylococcus aureus*: A Modern-Day 'Leprosy' and Hospital Menace," https://answersingenesis.org/natural-selection/antibiotic-resistance/the-genesis-of-methicillin-resistant-staphylococcus-aureus.
15. This check will also apply to the other examples of "evidence for evolution" we'll examine, but I'll only mention it here to avoid repetition.
16. While we'll skip Check #5 in most of these examples for brevity, you can check for propaganda by asking why a message sounds persuasive and questioning whether those factors make the message true. For example, this message is not necessarily true just because it exists in a scientific textbook.
17. See Kevin Anderson, "Is Bacterial Resistance to Antibiotics an Appropriate Example of Evolutionary Change?" *Creation Research Society Quarterly* 41, no. 4 (2005): 318–326, https://www.trueorigin.org/bacteria01.php. (Recommended in Roger Patterson, *Evolution Exposed: Biology* [Hebron: Answers in Genesis, 2006].)
18. Bacteria can also pick up genes from other microorganisms and their environment through different mechanisms. But again, even though the gene might be new to that bacterium, it's not a completely novel gene; it had already been existing somewhere. And it's the origin of functional new genetic information which molecules-to-man evolution demands.
19. See Dr. Georgia Purdom and Dr. Kevin Anderson, "A Creationist Perspective of Beneficial Mutations in Bacteria," Answers in Genesis, May 27, 2009, https://answersingenesis.org/genetics/mutations/a-creationist-perspective-of-beneficial-mutations-in-bacteria.

20. Mariana Pinho, Hermínia de Lencastre, and Alexander Tomasz, "An Acquired and a Native Penicillin-Binding Protein Cooperate in Building the Cell Wall of Drug-Resistant Staphylococci," *Proceedings of the National Academy of Sciences* 98, no. 19 (2001): 10,886–10,891.

21. Julie Perry, Nicholas Waglechner, and Gerard Wright, "The Prehistory of Antibiotic Resistance," *Cold Spring Harbor Perspectives in Medicine* 6, no. 6 (2016): a025197.

22. Robert Kofahl, "A Serious Problem for Homology," Creation 14, no 2. (1992): 31, https://answersingenesis.org/biology/a-serious-problem-for-homology.

23. Günter Wagner, *Homology, Genes, and Evolutionary Innovation* (Princeton University Press, 2018).

24. Ibid., 90.

25. James DiFrisco and Johannes Jaeger, "Beyond Networks: Mechanism and Process in Evo-Devo," *Biology & Philosophy* 34, no. 6 (2019): 54.

26. See Gary Parker, "Comparative Similarities: Homology," in *Creation: Facts of Life: How Real Science Reveals the Hand of God* (Green Forest: Master Books, 2006), https://answersingenesis.org/biology/homology-comparative-similarities.

27. Douglas Futuyama, *Evolution*, 3rd ed. (Sunderland: Sinauer Associates, 2013), 54.

28. E.g., the articles and videos at https://answersingenesis.org/human-body/vestigial-organs.

29. Incidentally, limbs on snakes don't appear in the "oldest" fossils anyway, like you'd expect from a straightforward evolutionary scenario. (Philip Bell, "'Oldest Snake' Fossils Found Evolution? The Fossils *Still* Say No!" Creation Ministries International, March 1, 2015, https://creation.com/oldest-snake-fossils; see also Elizabeth Mitchell, "Four-Legged Snake Fails as a Transitional Form and Perhaps Even as a Snake," Answers in Genesis, November 22, 2016, https://answersingenesis.org/reptiles/four-legged-snake-fails-transitional-form-and-perhaps-even-snake.)

30. James Dines, et. al., "Sexual Selection Targets Cetacean Pelvic Bones," *Evolution*, 68, no. 11 (2014), 3,296–3,306.

31. James Trexel, "Are Wisdom Teeth Evidence for Evolution?" Answers in Genesis, January 27, 2018, https://answersingenesis.org/human-body/vestigial-organs/are-wisdom-teeth-evidence-evolution.

32. Douglas Futuyama, *Evolution*, 3rd ed. (Sunderland, MA: Sinauer Associates, 2013), 54.

33. Biblical creationist models infer that today's continents once belonged to a larger landmass, too, which would most likely have divided during the global flood.

34. John Fleagle and Christopher Gilbert, "The Biogeography of Primate Evolution: The Role of Plate Tectonics, Climate and Chance," in *Primate Biogeography* (Boston: Springer, 2006), 375–418.

35. Alan De Queiroz, "The Resurrection of Oceanic Dispersal in Historical Biogeography," *Trends in Ecology & Evolution* 20, no. 2 (2005): 68–73.

36. Kurt Wise and Matthew Croxton, "Rafting: A Post-flood Biogeographic Dispersal Mechanism," *The Proceedings of the International Conference on Creationism*, vol. 5, no. 1 (2003): 37. Cited in Harry Sanders and Troy Lacey, "Floating Log Rafts: A Model for Post-flood Biogeography," Answers in Genesis, August 31, 2019, https://answersingenesis.org/the-flood/global/floating-log-rafts.

37. Michael J. Oard, "Marine Fossils in Amber Support the Flood Log-Mat Model," *Journal of Creation* 24 no. 1 (2010): 9–10, cited in Sanders & Lacey (2019).

38. Or a cheeky evolutionist who doesn't draw conclusions beyond the observational science for these fossils

39. David Menton, "Did Feathered Dinosaurs Evolve into Birds?" Answers in Genesis, September 7, 2018, https://answersingenesis.org/dinosaurs/feathers/did-dinosaurs-evolve-into-birds.

40. David Menton, "*Tiktaalik* and the Fishy Story of Walking Fish," Answers in Genesis, March 7, 2007, https://answersingenesis.org/extinct-animals/tiktaalik-and-the-fishy-story-of-walking-fish.

41. "*Tiktaalik*—Walking Off Stage," Answers in Genesis, July 1, 2010, https://answersingenesis.org/fossils/transitional-fossils/tiktaalik-walking-off-the-stage.

42. Jane Reece et. al., *Campbell Biology*, Canadian ed. (Don Mills: Pearson Canada, 2014), 548.

43. John Woodmorappe, "Mammal-Like Reptiles: Major Trait Reversals and Discontinuities," *Journal of Creation,* 15, no. 1 (April 2001): 44–52, https://answersingenesis.org/fossils/transitional-fossils/mammal-like-reptiles-major-trait-reversals-and-discontinuities.

44. You can learn how to apply Critical Thinking Check #6 to other common examples of evolutionary evidence in my video series *CT Scan* or with the help of other resources at AnswersInGenesis.org.

EVALUATING ARGUMENTS

12

How to handle remaining errors in logic

I opened the refrigerator door and peered into the wonderworld beyond, never suspecting that what was about to happen would scar my memory forever. It all began when I spotted the bag of Granny Smith apples. *Apple slices with cinnamon—perfect.*

My anticipation soared as I gutted one apple, seasoned it with a dash of powdery goodness from the spice rack, and tucked into the first slice. I paused, mid-chew. Something about that cinnamon didn't seem right. Another bite. *This is certainly not cinnamon.* Perturbed, I inspected the spice's label. Paprika. No wonder my taste buds had freaked! Do you have any idea what a bizarre flavor *paprika* lends a Granny Smith?

"Nibbling a nightmarish nugget"

Like my taste buds discovered the hard way, subtle mistakes can have salient consequences. Forgetting to read one little spice label can mean the difference between savoring a satisfying snack and nibbling a nightmarish nugget. So it goes with mistakes in logic. One little fallacy can produce an argument which *looks* persuasive, the way a paprika-covered apple might look delicious. But the longer you chew on the apple or argument, the more you grow convinced that something isn't right.

How can you recognize subtle fallacies before swallowing a faulty argument? That's what we'll examine in this chapter. Numerous flawed arguments could exist for any sound one—the way countless unpleasant substances could replace the cinnamon on any "cinnamon apple." But by learning to recognize the most common logical mistakes, you'll be far better equipped to identify the not-quite-right parts of messages from secular classrooms and cultures.

You will have caught many such fallacies during the first 6 Checks of Critical Thinking by filtering out equivocations, propaganda, interpretations, and assumptions from genuine facts. Yet like paprika particles slipping through the filter, other types of faulty logic may still linger in the message.

Three classes of potentially lingering logical errors include fallacies of unacceptable premises, faulty analogies, and formal fallacies. Let's see how to recognize each of these as part of Check #7: Check the Logic. Then we'll consider how to step back and identify big-picture questions, which reveal that arguments against the Bible often borrow biblical concepts. To begin, we'd better unpack what an argument is.

ANATOMY OF AN ARGUMENT

When we talk about arguments in everyday life, we're often referring to disagreements between people. But in logic, an argument is a set of statements called premises, which are meant to support another statement called the conclusion. Take the following argument:

Premise 1: DNA contains information.

Premise 2: Information comes only from intelligent sources.

Conclusion: Therefore, DNA originated from an intelligent source.

This is a *deductive* argument. Deductive arguments try to prove a conclusion is certainly true, while *inductive* arguments try to imply a conclusion is probably true. For example,

Deductive

Premise 1: All fossils are dead things.

Premise 2: *Tiktaalik* is a fossil.

Conclusion: Therefore, *Tiktaalik* is certainly a dead thing.

Inductive

Premise 1: The global flood buried most fossils.

Premise 2: *Tiktaalik* is a fossil.

Conclusion: Therefore, the global flood probably buried *Tiktaalik*.

We call a deductive argument *valid* if its conclusion logically follows from its premises. If the premises are true, the conclusion must be true. The conclusions of *invalid* arguments, however, do not logically follow from the premises, resulting in fallacies. But not even all valid arguments are worth believing. For example,

Premise 1: All mammals are fire-breathing creatures.

Premise 2: Squirrels are mammals.

Conclusion: Therefore, squirrels are fire-breathing creatures.

Although Premise 1 is (thankfully) false, this argument is logically valid because if both its premises were true, its conclusion would also be true. If an argument is valid and all its premises are true, we call the argument *sound*. However, if a valid deductive argument has even one false premise, the argument is *unsound*.

Instead of being valid or invalid, inductive arguments are called *strong* or *weak*. The more probable the conclusion (assuming all true premises), the stronger the inductive argument. For example,

Inductively Strong	**Inductively Weak**
Premise: 99% of patients say Vitamin X improved their symptoms.	**Premise:** 49% of patients say Vitamin X improved their symptoms.
Conclusion: So if you have symptoms, you'll likely benefit from Vitamin X, too.	**Conclusion:** So if you have symptoms, you'll likely benefit from Vitamin X, too.

If an inductive argument is strong and its premises are true, the argument is *cogent*. One or more false premises, however, make inductive arguments *uncogent*. This might seem like a lot to keep straight. But have no fear—Figure 12.1 is here:

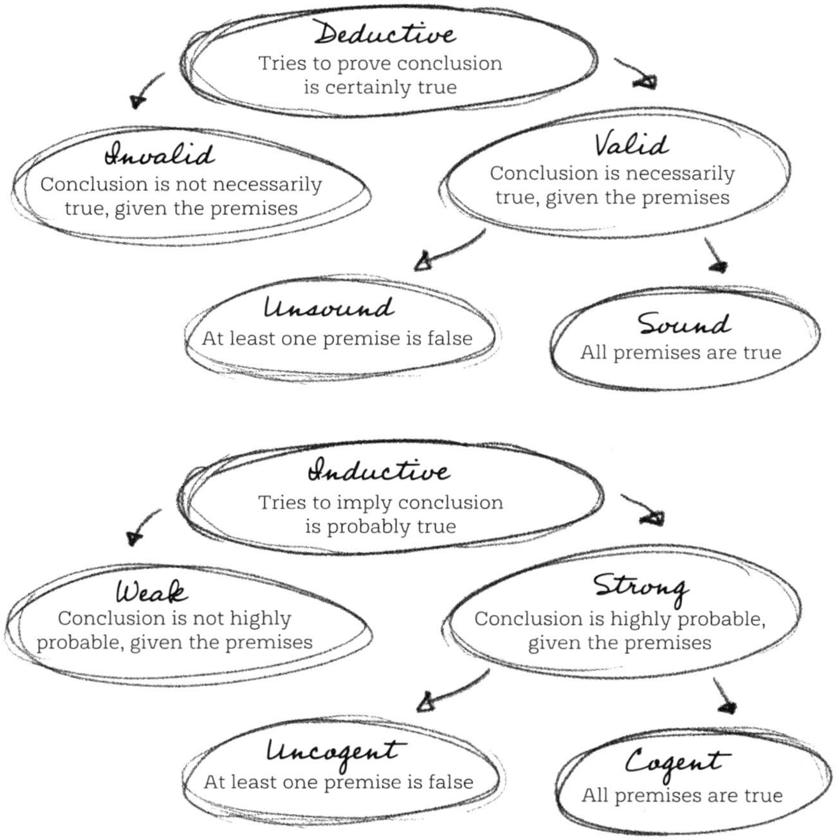

Figure 12.1: A summary of deductive and inductive arguments

TWO TYPES OF REASONING

While inductive and deductive *arguments* try to imply or prove a conclusion, inductive and deductive *reasoning* work a little differently. By understanding the difference between inductive and deductive reasoning, you can not only avoid being taken in by overstatements about what science can do but also recognize further types of faulty logic—and false teaching.

Inductive vs. Deductive Reasoning

Induction involves piecing together little facts which we already know to try constructing a larger picture of reality which we don't already know. It's like beginning with a few puzzle pieces and trying to imagine how the rest of the puzzle might look.

Deduction, however, involves drawing smaller conclusions from a known big picture of reality. It's like starting with the picture on a puzzle box, so we can look at its little pieces knowing where they fit within the bigger picture.

For an example of how deductive reasoning works, let's say our big picture is dinosaur. From that known big picture, we can draw conclusions about little facts which we know are part of the dinosaur, like its tail, feet, or toes. We could deductively argue,

All dinosaurs have toes.

T. rexes are dinosaurs (big picture).

Therefore, *T. rexes* have toes (little detail).

We know what the big picture (dinosaur) looks like, so we know what the little facts (toes) look like. Inductive reasoning, however, might argue,

All dinosaurs have toes.

T. rexes have toes (little detail).

Therefore, *T. rexes* are dinosaurs (big picture).

This might sound pretty smooth if you say it quickly while standing on your head. However, the problem with inductive reasoning is that little pieces aren't always enough to lead us to the right big picture. For example, we could inductively argue,

All dinosaurs have toes.

Kittens have toes.

Therefore, kittens are dinosaurs.

As cool as dino-kittens might be, the point is that induction doesn't always work.[1] But science is based on inductive reasoning. With enough details and data points, we can use the scientific method to reach a pretty reasonable conclusion. But we can't necessarily prove that conclusion is absolutely true.[2] That's why one of the first things I learned in my science classes was to never write "prove" on a lab report, even though we often find this word in the media.

No matter how many little facts, measurements, and observations we have, we can never be sure we're constructing the right big picture from them because we cannot know everything. We may piece together facts until we think we have a good idea of what the larger puzzle looks like. But the next day, another bit of evidence might come along which throws off our interpretation.

Deduction and the Bible

Fortunately, there is Someone who knows how all the pieces of reality fit together because he created the puzzle. And he's given us a puzzle box that shows us the big picture of reality through his Word. That's why Scripture is the surest foundation for our thinking.

Beginning with God's Word as our big picture of truth, we can deductively conclude that little statements in Scripture are also true. Drawing our ideas from Scripture this way is the proper way to interpret the Bible, a method called *exegesis*. Often, however, false teachers take individual verses (little details) out of context to inductively construct their own larger pictures of theology, a faulty method called *eisegesis*.

One common example of eisegesis happens when people try inserting human interpretations of science (like millions of years) into Genesis. Similarly, if professing Christians try quoting the Bible to justify wrongdoings, you can be pretty sure they're using eisegesis to do so.

To recognize eisegesis, you can ask the same doctrine-detection questions from Critical Thinking #2: Check the Challenge:

- Does this message conflict with a clear teaching from Scripture?
- Does this message conflict with the big picture of what the Bible teaches?
- Does this message conflict with the way most Christians have interpreted the Bible for thousands of years?

If you answer yes to any of these, there's a good chance you're dealing with eisegesis.

FALLACIES OF UNACCEPTABLE PREMISES

With those basics of biblical logic covered, it's time to examine the mug shots of Check #7's most wanted fallacies. They're a gang known as the *fallacies of unacceptable premises*,[3] with members including straw man arguments, motte-and-baileys, either-or fallacies, circular reasoning, and faulty analogies. Let's tackle each.

Straw Man Arguments

Beware of straw men. I'm not talking about the *Wizard of Oz* kind, with their burlap grins and cozy flannel (though if one starts arguing with you, then sure, be suspicious). Rather, straw man arguments happen when someone tries to weaken an opposing perspective by making it look unreasonable—and as easy to knock over as a scarecrow. To catch a straw man, simply bring a discussion back to what the attacked perspective really states. For example:

> **Person #1:** FAH LA-LA-LA-LAAAAAAAAAAA, LA-LAAAA-LAAAAAAA-LAAAAAAAAAAA—
>
> **Person #2:** Would you mind singing quieter, please?
>
> **Person #1:** Oh, you think I should never speak another word again?
>
> **Person #2:** That's not what I said—
>
> **Person #1:** You don't appreciate the arts?
>
> **Person #2:** That's also not what I said—
>
> **Person #1:** You think the whole world should be silent at your request?
>
> **Person #2:** That's also not what I said.

For every straw man Person #1 sets up to make Person #2's request sound unreasonable, Person #2 can respond by clarifying what was actually stated. Look out, though—straw men may be subtle. For instance, I've read textbooks that argue the following:

> Creationists believe that organisms never change.
>
> But organisms do change.
>
> Therefore, creationists are wrong.

But wait a minute . . . do most biblical creationists say that organisms never change? No. We do observe variation within created kinds of living things, like dogs changing into other varieties of dogs (see chapter 7). Such variation factors strongly into biblical creation models. However, by saying that creationists believe nothing ever changes, this argument tries to weaken the biblical perspective by making it sound ridiculous—a classic straw man.

Motte-and-Bailey Arguments

Straw man arguments aren't the only villains in town. Their counterparts, known as motte-and-bailey fallacies, work the opposite way straw men do, disguising weak perspectives as strong ones.

Why motte-and-bailey? The term traces back to a type of medieval castle built on a mount called a motte, overlooking a courtyard known as the bailey. Motte-and-bailey fallacies begin when someone presents a controversial, hard-to-defend point—the bailey. Then, when another person challenges that position, the arguer replaces the weak point with a more defensible one, representing the fortified motte. For example:

"The fortified motte"

Person #1: Churches indoctrinate children with outdated rules and myths, so youth under 18 shouldn't be allowed to attend church. (Bailey)

Person #2: Actually, denying minors the right to decide whether and where they worship would be a serious breach of religious freedom.

Person #1: I just believe in defending the intellectual rights of children! (Motte)

Did you catch what happened? Person #1's argument didn't change. But instead of admitting what they were really advocating for, they conflated their position with a better sounding one.[4]

To summarize, while a straw man reframes a strong position as a weak position, a motte-and-bailey reframes a weak position as a strong position. In both cases, you can respond simply by bringing the discussion back to what was originally said.

Either-or Type Fallacies

The next fallacies to beware of involve false either-or claims. To understand these fallacies, let's start by examining a true either-or claim, which does not contain a logical error: "Either a personal God created the universe, or a personal God did not create the universe." These options cannot both be true at the same time in the same way. In other words, they're mutually exclusive.

Logical either-or claims always contain two mutually exclusive options. If one option is true, then the other must be false. But either-or fallacies (alias, false dilemmas or fallacies of bifurcation) present two options as though they're mutually exclusive, when really, both might be true, both might be false, there could be middle ground between them, or there may be alternative options. For example, I was taught in the university that insect wings evolved from either gills or exoskeleton lobes, when the third (and correct) option is that God created insects' wings.

But watch out—not all either-or fallacies contain the word *or*. Sometimes, messages which can be rephrased as "if-then" statements imply false either-or situations, as these equivalent sentences show.

"Because you're a creationist, you're not a real scientist."

"If you're a creationist, then you're not a real scientist."

"Either you can be a creationist or a real scientist, but not both."

These statements contain a type of either-or fallacy called *affirming the disjunct*, which claims that if one option is true, the other must be false, when both may be true. In this case, the claim that you can either be a creationist or a scientist affirms a faulty disjunct because many people are both creationists and scientists at the same time.

Of course, either-or arguments do not contain fallacies if there really are only two options. Claiming a third possibility exists when it doesn't is itself a fallacy called *denying the correlative*. For example, some may argue that instead of believing in either creation or evolution, we can believe God used evolution to create humans. But as chapter 2 explained, that's not a biblically feasible option. Ultimately, the key to catching either-or type fallacies is to ask, "Are there really (only) two mutually exclusive options?"

Slippery Slopes

Like either-or fallacies present only two options when another may exist, *slippery slope arguments* present only one scenario when others may be possible. To illustrate, let me tell you about a series of decisions which led to my own "slippery slope" experience while skiing with a friend:

> **Decision #1:** Agree that it's a good idea to try the most difficult route on the hill.
>
> **Decision #2:** Ride the chairlift uphill, knowing that what goes up must come d-o-o-o-o-own.
>
> **Decision #3:** Ski to the route's entrance, behold the steep, icy mounds (moguls) below, and contemplate whether to back out. . . . Nah.
>
> **Decision #4:** Start skiing down the moguls, no turning baaaAAAAaaaAAAAaaaAAAAaaaAAACK! *crash*

Once we'd peeled ourselves off the snow, found our skis, and assured wide-eyed onlookers that we were still alive, my friend and I made one final decision: "Let's never try that again."

Just as that first decision launched my friend and me into a chain of events from which there was eventually no return, slippery slope arguments suggest that one choice, action, or belief will inevitably (or at least very likely) lead to another . . . and another . . . resulting in dire consequences. For example:

> If you leave the gate open, then the dog will escape.
>
> If the dog escapes, it will attack the mail carrier.
>
> If it attacks the mail carrier, then important mail will be delayed.
>
> If important mail is delayed, society will collapse.
>
> Therefore, if you leave the gate open, society will collapse.

This is a logically valid argument because if the premises are true, the conclusion must be true. However, the problem with slippery slope arguments is that it's sometimes hard to tell how true the if-then premises really are. Will society collapse if the mail gets delayed? That doesn't seem likely.

Because of the uncertainties involved, slippery slope arguments aren't usually meant to be deductive so much as inductive. So slippery slope arguments are only considered fallacies if the outcome isn't necessarily likely, given the premises. Two questions can help you discern the outcome's likelihood, and therefore the argument's strength.

1. **How probable is each if-then statement?**
   For example, how likely would the dog escape if the gate were left open, and how likely would the mail carrier be attacked if the dog

escaped? To estimate outcomes' likelihoods, it's often helpful to question how logically each event connects to its supposed consequence and consider whether other factors could likely alter or prevent that consequence. The less probable each consequence, the weaker the argument.

2. **How many if-then statements are there?**
   The longer the chain of events, the less likely the argument's conclusion will be if each event has an associated uncertainty. For instance, if it's only 50% likely the dog would escape if the gate were open and 50% likely that the mail carrier would be attacked, then there's only a .5 x .5, or 25%, chance the mail would be delayed. However, if you can show that each if-then statement is highly likely or certain, the resulting argument is inductively strong and therefore not a fallacy.

I've read skeptics say creationists use slippery slope fallacies when pointing out consequences which are consistent with evolutionary beliefs, including relative morals and decreased regard for every human life. For example, if humans are merely evolved animals, then we're logically justified in treating humans like animals, destroying the ones we don't believe are worth keeping alive.

Naturally, not every evolutionist will want to act on such reasoning. So it would be a slippery slope fallacy to claim, "If someone holds an evolutionary worldview, then they're guaranteed to behave consistently with that worldview and murder others to further their own evolutionary success." A more reasonable statement would be, "If someone holds an evolutionary worldview, then they may have no reason not to act consistently with that worldview, opening the door to negative outcomes."

It's no slippery slope fallacy to document the negative outcomes of an evolutionary worldview which are unfolding in society.[6] Of course, showing that evolutionary beliefs logically justify negative social outcomes doesn't prove evolution is false. But it does show the societal importance of defending the truth of God's Word, beginning in Genesis.

Circular Reasoning

To summarize the next fallacy, you should beware of circular reasoning because you should beware of circular reasoning.

If you're thinking the above (circular) explanation seems about as useful as a hollow, porcelain sledgehammer, you've just "nailed" the issue with circular reasoning: it's not a meaningful persuasion tool.

Also known as *begging the question*, circular reasoning happens when an argument assumes what it's trying to prove. In other words, the argument's premise is the same as (or presupposes) its conclusion, even if they're stated differently. For instance, the argument "Critical thinking is important for Christians because logically evaluating messages is a crucial skill for every believer" is just another way of saying, "Christians need critical thinking because Christians need critical thinking."

Now for a plot twist: while circular reasoning is considered an informal fallacy, circular arguments are not technically illogical. Remember, an argument is logically valid when the conclusion must be true if the premises are true. And in a circular argument, the conclusion is the premise. So an argument like "Christians need critical thinking because Christians need critical thinking" is formally logical; it's just not useful as a persuasive argument because there are no other premises to support why the conclusion is true. We'd have to believe it arbitrarily.

If you can show there are other good reasons to believe the conclusion, those extra premises remove the arbitrariness and prevent circularity. For example, you could say Christians need critical thinking because those skills help us defend our beliefs, strengthen our faith, and avoid being deceived.

Do Christians Use Circular Reasoning?

According to my critical thinking textbook, the classic circular argument states:

> The Bible says that God exists.
>
> The Bible is true because God wrote it.
>
> Therefore, God exists.

Worded that way, this argument is circular because its second premise assumes the conclusion, *God exists*, is true. Does that mean Christianity rests on a fallacy? Let's think about it.

As chapter 10 explained, a quick way to spot flawed logic is asking, "Is this message true or false because . . .?" Here, we'd ask, "Is it false that God exists because it's possible to defend his existence with circular reasoning?" Clearly, the answer is no. One circular argument cannot subtract from the plethora of sound reasons to accept the Bible's message. In fact, if the argument mentioned those reasons, it wouldn't be circular. So we could make this argument nonarbitrary by saying,

> The Bible says God exists.

We have both internal and external reasons to accept the Bible's claims as true.

Therefore, it's reasonable to accept the claim that God exists.

As you might have noticed, we could swap out the statement "God exists" with any statement the Bible teaches. Some might suggest the real circularity lies in why Christians believe the Bible is authoritatively true. The circularity states,

The Bible is true because it's God's Word.

We know it's God's Word because the Bible says so.

Again, you can break this circularity by adding the premise "We have both internal and external reasons to accept the Bible's claims as true." That's the shortcut to answering this objection against Christianity, using a couple of critical thinking hacks. Now, let's take a step back to see why this shortcut works.

Circular Reasoning and Axioms

We've already seen that while circular reasoning produces unpersuasive arguments, it's not a formal fallacy because it's technically logical. And when you think about it, some circular reasoning is not only logical but also necessary to establish starting points for our thinking. These starting points are called *axioms*, or *presuppositions*. Axioms are statements which we can't necessarily prove are true, but which we assume are true so we can reason about other things.

The laws of logic are axioms—and so is the statement that logic exists. Like apologist Dr. Jason Lisle has pointed out, we must assume that logic exists to logically argue that logic exists.[7] That's technically circular. Yet it's not a fallacy because we don't believe in logic's existence arbitrarily. In fact, the world only makes sense because this axiom is true.

"yet it's not a fallacy."

Other apologists have explained that the test of a trustworthy axiom is whether it's coherent with itself and consistent with observable reality. In other words, valid axioms lead to statements which don't contradict themselves and which real-world facts affirm. The axiom that logic exists passes both tests: the laws of logic don't contradict each other and the physical order we see in our universe—along with the facts that math and science are possible—affirm logic's existence. The laws of logic also provide a coherent basis for our thinking.

If an axiom passes the external and internal consistency tests, we don't need to believe it arbitrarily. So basing our thinking on such axioms is not a fallacy, even if it requires circular reasoning.

Axioms and Worldviews

Why does all this talk about testing axioms matter? Because all worldviews begin with axioms. Christianity begins with the axiom "God exists, so his Word is our authority." Secular humanism, however, begins with the axiom "There is no God, so human reasoning is our authority."

In the case of Christianity, it's fairly straightforward to show that the axiom "God's Word is our authority" leads us to conclusions that are consistent with themselves and the world around us. For example, if the Bible is right that God, whose character is the source of truth, created a logical universe and designed humans in his image with faculties for reasoning, then we have an absolute foundation for objective knowledge, morality, and logic. But if human reasoning is the authority, then knowledge, morality, and logic are ultimately meaningless chemical reactions happening in our accidentally evolved brains. This logically leads to conclusions which conflict with themselves and with the world around us—including the assumption that immaterial things like logic exist in a material universe without a consistent foundation for that assumption.[8]

Ultimately, it's Christianity, not humanism, which passes the test of a trustworthy axiom and is therefore not founded on a fallacy. Besides, while humans are fallible, God is not. He can rightly and nonarbitrarily claim to be the authority regarding the truth of his Word.

FAULTY ANALOGIES, BLIND MEN, AND ELEPHANTS

Those were some heavy concepts we just thought through, so let's shake things up with a story.

Have you heard the one about the three blind men who were feeling an elephant? The first guy touched the elephant's trunk and declared, "An elephant is a thin cylinder with two nostrils!"

"No, no," objected the second blind man, whose fingers examined the elephant's foot. "Anyone could tell that an elephant is a *thick* cylinder with toenails."

"Clearly, you're both wrong," remarked a third blind man, flapping the elephant's ear. "An elephant is merely a membranous disk."

Just like the three men were feeling the same elephant, different religions might seem to disagree but describe the same God.

Right?

Let's think about it.

Answering Faulty Analogies

To see how we can respond to this and other arguments by analogy, let's back up and examine how analogies work. Analogies, of course, are illustrative comparisons between two things—in this case, world religions and persons palpating a pachyderm. Engaging and memorable, analogies can be incredibly helpful for explaining abstract concepts. Jesus himself frequently taught with analogies, comparing the kingdom of heaven to everything from a pearl merchant to a mustard seed.

Because of their ability to explain, describe, and simplify, analogies often make for persuasive arguments. But as compelling as analogies may be, remember they can only illustrate. Analogies can never prove anything. And if an analogy argues against a biblical teaching, you know that analogy must harbor some weakness.

The key to identifying that weakness is to look for an important difference between the items the analogy compares. If you spot the analogy's weakness, you've spotted the argument's weakness. Sometimes, you can even turn the analogy around to promote a biblical perspective. To do so, it's often helpful to bring the argument back to an underlying big-picture concept, like what truth is and where it comes from.

Turning the Elephant Around

Let's try applying these techniques to the elephant analogy. First, what's an important difference between the two things being compared? The analogy is comparing different parts of an elephant to different religions comprised of different belief statements. The comparison suggests that just as we can discuss different body parts to describe the same elephant, we can use different religious statements to describe the same spiritual realities.

We know that different body parts can coexist on the same elephant. But can different—and extremely contradictory—religious statements about the nature of God, the universe, and human souls really coexist as truth within the same reality? Not if reality is logical. The fact that different body parts can coexist on one elephant but contradictory statements cannot logically coexist in one reality is a major difference between the items being compared.

"Coexist on the same elephant"

Now that we've identified this weakness, let's try turning the analogy around to enforce a biblical perspective. To begin, we can look for a big-picture question behind the analogy. For example, "How do we know the truth?"

Specifically, how would anyone talking about the blind men know the men were feeling the same elephant? That person would need to have open eyes. They'd need the ability to perceive the entire elephant and all the blind men touching it. So is anyone who claims that all religions are equal the only human who can see the grand scheme of reality, observing the form of truth which everyone else is groping to discover? Such a person would be God. And interestingly, God has revealed reality to us through his Word.

Aren't analogies awesome?

FORMAL FALLACIES

Most of the fallacies we've investigated so far are called informal fallacies because the errors lie in arguments' content rather than structure (form). Now let's turn to catching formal fallacies.

Some of the most common formal fallacies involve *conditionals*, or if-then statements, like, "If God created humans in his image, then every human life has value." Logicians nickname the "if" part of a conditional the *antecedent* and the "then" component the *consequent*. In this case, the antecedent is "God created humans in his image," and the consequent is "Every human life has value."

To see the structure of conditional arguments more clearly, we can symbolize their statements with letters—typically *p* for the antecedent and *q* for the consequent. So, every conditional statement follows the formula "If *p*, then *q*."

Valid Conditional Arguments

With these basics in mind, let's look at two common structures for valid if-then arguments to better spot fallacious ones. The first structure goes by the title affirming the antecedent (or *modus ponens* if you're a fan of Latin). This type of argument proves a consequent is true by showing its antecedent is true, using the structure

If *p*, then *q*.

p.

Therefore, *q*.

For example,

If God created humans in his image, then every human life has value.

God created humans in his image.

Therefore, every human life has value.

The opposite of affirming the antecedent is another valid structure called *denying the consequent*, or *modus tollens*. This structure proves an antecedent is false by showing its consequent is false:

If *p*, then *q*.

Not *p*.

Therefore, not *q*.

For example,

If life evolved through natural processes, then the information in genes must have appeared by chance.

The information in genes could not have appeared by chance.

Therefore, life could not have arisen through natural processes.

Again, this argument is both logically valid and intellectually sound.

Unsound Conditional Arguments

Alright, practice time. What are the following arguments' structures?

1. If dinosaurs evolved into birds, then birds are dinosaurs.
   Dinosaurs did evolve into birds.
   Therefore, birds are dinosaurs.
2. If a loving God exists, then the world would not be full of suffering.
   The world is full of suffering.
   Therefore, a loving God must not exist.

Hopefully, you answered *affirming the antecedent* for Argument #1 and *denying the consequent* for Argument #2. Both forms are logically valid. Does that mean we should believe these arguments' conclusions? Not necessarily.

Remember, trustworthy arguments are not only valid but also sound, containing no false premises.[9] For example, one of the premises in Argument #1 claims that dinosaurs evolved into birds. Although stated as a fact, this idea is really an interpretation about the past which faces multiple challenges from observational science.[10]

What about Argument #2? The premise "The world is full of suffering" is clearly true. But notice the other premise makes an either-or claim by suggesting that the existence of suffering and a loving God are mutually exclusive. As with any either-or statement, we can test this claim by asking if other options are possible—or if both options can be true at once. And sure enough, Genesis teaches that God exists and suffering exists because of sin. So the argument's first premise contains a hidden *affirming the disjunct* fallacy. Therefore, the argument is unsound.

"False premises"

Denying the Antecedent

What's wrong with the following argument?

If you have a dog, then you are a pet owner.

You do not have a dog.

Therefore, you are not a pet owner.

As you probably noticed, there are other ways to be a pet owner besides having a dog. You might own a cat, a chinchilla, or a small albino armadillo. So the conclusion "You are not a pet owner" isn't necessarily true given the premises. That's the problem with arguments which follow this structure, known as *denying the antecedent*:

If *p*, then *q*.

Not *p*.

Therefore, not *q*.

For example,

"If we found dinosaurs and humans in the same rock formation, then they lived at the same time.

We do not find them next to each other in the same rock formation.

Therefore, they did not live at the same time."[11]

This argument might sound persuasive, but it fallaciously denies the antecedent. There could be other reasons we don't typically find human and dinosaur fossils together—the lack of telltale fossils simply means they weren't buried together.[12]

Affirming the Consequent

Denying the antecedent has a villainous opposite nicknamed *affirming the consequent*:

If *p*, then *q*.

q.

Therefore, *p*.

For instance,

If humans and apes share a common ancestor, they should have similar DNA.

They do have similar DNA.

Therefore, they share a common ancestor.

This argument might seem convincing. But its conclusion isn't necessarily true because—like chapter 11 discussed—common design explains genetic similarities at least as well as common ancestry. Affirming the consequent involves a similar problem to denying the antecedent: there could be at least one way for the conclusion to be false, even if the nonconditional premise is true.[13]

The only case when both structures are not fallacies is if there are no other ways for the consequent (*q*) to be true without the antecedent (*p*) being true. For example,

> If God created life (*p*), then life should show irreducibly complex design features (*q*).
>
> Life does show irreducibly complex design features (*q*).
>
> Therefore, God created life (*p*).

This argument affirms the consequent. But is there any other way for the consequent to be true without the antecedent being true? No—there are no known mechanisms by which inanimate chemicals can realistically assemble themselves into even one living cell or for natural processes to produce functional genetic information for complex new features, because information comes only from intelligent sources. So it's not a fallacy to say that life's complexity necessarily points to a Creator, God.

Stolen Concept Fallacies

The last fallacy we'll consider, another informal error, goes back to the garden analogy from chapter 7, which compared a person arguing against the Bible to a gardener trying to prune a stone. Just as critical thinking is only possible because God's Word provides a foundation for logic, that gardener can only stand upright to hack against the stone because a foundation of bedrock is upholding everything. By simultaneously fighting against and relying on the same substance, the gardener acts in a self-defeating manner. In the same way, arguments become self-defeating when they assume the truth of the same principles they're opposing—a problem known as the *stolen concept fallacy*.

"God's Word provides a foundation for logic."

For example,

> **Person #1:** I don't believe in air. After all, I can't see it.
>
> **Person #2:** But you're using air to say you don't believe in air.

Like Person #1 required air to argue against air, people who want to attack biblical teachings must often borrow biblically based principles to do so. As others have documented in detail,[14] these principles include:

- Truth
- Logic
- Knowledge
- Science
- Morality
- The value of every human life

To identify these principles within an argument, it's helpful to ask why the argument's topic is worth raising. For example, imagine someone argues that the Bible condones slavery.[15] Before delving into the details of ancient systems of indentured servitude, how they compare with modern slavery, and how Scripture really addresses human exploitation, you could ask, "Why are we concerned about slavery?"

In answer, we're concerned about slavery because it devalues and exploits human life. But why are we concerned about exploiting human life? We're concerned because human life matters, so exploiting it is morally wrong. But why does human life matter and where do moral standards like "wrong" come from? A biblical worldview, not an evolutionary one, can consistently answer these questions. Ultimately, asking big-picture questions helps you not only identify stolen concept fallacies but point others to Jesus.

So Long, Paprika

By understanding the logical errors we just covered,[16] you'll be well equipped to recognize the paprika-like taste of fallacies before swallowing an argument. But there's more to surviving the battlefields of secular classrooms and culture than spotting faulty messages. You also need to combat brainwashing conditions that make those messages harder to resist. And that's what we'll talk about next.

Endnotes

1. That's not to say induction is not a useful tool when applied properly. It simply can't absolutely prove conclusions, and it possesses the potential to mislead (especially when based on limited data).
2. This doesn't mean Christians should shun science; in fact, a Christian worldview provides the philosophical foundation to make scientific reasoning possible. (See Dr. Jason Lisle, "Biblical Faith is Not "Blind"—It's Supported by Good Science," Answers in Genesis, April 7, 2006, https://answersingenesis.org/what-is-science/biblical-faith-is-not-blind-its-supported-by-good-science.)
3. Not to be confused with fallacies of *irrelevant* premises, which we examined in chapter 10
4. For more on responding to motte-and-bailies, see Patricia Engler, "Logical Fallacies: Motte-and-Bailey," Answers in Genesis, January 27, 2021, https://answersingenesis.org/blogs/patricia-engler/2021/01/27/logical-fallacies-motte-bailey-arguments.
5. The claim that no "real" scientist rejects evolution is a "no true Scotsman" fallacy. See "Only the Uneducated Reject Evolution," Answers in Genesis, November 8, 2017, https://answersingenesis.org/evolution/only-uneducated-reject-evolution, or *Critical Thinking Scan*, Season 2, Episode 6, on Answers TV.
6. E.g., see Dr. Jerry Bergman, *How Darwinism Corrodes Morality* (Joshua Press, 2017). See also AnswersInGenesis.org/sanctity-of-life.
7. Dr. Jason Lisle, "The Fallacy of Begging the Question," Answers in Genesis, August 17, 2009, https://answersingenesis.org/logic/the-fallacy-of-begging-the-question.
8. See Dr. Jason Lisle, "Atheism: An Irrational Worldview," Answers in Genesis, October 10, 2007, https://answersingenesis.org/world-religions/atheism/atheism-an-irrational-worldview.
9. Here's a handy rule for spotting structurally false if-then premises: a conditional statement is false if the antecedent is true and the consequent is false.
10. E.g., see Dr. David Menton, "Did Dinosaurs Turn into Birds?" *The New Answers Book 1* (Green Forest: Master Books, 2006).
11. Example given by Dr. Jason Lisle, "Formal Fallacies," Answers in Genesis, October 5, 2009, https://answersingenesis.org/logic/formal-fallacies.
12. See Bodie Hodge, "Why Don't We Find Human & Dinosaur Fossils Together?" *The New Answers Book 1* (Green Forest: Master Books, 2006).
13. That's one reason why it's always helpful to check for other alternative explanations when you hear an assumption from historical science presented as fact (see chapter 11).
14. E.g., Dr. Jason Lisle, *The Ultimate Proof of Creation: Resolving the Origins Debate* (Green Forest: Master Books, 2009). See also Patricia Engler, "Six Principles Skeptics Borrow from the Bible," Answers in Genesis, February 17, 2021, https://answersingenesis.org/blogs/patricia-engler/2021/02/17/6-principles-skeptics-borrow-bible.
15. See Bodie Hodge and Paul Taylor, "Doesn't the Bible Support Slavery?" *The New Answers Book 3* (Green Forest: Master Books, 2010).
16. A summary of these and other fallacies is available in appendix B.

COMBATING BRAINWASHING

13

How to take care of yourself and thrive on campus

Imagine being led every day to a room with white walls and fluorescent lights. There, a professionally dressed authority figure tells you the following messages for over an hour:

What you believe is wrong.

Nobody thinks like you do anymore.

Intelligent people accept a different way of thinking now.

You need to accept it, too, for society to move forward.

What you believe is wrong.

As you look around the room, you can't help suspecting that everyone else present has bought into these messages. They're even repeating the same words themselves. At first, you resist the pull to obey—to conform. But in between the hours you spend in the room, the authority figures are working you hard. You don't get as much sleep as you used to. You don't always eat as well as you should. You find yourself battling illnesses more often. Little by little, your defenses are wearing down.

"Steady winds erode a cliff."

I've just described what many political prisoners experience in labor camps—and what Christian students may experience on a less extreme level at a university.

Some call it brainwashing. It's a slow force that undermines your beliefs the way steady winds erode a cliff or raindrops dissolve a message in sidewalk chalk.

I felt the steady drip, drip, dripping of that force in my classes, where authoritative professors and textbooks repeatedly told me the Bible is wrong, earth is millions of years old, and no "real" scientist believes in Genesis. The demands of student life left little time and energy for responding to these claims as they accumulated. And everyone around me seemed to accept them.

I knew that statements which conflict with Scripture aren't true. I had apologetics training to defend why they aren't. Even so, consistently hearing them presented as facts for four years wore on me. This type of "brainwashing" was the hardest part of secular education.

A RATTLESNAKE WORD

Brainwashing is one of those emotionally charged words that sizzles with threat like the tail of a rattlesnake. Its hair-raising quality makes brainwashing the perfect word for propaganda by fear appeals. Instead of logically arguing against a message, propagandists can simply accuse the message source of brainwashing children. And *voila*. The source suffers instant discreditation, regardless of whether their message was true.

Because of the term's degradation into cheap arsenal for propaganda battles, it's wise to apply the word *brainwashing* cautiously. This is especially true because not everyone agrees about what brainwashing involves—or even whether it happens. Let's clear up the confusion by unpacking what brainwashing is, how it occurs, and where the boundary lies between teaching and indoctrination. We'll look at hallmarks of classic brainwashing environments so we can spot modern indoctrination when we see it. Then we'll explore practical strategies for resisting brainwashing at a university.

WHAT IS BRAINWASHING ANYWAY?

According to *Merriam-Webster's Dictionary*, a couple of definitions exist for *brainwashing*:[1]

1. a forcible indoctrination to induce someone to give up basic political, social, or religious beliefs and attitudes and to accept contrasting regimented ideas
2. persuasion by propaganda or salesmanship

The first definition captures the historical (and more controversial) view of brainwashing. Today, we often think of brainwashing as any intense, manipulative persuasion method. But around 1950,[2] the word *brainwashing* specifically described the "reeducation" processes communist governments practiced on dissidents. Authorities controlled everything from captives' sleeping to eating to social contact while indoctrinating them (including by torture) to embrace communism and renounce former beliefs.

Pastor Richard Wurmbrant, one among millions of Christians persecuted under twentieth-century communism, wrote:

> The methods vary, but brainwashing in my Romanian prison consisted essentially of this: we had to sit seventeen hours on a form which gave no possibility to lean, and you were not allowed to close your eyes. For seventeen hours a day we had to hear, "Communism is good, Communism is good, Communism is good, etc.; Christianity is dead, Christianity is dead, Christianity is dead, etc.; Give up, give up, etc."[3]

He described this as worse than the physical torture he experienced.

As similar atrocities unfolded throughout the twentieth century, people increasingly researched, discussed, and dreaded brainwashing. By the mid-1990s, ideas about how to define, measure, and respond to brainwashing became so muddied and politicized that many researchers dismissed the concept of brainwashing altogether.[4] Other researchers, however, argued that brainwashing (or "mind control") *does* exist as an extreme form of social influence, exploiting the psychological manipulation tactics we see in other contexts, like advertising, but to a greater extent.[5,6,7]

It gets a little more complicated than that, and the definition for *brainwashing* can become quite narrow. So, I want to be careful when describing Christians' experiences in secular classes and culture as "brainwashing." For example, most Western students (hopefully) aren't being forced at gunpoint to recant their former beliefs. However, I'd suggest the conditions Christian students face at university can share some parallels with what "brainwashing" victims experience—like being repeatedly told their beliefs are wrong while living under conditions that hamper critical thinking.

Ultimately, while universities don't necessarily involve what *Merriam-Webster's* would call "*forceful* indoctrination" under definition #1, they *are* ideal indoctrination centers.[8] There, intensive "persuasion by propaganda" (definition #2) can run full course, fueled by repetition, authority, conformity, and similar forces unpacked in chapter 10. So, when I say "brainwashing" in educational contexts, I mean it in the popular sense of *potentially subversive, one-sided indoctrination*.

TEACHING VS. BRAINWASHING

Okay, so what exactly does *indoctrination* mean? *Merriam-Webster's Dictionary* provides two definitions:[9]

1. to imbue with a usually partisan or sectarian opinion, point of view, or principle
2. to instruct, especially in fundamentals or rudiments: TEACH

Given that the second definition is basically *education*, where do the lines blur between teaching and brainwashing? I'd suggest the answer lies in the documentable truth of what's being taught and in students' freedom to question it.

After all, we wouldn't normally think of brainwashing someone into believing the truth. It'd technically be possible (albeit unbiblical) to try using brainwashing tactics to manipulate someone into accepting accurate beliefs, similar to how propaganda can promote true ideas. However, true truth should stand to reason itself without requiring that people be brainwashed into accepting it.

"But what counts as truth?"

But what counts as truth? Facts we can observe and agree about in the present are most clearly true, assuming our observations are accurate. Assumptions, interpretations, and beliefs based on those facts may or may not be true. But we can test those beliefs by asking whether they're consistent with themselves and observable reality.

With these points in mind, it's easier to tell the difference between indoctrination and instruction. Instruction communicates observable (or previously observed[10]) facts. It explains what different people believe about those facts. And it equips students to reason about whether those beliefs are likely true. But indoctrination expresses only dogma—beliefs which aren't necessarily fact, but which indoctrinators expect people to accept without question.

Test Your Skills: Which of these statements contains indoctrination?

A. "The Bible teaches that God created the universe in six days."

B. "Evolutionists believe that humans are closely related to apes."

C. "Jesus fulfilled every Old Testament prophecy about the death of the Messiah."

D. "The evolutionary changes in the fossil record are an observable fact."[11]

As you probably noticed, statements *A*, *B*, and *C* present observable (or previously observed) facts—including facts about what evolutionists believe. These statements are examples of instruction. But the last statement, a quote from one of my textbooks, is an interpretation presented as an unquestionable fact. So if you answered *D*, you'd be right.

As this textbook statement illustrates, education often includes both instruction and indoctrination as educators present facts through specific worldview lenses. One-sided indoctrination only teaches students to interpret the facts through a single lens. Students rarely encounter other viewpoints or interpretations—even for instructional purposes.[12] This kind of indoctrination grows more subversive the more it relies on subconscious forces like repetition, authority, and conformity.

All these factors were present in the secular university as I experienced it. So if brainwashing is defined as subversive, one-sided indoctrination, then yes, universities can certainly be brainwashing centers.

Do Churches Brainwash, Too?

Hang on a second. If one-sided indoctrination involves only presenting facts through a single lens, does that mean churches and Christian families brainwash kids? Voices in secular classrooms and cultures might tell you so. But let's take a minute to think about whether that's true.

Churches do teach specific worldview doctrines, like my university classes did. Secular schools teach humanistic doctrines, but churches (hopefully) teach doctrines based on a biblical worldview. These teachings are not unsupported dogmas, but facts grounded in the eyewitness testimony of God and the authors he inspired.

> *"Unnecessary and unhelpful"*

As Peter wrote to early Jewish believers, "For we did not follow cleverly devised myths when we made known to you the power and coming of our Lord Jesus Christ, but we were eyewitnesses of his majesty."[13] A few verses later, he added, "We also have the prophetic message as something completely reliable. . . . For prophecy never had its origin in the human will, but prophets, though human, spoke from God as they were carried along by the Holy Spirit."[14]

Paul also affirmed that the gospel's persuasiveness stems from its truth, requiring no manipulation tactics. When writing to the Thessalonians, Paul explained, "For our appeal does not spring from error or impurity or any attempt to deceive, but just as we have been approved by God to be entrusted with the gospel, so we speak, not to please man, but to please God who tests our hearts."[15]

Real-world observations and historical records confirm the apostles' testimony—and Scripture as a whole.[16] Even so, students may feel indoctrinated if their churches teach them to dogmatically accept everything they're told—to "just have faith" without ever asking questions, discovering why biblical teachings are trustworthy, or learning what others believe. That does sound like one-sided indoctrination. And it's completely unnecessary and unhelpful.

Solid apologetics resources exist to help churches and families equip youth to tackle tough questions, understand why the Bible is reliable, and learn how other worldviews compare. God's Word is true, and truth does not require people to be indoctrinated into believing it. By teaching biblical critical thinking skills and encouraging youth to ask questions, churches can not only instruct rather than indoctrinate but equip students to avoid real indoctrination.

Recognizing Brainwashing Environments

Now that we've covered what brainwashing is and how it differs from teaching, let's move on to unpack some hallmarks of historical brainwashing. That way, we'll be able to recognize its modern forms in secular classrooms and cultures.

Hallmarks of Indoctrination

To understand classical brainwashing environments, we'll need to backtrack to the early 1960s. The Korean War ended about 10 years ago, remaining fresh in the minds of political prisoners who survived. Some of them have been sharing their stories in interviews with psychiatrist Robert Lifton, the first researcher to describe the brainwashing (or "thought reform") process. Based on his conversations with these prisoners and others, Lifton suggested that "thought reform" environments involve eight features.[17]

1. Milieu control

The first hallmark of brainwashing, milieu control,[18] involves censorship of what information people can access, communicate, and think about. This ensures people only hear one side of the story—one interpretation of the facts.

You can probably think of some modern examples. For instance, chapter 3 described how the Parliamentary Assembly of the Council of Europe has urged nations to censor even remotely creationist teachings from all but religious studies classrooms,[19] despite the observational support for creation.

2. Mystical manipulation

The next hallmark, mystical manipulation, happens when indoctrinators use whatever means necessary to manipulate others' emotions and behaviors—without necessarily looking like it. Typically, the manipulation unfolds in the name of serving some higher purpose. The public can't openly question this process; instead, as Lifton observed, "One is asked to accept these manipulations on a basis of ultimate trust (or faith)."[20]

3. A demand for purity

At this stage, indoctrinators define the pure (or "good") as everything inside their ideology, and the impure (or "bad"), as everything outside their ideology. They reinterpret morality this way, claiming, as Lifton noted, that "anything done to anyone in the name of this purity is ultimately moral."[21]

On campus, for instance, you may notice that concepts which fit with humanism—like abortion, relative morals, and Marxism—are celebrated as "good," while biblical beliefs tend to be labeled as "hateful, oppressive, antiscientific, and evil." Research has also confirmed that universities in Canada, America, and Britain discriminate against students and professors who don't conform to leftist ideologies, further illustrating a demand for purity.[22]

4. A cult of confession

By cult of confession, we're not talking about some secretive religious ritual. We're talking about situations where indoctrinators create a culture obsessed with confessing breaches of the newly defined "purity." In such cultures, people may feel forced to repent of "crimes" they never committed.

5. Sacred science

Indoctrinators impose a sacred science on society when they—like the textbook I quoted earlier—promote human ideology as the unquestionable truth. Lifton explained,

> Thus the ultimate moral vision becomes an ultimate science; and the man who dares to criticize it, or to harbor even unspoken alternative ideas, becomes not only immoral and irreverent, but also "unscientific." . . . The assumption here is not so much that man can be God, but rather that man's ideas can be God.[23]

That sounds like something Answers in Genesis has warned about for years: setting human reasoning above God's Word as the ultimate authority for society's thinking.

6. Loading the language

To keep their ideas cemented in the public's minds, indoctrinators load the language by creating clichés that promote the sacred science while silencing argument.[24] The example Lifton cited of language-loading from communist regimes decades ago—which we're seeing again today—involves stamping anyone who agrees with an indoctrinated agenda as "progressive" and painting anyone who disagrees as essentially "oppressive." The effectiveness of loading the language lies in propaganda techniques, including labeling, association, conformity, and repetition.

7. Doctrine over person

At this point, preserving a group's sacred science grows so important that if any member personally observes or experiences something which doesn't fit that ideology, those experiences are either dismissed or reinterpreted to fit the sacred science. For example, in his book *Slaughter of the Dissidents*, Dr. Jerry Bergman documents how frequently scholars who question evolution have lost positions at universities or been denied degrees.[25]

8. Dispensation of existence

Brainwashing hits its zenith when indoctrinators set themselves up as "God" to the point where they can decide which people count as "real persons" with human rights. Often, the real persons are those who (surprise, surprise) conform to the indoctrinators' agenda. Those who dare dissent, however, risk relinquishing their rights to personhood.[26] Again, this is one logical extension of making humans' word the authority for truth—including the truth about what it means to be human.

Recognizing Brainwashing Messages

These eight criteria can help us spot aspects of indoctrination in today's secular classrooms and cultures. But how can you tell if you're being indoctrinated by a specific message in these environments? Based on the 7 Checks of Critical Thinking, here are a few questions you can ask to recognize brainwashing messages.

Is this information likely true?

Since we normally wouldn't associate truth with brainwashing, we'd expect that most brainwashing involves messages which aren't necessarily true. The first way to test a message's truth is asking whether it challenges a clear teaching from Scripture, using Critical Thinking Checks #1–2. The next way is to consider the message's reliability by applying Check #3: Check the Source.

Where does this information come from?

Remember, part of checking the source involves asking how the data in a message was collected. Does it come from reputable studies featuring careful, meticulous observations? If so, are the studies' methods, results, and implications being accurately reported? Do other careful, reputable studies agree? The more vague the information's reliability, the more wary you can be of anyone insisting you should believe it.[27]

Are words being redefined to promote a certain agenda?

For Check #4: Check the Source, you can ask whether the message source is redefining key words in ways which resemble Lifton's "thought reform" hallmarks. For instance, a *demand for purity* may be afoot if people are redefining "goodness" as "conformity to a certain ideology."

Another red flag starts waving if you notice certain terms are being redefined to load the language. Words like *scientist*, *evolution*, *truth*, or *tolerance* might help you think of some examples.

Why does this message sound persuasive?

To check whether the message involves subversive persuasion, you can apply Critical Thinking Check #5 by asking, "Why does this message seem convincing?" For example, does the message share logically sound arguments grounded in observational fact? Or does its persuasive oomph lie more in the way authority figures are harnessing the powers of repetition, emotion, public consensus, and other propaganda forces to promote a specific agenda?

Often, both fact and propaganda work together to make messages convincing. But the more propaganda techniques factor into making a message persuasive, the wiser you are to guard against subversive manipulation.

What parts of this message are instruction and which are likely indoctrination?

With propaganda identified, you can apply Check #6 to separate instruction from indoctrination. To recognize instruction, ask, "What parts of the message communicate observed or observable facts? Are those observations accurate?"

To spot potential indoctrination, ask, "What interpretations, assumptions, conjectures, or speculations am I being told to believe, which may or may not be true?"

These interpretations result from viewing facts through a particular lens. To identify that lens, ask, "What presuppositions or worldview is the message source's starting point? Are those presuppositions reliable?"[28]

Is this one-sided indoctrination?

Now it's time to unmask the true nature of any indoctrination you've identified. For instance, do you only hear facts interpreted through one lens (like evolutionary naturalism) when there could be alternative explanations which are at least as valid? Are you ever accurately taught interpretations from other viewpoints, even for educational purposes? Can you raise honest questions about the viewpoint's validity without being shot down?

If you answered no to these questions, there's a strong chance you're experiencing one-sided indoctrination.

This is especially bad news if you're in an isolated environment (say, a university lecture hall), which offers few opportunities to encounter other viewpoints. Separated from friends and family who don't embrace the sacred science, you're more likely to feel alone in your beliefs—and less likely to receive a reality check if you begin accepting the indoctrination. For these reasons, cult researchers recognize isolation as a feature of brainwashing environments.[29]

The good news? You can combat isolation—and therefore potential brainwashing—by maintaining strong interpersonal foundations.[30]

THREE WAYS TO RESIST BRAINWASHING

Along with fending off isolation, another way to guard against brainwashing is to ask, "Is there anything about this situation which makes critical thinking harder? If so, how can I boost my thinking abilities?"

Lower critical thinking defenses mean higher vulnerability to indoctrination. That's why classical brainwashing involves tactics like sleep deprivation, malnourishment, and verbal or physical abuse. Three strategies, however, will help you sharpen your defenses to resist potential brainwashing on campus.

1. Take Care of Yourself Spiritually

Caring for yourself spiritually involves maintaining the strong spiritual, intellectual, and interpersonal foundations which help Christian students worldwide keep their faith at a university. We've already seen how interpersonal foundations can promote students' walks with God while preventing isolation. But what about spiritual and intellectual foundations?

Pastor Richard Wurmbrand, who understood firsthand what Christians require to resist brainwashing, answered that. He emphasized spiritual foundations foremost, saying, "The preparation for underground work is deep spiritualization. As we peel an onion in preparation for its use, so God must 'peel' from us what are mere words, sensations of our enjoyments in religion, in order to arrive at the reality of our faith."[31]

Like chapter 6 explained, part of establishing strong spiritual foundations involves drawing personal boundaries. Pastor Wurmbrand echoed the importance of boundaries, illustrating that Christians must choose beforehand how they'll respond under pressure.[32]

Highlighting the need for strong intellectual foundations, Pastor Wurmbrand also described how the liberal theologians he knew caved easily under pressure. They asked,

> Why should I die for a dead God and a problematic Bible? If the stories of Adam and Eve are not true, if Joshua did not stop the sun, if the prophecies were written many years after they were fulfilled, if Jesus was not born of a Virgin and He did not rise bodily from the dead—then there are more lies in the Bible than in "Pravda."[33] Why should I go to death for what is not true or at least remains problematic?[34]

These liberal theologians' heartbreaking reactions remind us that to resist messages indoctrinating us that the Bible is false, we must be able to defend the Bible's truth.

2. Take Care of Yourself Physically

The brainwashing which Pastor Wurmbrand experienced involved both malnutrition and sleep deprivation. And though not enforced in universities, poor nutrition and limited sleep can hamper students' ability to think critically about indoctrinated messages.

For instance, remember from chapter 10 how the brain uses two channels—one for logical reasoning and another for intuitive thinking? As it turns out, the brain needs more glucose when reasoning logically.[35] Thinking is "sugar-powered."[36] Studies have shown that people who'd recently drunk sugary beverages relied less on mental shortcuts than people who'd drunk sugar-free beverages.[37] Keep in mind, however, that research suggests diets high in refined sugar and saturated fats negatively impact the brain.

Not only does the brain require proper nutrition, but it also needs enough sleep. One study showed sleep-deprived college students performed significantly worse on a critical thinking appraisal compared to well-rested students. Notably, the tired students also overestimated their own critical thinking performance.[38]

Other researchers found sleep-starved students were more likely to rely on mental shortcuts than on careful, logical thinking.[39] Studies also suggest sleep deprivation affects people's ability to make moral judgments.[40] Ultimately, pulling endless all-nighters at a university while living mainly on instant noodles will not support your critical thinking abilities.

3. Take Care of Yourself Mentally

Taking care of yourself spiritually and physically both contribute to taking care of yourself mentally. Eating well and racking up enough shut-eye, for example, predict lower risk of anxiety, depression, and other mental health struggles among young people.[41, 42]

Multiple studies have also linked church attendance and prayer to stronger mental health, with a close relationship with God especially predicting human flourishing. One research team recently concluded, "Theists securely attached to God were higher on every measure of well-being than were atheists, agnostics, and theists insecurely attached to God."[43]

Along with maintaining your physical and spiritual health, here are a few other practical, research-backed tips for boosting your mental well-being.

Take Breaks (Exodus 20:11)

Studying one subject for hours isn't only hard on the eyes. Extended, unbroken concentration can also be tough on the brain. You're more likely to remember information you've memorized in shorter, spaced-out study sessions than in one grueling marathon. Numerous studies suggest that short (less than 10-minute-long) "micro-breaks" can help students recharge, de-stress, refocus, and combat the physical and psychological side effects of focusing too long on one task.[44, 45, 46]

Understandably, some activities make for more effective breaks than others. While any break can help restore your energy, pausing to look at a smartphone doesn't reduce emotional exhaustion as much as taking a walk or talking to a friend.[47]

Research suggests that health-boosting breaks involve being in nature—or simply *looking* at something natural. One study, for instance, found that gazing at a grassy space for just 40 seconds significantly improved students' ability to focus on a task.[48]

Get Outside (Psalm 89:11)

Speaking of enjoying nature, a wealth of research suggests that spending time in God's creation is one of the best things a student can do. Studies repeatedly affirm that being in nature heightens mood, lowers stress, improves sleep, and reduces individuals' risk for anxiety and depression.[49] As an added bonus, experiencing nature also benefits your brain, promoting focus, memory, attention, and creativity.[50]

How can you spend time interacting with nature as a busy student? Personally, I loved studying outdoors whenever the weather cooperated. On rainy days, I'd head to the library early to find study spots by windows overlooking green spaces. Even working in indoor areas featuring plants, outdoor photography, or nature paintings beats studying in a blank cubicle when it comes to promoting well-being.

Exercise (1 Timothy 4:8)

Another advantage of spending time in nature is that outdoor activities often involve exercise. Scores of studies confirm that exercise packs a plethora of perks. Certainly, these benefits include increased physical health, strength, and endurance. But regular exercise also promotes and protects humans' mental health—for instance, by lowering stress, raising mood, and reducing risk of anxiety and depression. Physical activity can even bolster your brain, improving memory and attention.[51] (Sounds a lot like the benefits of experiencing nature, hey?)

"Integrate exercise into other activities."

How much exercise do students need? The World Health Organization recommends that adults score at least 30–60 minutes of moderate exercise (or 15–30 minutes of vigorous exercise) five days a week.[52] But apart from playing sports, how can students wrestle all that physical activity into their already-packed workloads?

One great way is to integrate exercise into other activities, like studying, taking micro-breaks, spending time with friends, and commuting. Personally, I'd integrate education with exercise by jogging while listening to recordings of myself reading terms and definitions for exams. Or I'd combine exercise with social activities by walking, running, or hiking with friends.

Spend Time with People (Hebrews 10:24–25)

While spending all your time at social gatherings probably won't improve your grades, isolating yourself behind a wall of textbooks isn't fantastic for your brain either. Activities that strengthen your interpersonal foundations—whether campus ministry nights, church events, mentorship meetings, small group studies, or simply hanging out with friends—all contribute to your social support system. And studies confirm social support to be a key factor promoting students' mental health.[53]

Ideally, much of your social support will stem from the strong interpersonal foundations you've been building. But you can also combine social support with academics by having a solid study buddy—a motivated classmate with a similar learning style and sense of humor as you. Meeting with my own #1 study pal to memorize notes, practice possible exam questions, or even work on separate assignments together led to productive (and often hilarious) memory-making.

Make Music (Psalm 33:1–3)

One spirit-lifting, mind-sharpening way to spend time with others is to jam or sing together. If you play an instrument, practicing a song also makes for an excellent micro-break from studying.

An entire field of psychology documents how music benefits the mind and brain all throughout life.[54] Among young adults, music interventions can help improve mood while decreasing anxiety and depression.[55] Some research even links musical training to quicker maturation in certain areas of the brain.[56]

Of course, different types of music will yield different effects. In fact, a form of brainwashing called *music torture* exists to wear down prisoners' defenses through loud, annoying, or offensive songs.[57] Lyrics themselves can be effective indoctrination tools, underscoring the importance of guarding what music you allow into your mind. On the flip side, I found that listening to biblical worship music was a valuable way to combat indoctrination, fortify my spiritual foundations, and recuperate from unbiblical lectures at the university.

MAXIMIZING YOUR TIME

As vital as it is to take care of yourself physically, mentally, and spiritually on the secular education battlefields, let's face it: student life doesn't leave much free time. How can you manage your time to maximize your overall well-being? Here are three field-tested tips.

1. Combine Health-Boosting Activities

You might have noticed that one secret to time management is combining activities which promote physical, spiritual, or mental well-being. For example, I mentioned in chapter 4 that some of my favorite university memories involved hiking with other Christians. A few friends and I started a social media group to help students from different campus ministries get outside together, which led to weekly sunrise hikes. We'd eat breakfast on a foothill overlooking campus, talk about life, and occasionally sing a few worship songs.

One of the churches in my university town also included a Saturday hiking group. My ukulele and I regularly joined these adventures, which often featured outdoor devotionals. While the Friday hikes contributed to my peer support, the Saturday hikes let me develop mentorship connections with older adults outside campus. Participating in these groups let me simultaneously combine the benefits of taking breaks, getting outside, exercising, making music, and spending time with friends—all while contributing to my spiritual and intellectual foundations.

Find what works for you. Maybe hiking's not your thing, but you love music. Why not gather some friends and jam together? You could plan a student-led worship night. You could take your instruments under the stars. Ask God for ideas, blend health-boosting activities, and combat campus brainwashing conditions—and bless others in the process.

2. Mix Self-Care with Academics

Like I've hinted earlier, it's often possible to associate health-boosting activities—like being outdoors or exercising—with studying. Take your books outside, listen to study notes while you work out, or find friends you can study alongside without distracting each other. Along the way, you'll not only be making the grade but creating lasting memories.

3. Beware of Pitfalls

Part of maximizing your physical, spiritual, and mental health involves looking out for pitfalls which could undermine your efforts. This includes watching what kind of screen time you're getting. Not only do some studies link lower internet, television, and social media use to higher mental well-being under certain conditions,[58, 59, 60] but, depending on what you watch, media itself is a form of indoctrination.[61]

Other possible pitfalls may look different for different people. Whatever the specifics, you can recognize potential hazards by asking, "What aspects of this activity are likely to *promote* my spiritual, physical, or mental well-being, and what aspects are likely to *harm* them?" If the potential downfalls outweigh the rewards, you may want to reconsider how you allocate your time.

OVERCOMING BRAINWASHING

While all these tips can help you keep your mind strong and your critical thinking defenses ready, indoctrination isn't something humans were meant to resist alone.

I remember learning this after one especially indoctrination-heavy lecture. Feeling slightly pummeled from the lecturer's barrage of anti-biblical messages, I walked outside, started listening to worship music, and realized that staying strong in secular classrooms and cultures isn't only a matter of holding on to God—but also of being held by him.

I couldn't trust in my own strength to stay a faithful Christian by "knowing enough." Instead, my job was to stay close to God, who is able to keep believers from falling.[62] As the Apostle Paul assured

Christians in the secular society of Corinth, "[He] will sustain you to the end, guiltless in the day of our Lord Jesus Christ."[63]

God is ultimately the one who enables us to survive the brainwashing environments of secular classrooms and culture. As we stay faithful in the little things, keep connected to God through continuous communication, and maintain our spiritual, intellectual, and interpersonal foundations through the resources he provides, he takes care of the big picture.

More amazing still, God can use those same three foundations to help you not only *keep* your worldview in secular classrooms but *apply* your worldview to transform culture.

How?

That's what we'll explore next.

Endnotes

1. "Brainwashing," Merriam-Webster.com Dictionary, *Merriam-Webster*, accessed December 1, 2020, https://www.merriam-webster.com/dictionary/brainwashing.
2. Many attribute the earliest reports of brainwashing to journalist Edward Hunter, but some researchers suggest the term appeared in slightly earlier documents likely written the same year (1950). (Marcia Holmes, "Edward Hunter and the Origins of 'Brainwashing,'" Hidden Persuaders, Birkbeck University, May 26, 2017, http://www.bbk.ac.uk/hiddenpersuaders/blog/hunter-origins-of-brainwashing/#_ftn2.)
3. Richard Wurmbrand, "Preparing for the Underground Church," Christian Mission to the Communist World, 1982, 27.
4. James Richardson, "Brainwashing Claims and Minority Religions Outside the United States: Cultural Diffusion of a Questionable Concept in the Legal Arena," *BYU Law Review*, 1996, no. 4 (1996): 873.
5. Dominiek Coates, "Life Inside a Deviant 'Religious' Group: Conformity and Commitment as Ensured Through 'Brainwashing' or as the Result of Normal Processes of Socialisation," *International Journal of Law, Crime and Justice* 44 (2016): 103–121.
6. Philip Zimbardo, "What Messages Are Behind Today's Cults?" *APA Monitor* 28, no. 5 (1997): 14.
7. What's *not* scientific is the caricature that brainwashing involves mysterious, irresistible forces by which authority figures hijack unsuspecting people's minds against their wills and turn them into robot-slaves. Instead, one cult researcher describes brainwashing as a specific process of changing people's belief systems so they become willing to do and believe whatever a brainwasher says—or face social and emotional consequences. (Benjamin Zablocki, "The Blacklisting of a Concept: The Strange History of the Brainwashing Conjecture in the Sociology of Religion," *Nova Religio* 1, no. 1 (1997): 96–121.)
8. For example, secular research has confirmed that many Western universities are heavily biased toward left-wing ideology and discriminate against right-wing professors and students. (Eric Kauffman, "Academic Freedom in Crisis: Punishment, Political Discrimination, and Self-Censorship," Center for the Study of Partisanship and Ideology, March 1, 2021, https://cspicenter.org/reports/academicfreedom.)

9. "Indoctrinate," Merriam-Webster.com Dictionary, *Merriam-Webster*, accessed December 1, 2020, https://www.merriam-webster.com/dictionary/indoctrinate.

10. By "previously observed facts," I mean historical events which someone witnessed and recorded in the past, but which we can't observe directly now. For instance, the Titanic struck an iceberg in the past and cannot be seen doing so today. Eyewitness testimony usually provides the most reliable information in such cases, especially when that testimony is confirmed by things we can observe in the present—like the sunken Titanic. Similarly, in a biblical worldview, God's eyewitness testimony provides an accurate account of the universe's beginning, confirmed by observational science.

11. Jane Reece et. al., *Campbell Biology*, Canadian ed. (Upper Saddle River: Pearson Education, 2012), 12.

12. Some of my textbooks did teach about creation in order to attack it, as I described in chapter 4. But the top scientific reasons why people believe creation were certainly not discussed in class.

13. 2 Peter 1:16

14. 2 Peter 2:19–21

15. 1 Thessalonians 2:3–4

16. This breaks any circularity in arguing the Bible is true because it's God's Word (see chapter 12).

17. Robert Lifton, "Ideological Totalism," *Thought Reform and the Psychology of Totalism: A Study of 'Brainwashing' in China* (New York: Norton, 1963), 419–437.

18. That is, control over the social environment within a culture

19. For example, the Parliamentary Assembly of the Council of Europe has urged its member nations to "firmly oppose . . . the presentation of creationist ideas in any discipline other than religion" in public schools, as chapter 3 explains. ("Resolution 1580: The Dangers of Creationism in Education," Parliamentary Assembly of the Council of Europe, Committee on Culture, Science and Education, October 4, 2007, http://assembly.coe.int/nw/xml/XRef/Xref-XML2HTML-EN.asp?fileid=17592&lang=en.)

20. Lifton (1963), 422.

21. In a tragic twist of irony, such "morality" may include violently exterminating anyone deemed "impure." (Ibid., 423.)

22. Eric Kauffman, "Academic Freedom in Crisis: Punishment, Political Discrimination, and Self-Censorship," Center for the Study of Partisanship and Ideology, March 1, 2021, https://cspicenter.org/reports/academicfreedom.

23. Ibid., 428.

24. Not to be confused with an informal logical fallacy called *loaded language* or *complex question*, which you can learn about in Dr. Jason Lisle, "The Complex Question," Answers in Genesis, August 31, 2009, https://answersingenesis.org/logic/the-complex-question.

25. Jerry Berman, *Slaughter of the Dissidents (Volume 1): The Shocking Truth About Killing the Careers of Darwin Doubters* (Southworth: Leafcutter Press, 2008).

26. *Personhood* as defined by the indoctrinators, that is—not by God

27. Another part of Check #3 in this context involves asking if the source may have a financial, political, or other personal motive for advancing a message using subversive, one-sided indoctrination. However, just because we might *think* of a motive doesn't guarantee whether that motive is really at play or whether there's brainwashing involved. Finding out that will require asking a few more questions.

28. By reliable, I mean "consistent with themselves and with the observable universe," like biblical presuppositions.

29. Dominiek Coates, "Life Inside a Deviant 'Religious' Group: Conformity and Commitment as Ensured Through 'Brainwashing' or as the Result of Normal Processes of Socialisation," *International Journal of Law, Crime and Justice* 44 (2016): 103–121.

30. Practical tips on how to do this are back in chapter 8.

31. Richard Wurmbrand, "Preparing for the Underground Church," Christian Mission to the Communist World, 1982, 11.

32. Ibid., 12.

33. The official newspaper of the Soviet Union

34. Ibid., 13.

35. Jacob Orquin and Robert Kurzban, "A Meta-Analysis of Blood Glucose Effects on Human Decision Making," *Psychological Bulletin* 142, no. 5 (2016): 546.

36. E.g., Heather Francis and Richard Stevenson, "The Longer-Term Impacts of Western Diet on Human Cognition and the Brain," *Appetite* 63 (2013): 119–128.

37. E.g., Emer J. Masicampo and Roy F. Baumeister, "Toward a Physiology of Dual-Process Reasoning and Judgment: Lemonade, Willpower, and Expensive Rule-Based Analysis," *Psychological Science* 19, no. 3 (2008): 255–260.

38. June Pilcher and Amy Walters, "How Sleep Deprivation Affects Psychological Variables Related to College Students' Cognitive Performance," *Journal of American College Health* 46, no. 3 (1997): 121–126.

39. Mindy Engle-Friedman et. al., "The Role of Sleep Deprivation and Fatigue in the Perception of Task Difficulty and Use of Heuristics," *Sleep Science* 11, no. 2 (2018): 74.

40. William Killgore et. al., "The Effects of 53 Hours of Sleep Deprivation on Moral Judgment," *Sleep* 30, no. 3 (2007): 345–352.

41. Felice Jacka et. al., "A Prospective Study of Diet Quality and Mental Health in Adolescents," *PloS One* 6, no. 9 (2011): e24805.

42. Daniel Freeman et. al., "The Effects of Improving Sleep on Mental Health (OASIS): A Randomised Controlled Trial with Mediation Analysis," *The Lancet Psychiatry* 4, no. 10 (2017): 749–758.

43. David Njus and Alexandra Scharmer, "Evidence that God Attachment Makes a Unique Contribution to Psychological Well-Being," *The International Journal for the Psychology of Religion* (2020): 1–24.

44. Kate Lee et. al., "Green Micro-Breaks: Viewing Workplace Nature Improves Mood and Performance," *Academy of Management Proceedings*, vol. 2017, no. 1 (2017).

45. Hannes Zacher, Holly Brailsford, and Stacey Parker, "Micro-Breaks Matter: A Diary Study on the Effects of Energy Management Strategies on Occupational Well-Being," *Journal of Vocational Behavior* 85, no. 3 (2014): 287–297.

46. Linda McLean et. al., "Computer Terminal Work and the Benefit of Microbreaks," *Applied Ergonomics* 32, no. 3 (2001): 225–237.

47. Hongjai Rhee and Sudong Kim, "Effects of Breaks on Regaining Vitality at Work: An Empirical Comparison of 'Conventional' and 'Smart Phone' Breaks," *Computers in Human Behavior* 57 (2016): 160–167.

48. Kate Lee et. al., "40-Second Green Roof Views Sustain Attention: The Role of Micro-Breaks in Attention Restoration," *Journal of Environmental Psychology* 42 (2015): 182–189.

49. David Pearson and Tony Craig, "The Great Outdoors? Exploring the Mental Health Benefits of Natural Environments," *Frontiers in Psychology* 5 (2014): 1,178.

50. Gregory Bratman et. al., "Nature and Mental Health: An Ecosystem Service Perspective," *Science Advances* 5, no. 7 (2019): eaax0903.

51. D. Lubans et. al., "Physical Activity for Cognitive and Mental Health in Youth," *Pediatrics*, vol. 2016, 1,642.

52. "Physical Activity," World Health Organization, November 26, 2020, https://www.who.int/news-room/fact-sheets/detail/physical-activity.

53. E.g., Jennifer Hefner and Daniel Eisenberg, "Social Support and Mental Health Among College Students," *American Journal of Orthopsychiatry* 79, no. 4 (2009): 491–499.

54. Nikki Sue Rickard and Katrina McFerran, *Lifelong Engagement with Music: Benefits for Mental Health and Well-Being* (Hauppauge: Nova Science Publishers, 2012).

55. Norma Daykin et. al., "What Works for Wellbeing? A Systematic Review of Wellbeing Outcomes for Music and Singing in Adults," *Perspectives in Public Health* 138, no. 1 (2018): 39–46.

56. James Hudziak et. al., "Cortical Thickness Maturation and Duration of Music Training: Health-Promoting Activities Shape Brain Development," *Journal of the American Academy of Child & Adolescent Psychiatry* 53, no. 11 (2014): 1,153–1,161.

57. Jonathan Pieslak, "Cranking Up the Volume: Music as a Tool of Torture," *Global Dialogue* (online) 12, no. 1 (2010): 1.

58. Holly Scott and Heather Cleland Woods, "Understanding Links Between Social Media Use, Sleep and Mental Health: Recent Progress and Current Challenges," *Current Sleep Medicine Reports* 5, no. 3 (2019): 141–149.

59. Amber Barthorpe et. al., "Is Social Media Screen Time Really Associated with Poor Adolescent Mental Health? A Time Use Diary Study," *Journal of Affective Disorders* 274 (2020): 864–870.

60. Jean Twenge and Eric Farley, "Not All Screen Time is Created Equal: Associations with Mental Health Vary by Activity and Gender," *Social Psychiatry and Psychiatric Epidemiology* (2020): 1–11.

61. Interestingly, the Barna researchers' *Faith for Exiles* study cited in chapter 6 found that the 10% of American Christian young people who had the strongest biblical worldviews tended not only to rack up less screen time but allocate proportionately more of their screen time to viewing Christian content. (David Kinnaman and Mark Matlock with Aly Hawkins, *Faith for Exiles: 5 Ways for a New Generation to Follow Jesus in Digital Babylon,* ebook ed. [Grand Rapids: Baker Books, 2019], accessed on Hoopla, 138–147.)

62. Jude 1:24

63. 1 Corinthians 1:8

14

THE NEXT LEVEL

Applying these skills and foundations to fulfill your God-given purpose

"Hans, Hans, wake up! Put your clothes on and come downstairs. You have to go on an urgent mission."[1]

Corrie ten Boom, a watchmaker whose family home had become a refuge for Jewish people in Nazi-occupied Holland,[2] wrenched Hans from a deep sleep. He awoke to the familiar ten Boom house where he, too, had sought shelter—not as a Jew, but as a Christian student.

A year earlier, the Nazis had decreed that all university students must submit a signed declaration of loyalty to Hitler—or cease studying. At that point, 18-year-old Hans Poley was already on the run.

Hans hid at the ten Boom's house for nine months, where the family integrated him into their lifestyle of prayer, Scripture reading, and dedication to biblical authority. It was this dedication which translated into the ten Boom's life-risking actions assisting Jews.[3]

"Underground resistance"

With their deeply grounded *spiritual* foundations, the ten Booms became ideal mentors for strengthening Hans' *interpersonal* foundations. Corrie's elderly father, Opa, especially influenced Hans. Hans wrote, "For all of us under Opa's roof, his prayers became a continuing powerful source of trust and hope. Without this, we might not have survived emotionally and spiritually."[4]

During his stay with the ten Booms, Hans began participating in underground resistance activities—delivering messages, giving ration cards to refugees, and keeping track of gestapo[5] movements. His final mission unfolded on the morning of February 5, 1944, shortly after Corrie woke him with urgent news. The gestapo were coming to arrest a certain resistance worker—unless Hans could warn him first.

Hans raced to the man's house, delivered the warning, and turned to depart. But before he had fled the man's driveway, the gestapo arrived and arrested them both. Hans records his subsequent experiences in concentration camp (and his miraculous release) in his book, *Return to the Hiding Place*. A film by the same name retells his story, along with those of others in Corrie ten Boom's clandestine resistance army.

Do you know who comprised the bulk of this army, which posed a formidable force against the Nazis? *Ordinary Christian young people*.

A RECURRING THEME

Hans and his fellow students weren't the only Christians whose biblical worldviews and personal foundations allowed them to influence history. Not by a long shot.

Let's rewind the clock another couple of centuries to meet two other world-changing believers: Hannah and William. We'll see how their stories, like Hans', show that the same foundations which apply to surviving universities also apply to impacting culture. Then we'll unpack practical ways you can prepare—and begin—to impact your culture by stepping into the unique missions God created you to fulfill,[6] even beyond the university.

The Story of Hannah and William

Hannah's story begins near Bristol, England, in 1745. Born a commoner, the fourth daughter of a schoolmaster, Hannah More grew up in nineteenth-century England's equivalent of a Christian homeschool family. Her love of writing developed into such a penchant for penning plays, poems, and stories that in those days her writings far outsold even those of Jane Austen.[7]

Despite her Christian upbringing, Hannah did not begin to embrace a biblical worldview until adulthood in a way that would profoundly influence her writing—and her world. What sparked this transformation? Hannah read a book by John Newton, the slave trader-turned-minister who wrote the hymn "Amazing Grace."

Unlike England's fashionable liberal theologians, who compromised with humanism, Newton preached a living Christianity founded on the authority of God's Word. He proclaimed, "We have the Scripture in our hands and are not bound to abide by the decisions of any man, farther than as they agree with this standard."[8]

In 1787, Hannah met both Newton and another Englishman whom Newton had impacted—a young politician named William Wilberforce. Upon converting to biblical Christianity, William had written at age 26, "God almighty has set before me two great objects: the suppression of the slave trade and the reformation of manners."[9]

By "reformation of manners," William meant tackling the social issues which sprang from English culture's departure from God's Word. Although England maintained a religious veneer, scriptural values largely remained locked inside closed Bibles rather than pouring from churchgoers' hearts into England's streets. As biographer Eric Metaxas described:

> Britain was particularly brutal, decadent, violent and vulgar. Slavery was only the worst of a host of societal evils that included

> epidemic alcoholism, child prostitution, child labor, frequent public executions for petty crimes, public dissections and burnings of executed criminals, and unspeakable public cruelty to animals.[10]

From their shared foundation of biblical authority, William and Hannah began working together to transform this cancerous culture. While William drafted bills and delivered speeches in parliament, Hannah penned her influential poem "Slavery" to sway public opinion in favor of abolition.

Hannah and William teamed up to fight injustice on countless other fronts as well, including by helping open Sunday schools to combat rampant poverty. Meanwhile, as the nearby French revolution rained murder like brimstone on thousands, Hannah's pseudonymously published pamphlet *Village Politics* helped prevent the revolution from spreading to England. Both Hannah and William also called England's mainstream, superficial Christians back to the foundation of biblical authority with their respective books, *An Estimate of the Religion of the Fashionable World* and *Real Christianity*.[11]

"Mainstream, superficial Christians"

After decades of setbacks and controversies, England finally passed a Slavery Abolition Act in 1833—the year both Hannah and William died. Summarizing the results of their efforts, Metaxas observed, "It was [Hannah's] friendship with Wilberforce that fueled their collaborations against the slave trade and a host of other social evils. Between them, they would quite literally change the world."[12]

The Secret to Hannah and William's Success

How did this daring duo accomplish such a feat? First, they began with an uncompromised stance on God's Word. As Wilberforce wrote in *Real Christianity*, "It must be conceded by those who admit the authority of Scripture . . . that from the decision of the word of God there can be no appeal."[13]

Second, Hannah and William excelled in the same personal foundations which help Christian students survive universities. Regarding the importance of William's spiritual foundations, for example, Metaxas noted, "It's important to say that Wilberforce wasn't just 'religious,' but actually had a personal relationship with God. He seems to have been motivated by love—love of God and the love of his fellow man. . . . This is probably the single most important factor in what he was able to do."[14]

William maintained a vibrant devotional life of Bible study and prayer, both alone and with others. He decried the apathy toward Scripture he saw in the professing Christians of his day, asking, "Is it not undeniable that with the Bible in our houses, we are ignorant of its contents; and that hence, in great measure, it arises, that the bulk of the Christian world know so little, and mistake so greatly, in what regards the religion which they profess?"[15]

In other words, William saw that while people had access to the Bible, they weren't opening it up, taking it in, and living it out in a way that transformed their lives and surroundings. They lacked spiritual foundations—and their culture suffered for it.

Given that so few Christians really seemed to read or understand the Bible, it's hardly a shock that William realized many Christians could not defend the Bible either. That is, they lacked intellectual foundations. As a result, William noted that Christianity had come under strong attack in nearby Europe because professing Christians were "wholly unarmed" to defend a biblical worldview against opponents' flawed arguments.[16]

"He warned the church in England."

He warned the church in England, "Let us be aware, less we also suffer from a like cause [the inability to defend the faith]; nor let it be our crime and reproach, that in schools, perhaps even in Colleges, Christianity is almost if not altogether neglected."[17]

Clearly, William recognized the dire straits that result when cultures and churches forsake the authority of God's Word. In response, he called Christians back to strong spiritual and intellectual foundations. And he possessed these foundations himself.

Even then, William Wilberforce couldn't change the world alone. He needed a network of like-minded believers, including friends like Hannah More. This core network came to be known as the Clapham Sect—not a sect so much as a collection of passionate Christians committed to abolition and social reform. The Clapham Christians lived near each other to meet regularly, pray together, strategize, and encourage one another. As a result, Hannah and William shared strong interpersonal foundations, which played a key role in the abolitionists' success.

Ultimately, strong spiritual, intellectual, and interpersonal foundations positioned Hannah and William, beginning from the starting point of biblical authority, to impact their world as God enabled them.

OVERCOMING GIANTS

As these stories illustrate, confronting the giants of unbiblical cultures is nothing new for believers who stand on God's Word. Never mind if they stand alone. Never mind if the odds seem insurmountable. Whether resisting Nazis, battling slavery, or preventing revolution, it's not unusual for people who walk with God to accomplish impossible things.

Hans, Hannah, and William could tell you. They wouldn't tell you it was easy, but they'd tell you it was worth it. Their stories remind us that spiritual, intellectual, and interpersonal foundations pertain not only to surviving college (and other challenging or hostile environments) as a Christian but also slaying giants. The key is knowing, believing, and obeying Someone bigger than the giants.

"Someone bigger than the giants"

That's great news for today's generation because giants clearly swarm our fallen planet. Abortion, euthanasia, human trafficking, attacks on the institution of family, compromised theology, youth leaving the church, the decline of Western Christianity . . . these are just some of the giants born to a culture founded on man's word rather than God's Word. Other giants, like poverty, disease, and addiction, also roam as effects of our sin-shattered world.

Such giants are hounding billions of humans made in God's image—individuals for whom Jesus died to offer abundant life.[18] Look outside in the shadows of forgotten steeples, and you'll see throngs of faces, hearts, and souls who need the hope we have in Christ.

Yes, we live among giants. The point is not to be overwhelmed by them but rise like David and ask, "Is there not a cause?"[19] Then, empowered by the God who guided David's stone, we, too, can take the slingshots God gives us and run into battle—not just the battlefield of a secular university, but the war zone of our giant-riddled world.

ON YOUR MARK . . .

Where do we begin? First off, we begin by recognizing that *we do not have what it takes to overcome the giants of our world*. On our own, we're already defeated by the sin nature inside us, never mind the monsters *outside*.

Jesus wasn't exaggerating when he said that apart from him, we can do nothing (John 15:5). That's why he said to "abide" in him the way a branch abides in a vine. The branch can bear the fruit it's created to produce only because it's connected to its life source. Similarly, we can't fulfill our God-given purposes without Jesus' life bearing fruit in us.

To demonstrate it's his power that overcomes, God often chooses insignificant people to accomplish his purposes—people like David, the youngest of his household. As I mentioned in chapter 4, David had developed his giant-slaying slingshot skills by being faithful to the ordinary shepherding tasks God gave him. But David recognized that it wasn't his own skills that would ultimately defeat Goliath. As David told King Saul, "*The LORD* who delivered me from the paw of the lion and from the paw of the bear will deliver me from the hand of this Philistine"[20] (emphasis added).

David knew that Goliath wouldn't stand a chance because David knew God. David's actions remind us that the secret to giant-slaying is drawing close to the Creator who loves us, remembering that "we are weak, but he is strong."[21] As we seek his heart, growing to love what he loves and be angered by what angers him, God provides us with everything we need to obey him—even when that means confronting giants.

GET SET . . .

If God places a particular giant in your sights,[22] what are some steps you can take to become better equipped to fight it? God understands exactly which tools you'll need, so being faithful to the tasks he's given you now is one way. But sometimes picking up other tools God makes available can require a little extra initiative.

For instance, when I first felt called to defend Genesis as a teenager, I recognized that becoming an apologist would require years of education and experience. But I also knew the process would involve a long series of little steps, many of which I could begin taking right away. These included researching apologetics topics, connecting with my mentor, volunteering at conferences with apologetics speakers, taking a public speaking course, and selecting subjects in high school that would help me study science at a university.

"Dream houses or apologetics careers"

Along the way, I drew motivation from Proverbs 24:27: "Prepare your work outside; get everything ready for yourself in the field, and after that build your house." This verse reminded me that, while end results like dream houses or apologetics careers might be fun to envision, a ton of groundwork needs to happen first.

On that note, if you think God might be calling you in a certain direction, you may want to consider what tools he's laid within your reach to "prepare your outside work." Could you begin to learn another language, attend certain classes, develop specific skills, or gain relevant volunteering experience? Could you serve, talk to, job shadow, or read books written by people who are doing the work you're interested in pursuing? Ask God what steps you can start taking now, remembering that drawing close to him is the greatest one.

GO!

As you walk with God, align your life to his Word, and faithfully perform each task he shows you (Colossians 3:23–24), he directs your steps (Proverbs 3:5–6; Psalm 37:23). This process may look different for different people. Personally, looking back at times where I can see that God was leading me, I find he often began by impressing a clear inclination on me—for instance, becoming an apologist, studying science at a particular college, or traveling and interviewing students.[23]

Not every dream I've ever held, of course, originated from God. How can we tell which desires are God-given and which ones likely stem from ourselves? The first test involves comparing our dreams against Scripture because *God-given desires will always line up with his Word* (Critical Thinking Check #1, right?).

Godly mentors can help us discern whether our inclinations, plans, and motivations align with Scripture. Plus, mentors will likely be able to lend specific advice and wisdom based on their own experience, insights, and knowledge of us personally. So seeking wise counsel is another helpful test of a God-given dream.

But the ultimate test is surrender.

Going . . . by Letting Go

Surrender involves letting go of our desires, releasing them into God's hands where they belong. Essentially, we're saying, "Lord, here's a dream for something I think I'd like to do. If it's your dream, please guide my steps and open the doors to help it happen. But if not, that's okay. I trust you."

The "but if not, that's okay" part is the hard bit. Yet that's where real surrender happens. If God gives back the dream, allowing the right doors to open in his perfect timing, then the dream becomes his to look after. This means we can trust him with any problems that arise along the way. We've relinquished our "right" to worry because the dream is no longer in our hands. And if God doesn't ever give it back, then it was likely never his "Plan A" for us in the first place.

"Witness his faithfulness."

An example of a dream God gave back to me was 360° in 180. Doors opened as I prayerfully knocked on them. Godly people around me encouraged the endeavor. And traveling to interview students simply seemed like the right thing to do. Issues which arose along the journey became opportunities to trust God—and witness his faithfulness in action.

But do you know a dream which God didn't give back—at least, not in the way I'd planned? It might seem eccentric, but when people asked me what I wanted to do after college, I usually rattled off a grand plan about living as a nomad in a converted camper van. I'd teach English overseas for half the year (preferably the snowy half) and rove across North America in my van the other half, speaking about apologetics to whomever would listen.

I was so determined to follow the "van plan" that when I returned from 360° in 180 and heard a friend say she'd been praying that God would connect me with the right organization to work for, I "corrected" her. I wasn't planning to join an organization, I said. I wanted flexibility to speak, write, and live in a van.

But a month later, God said something else. Suddenly and unexpectedly, he opened the door for me to join the Canadian branch of Answers in Genesis—the organization which first kindled my enthusiasm for apologetics. Again, the open door, godly counsel, and inner conviction affirmed, "Go."

But there were a few things I had to give up first, including my best-laid van plan. God did not give back that dream—not in the sense I'd expected anyway. But he gave me something else, beyond what I had asked or imagined: the chance to fight the giants of secular culture full time by calling other students to stand on the authority of God's Word.

Tools for the Mission

Whatever giants God may inspire you to fight, a few strategic weapons will likely come in handy. The greatest are worship, prayer, and the sword of the Spirit.[24] Honing these weapons involves building the spiritual foundations we discussed in chapter 6. But there's another kind of weapon, too—one which has turned the tide of many a cultural battle. What am I talking about?

Just this: have you ever heard the expression "The pen is mightier than the sword"?[25]

Words pack unbelievable power. For better or worse, words serve to sway hearts, change minds, rally action, and influence history.[26] Words help culture's giants rise—and fall.

I can attest to the power of spoken words firsthand because hearing an Answers in Genesis speaker at age 14 revolutionized my life. Written or recorded words exert an even greater impact still, as they can last indefinitely. Phrases penned by Hans Poley, William Wilberforce, and Hannah More are still influencing generations today, even though their authors have long ceased writing.

These authors fought their cultures' giants using the communication slingshots available at the time. Hannah penned poems, plays, and pamphlets to reach nineteenth-century England. William crafted speeches, composed letters, and compiled his book. Centuries later, while hiding in Corrie ten Boom's house, Hans copied underground newsletters for distribution to other resistance workers.

Along with the types of media which Hans, Hannah, and William leveraged, Christians today have unprecedented potential to engage their world through digital technologies. How can modern young people hone their own communication slingshots "for such a time as this"?[27]

Writing Tips

With today's online resources and education opportunities, it's easier than ever to learn how to wield words effectively. The internet bourgeons with masterful advice on writing, blogging, designing websites, delivering presentations, producing videos, and communicating from a biblical foundation. I'd encourage you to dive into any such resources which interest you, as communicational dexterity comes in handy not only for combating giants but for excelling at a university. To give you a head start, I've listed many of the top writing tips which I've personally found most useful in appendix D.

Research Skills

If communication is a giant-slaying slingshot, then quality research findings are an especially useful type of stone. Here are just some advantages of knowing how to find and read scientific studies:

- Backing your arguments with observational data lets you persuade from fact rather than propaganda.
- Going back to original research helps you ask critical thinking questions like "Where did this information come from? How was the data collected? Is it being reported accurately? What assumptions did the researchers use? Are there other ways to interpret the results? What have other experts said? Does newer research say anything different?"
- Efficiently tracking down research gives you an edge in a university.
- Familiarity with recent research helps you respond to current issues from an informed Christian perspective.
- Real-world observations confirm the Bible's teachings are true. Reading those observations not only encourages your own faith but strengthens your ability to defend the hope you have in Christ (1 Peter 3:15).

Of course, relatively few researchers will interpret their observations through a biblical lens. Secular interpretations may sound persuasive at first—especially given researchers' intellectual writing styles.[28] But with the foundation-building tools we've examined, including how to think critically, study apologetics, and find mentors who can answer questions that arise, you have the resources you need for thinking through research papers.

You can learn about how to find, read, and report results from research papers in appendix E, where I share the top research tips that I wish I had known as a first-year student.

BEWARE OF PITFALLS

While preparing to combat culture's giants may seem exciting, remember that battlefields are never safe. We have a real enemy, and as 2 Corinthians 2:11 says, we are not unaware of his schemes. We're also human beings with sinful natures, prone to weaknesses which the devil will not hesitate to exploit.

Accordingly, anything which begins disrupting our spiritual foundations—our stances on biblical authority or our relationship with God—demands our immediate correction. As chapter 6 discussed, guarding our spiritual foundations requires resisting little compromises, setting boundaries beforehand, stewarding our time, and individualizing our action plans.

Protecting our spiritual foundations also means *not getting so caught up in slaying giants that we neglect to spend time with God*. This potentially fatal mistake can unfold if we pour so much time and energy into serving that, like Martha in Luke 10, we miss recharging at the feet of Jesus.

"Potentially fatal mistake"

The enemy can also leverage our ministries against us if giant-slaying becomes our foremost identity. As chapter 6 mentioned, grounding our identity in anything transient (including ministry) entails crossing a dangerous line. Guarding against both these pitfalls requires prioritizing our personal walks with Christ—that is, maintaining strong spiritual foundations.

Strong interpersonal foundations assist with this process, as godly friends and mentors can let us know if they spot something amiss in our lives. That's just one more example of how the foundations that apply to surviving a university also apply to surviving *life after a university*.

The Battle Plan

In the end, we've seen that both life and university represent a spiritual battlefield. We've glimpsed how we're caught in the crossfire of a war as old as time—a rebellion to coronate human reasoning above God's Word. It's a war for the future of culture, the church, and immortal souls—a war with eternal stakes. The winning side has already been determined. But until our Victor comes, skirmishes will continue unfolding.

When we're surrounded by the clash of battle, it's easy to feel overwhelmed. Every direction we glance, we see another giant which has arisen from humanity's futile revolution against its Creator. We see giants wrought by Adam's fall, contemporary sinful decisions, and the culture abandoning the foundation of God's Word. But like history has proven repeatedly, those who know their God can effectively "fight the good fight"[29] by enacting the following battle plan.

Return to Biblical Authority

As many before us have discovered, standing up to giants starts by standing up for biblical authority. For example, only when he had discovered real Christianity himself could Wilberforce call others to confess the authority of Scripture—the foundation for combating slavery. From an uncompromised position on the same foundation of biblical authority, we, like Wilberforce, can confront our culture's giants in truth and love.

Develop Personal Foundations

Staying uncompromised, alert, and effective in battle requires having strong spiritual, intellectual, and interpersonal foundations to know God, defend his Word, and thrive alongside our fellow fighters. These are the foundations which Christian students worldwide have found essential for surviving the battlefields of secular universities. They're also the foundations which impactful Christians like Hans, Hannah, and William required to help stem tides of battle in their secular cultures.

Be Faithful

Preparing for—and waging—our parts of the battle involves being faithful in the missions God gives us. Our overall mission is to fulfill God's commandments to love him, love others, and make disciples, which he enables us to do as we walk with him. Individually, however, our missions also include specific assignments God sets before us, whether they seem important (like facing a giant) or insignificant (like watching sheep).

When God does set a certain Goliath in our sights, we can surrender the desire to fight it, placing our dreams in God's hands. If God defers or redirects those dreams as we continue seeking him, we can trust they weren't the best dreams for us right now. But if they do turn out to be God-given dreams, we can begin stepping into them by honing the slingshots available to us—including communication and research skills. All along, we must guard against anything which may disrupt our walks with God.

Bring Others Along

As we fulfill the missions God calls us to, we're wise to remember this war is far greater than we are. You and I only have one lifetime, whatever days God lends us. But the timeline of the war we're in extends from Genesis to Revelation.

Unless Jesus returns in our lifetimes, others will be coming to take our places after us. And it's our job to disciple them. This means that as we uphold biblical authority, maintain our foundations, and complete the tasks God gives us, we must also mentor others who will do the same. Paul modeled this process by discipling Timothy after "fighting the good fight" himself.

There it is—the battle plan history has witnessed in action time and time again, from the prophets to the apostles to giant-slayers like Hans, Hannah, and William. Throughout the ages, men and women of God have called their nations back to biblical authority. They've armed themselves with strong spiritual, intellectual, and interpersonal foundations to remain standing in battle. They've held an unwavering stance on God's Word. And through him, they've impacted the chapters of history in which God had placed them.

Now it's our turn.

Endnotes

1. As recounted in Hans' autobiography, *Return to the Hiding Place* (Elgin: LifeJourney Books, 1993), 125
2. Corrie ten Boom records these experiences in her well-known autobiography, *The Hiding Place* (Chosen Books, 1971).
3. As Hans observed, "Not only did the family take a fervent biblical stand against the current modernistic theology that had become mainstream in the Reformed Church, but they witnessed of the Old Testament promises of God for the dispersed Jews." (Hans Poley, *Return to the Hiding Place* [Elgin: LifeJourney Books, 1993], 25.)
4. Ibid., 26.
5. The Nazi secret police
6. Ephesians 2:10
7. Eric Metaxes, *Seven Women and the Secret of Their Greatness* (Nashville: Thomas Nelson, 2015).

8. "Job's Faith and Expectation," sermon by John Newton, available at biblehub.com.

9. William Wilberforce, 1787 (journal entry), quoted in Robert Isaac Wilberforce and Samuel Wilberforce, *The Life of William Wilberforce,* Vol. 1 (John Murray, 1838), 149.

10. Eric Metaxas, *Amazing Grace: William Wilberforce and the Heroic Campaign to End Slavery* (Grand Rapids: Zondervan, 2007), 69–70.

11. The original title is much longer (see reference 13).

12. Eric Metaxas, *Seven Women and the Secret of Their Greatness* (Nashville: Thomas Nelson, 2015), 59–60.

13. William Wilberforce, *A Practical View of the Prevailing Religious System of Professed Christians, in the Higher and Middle Classes, Contrasted with Real Christianity* (London: T. Cadell, 1797), 5. (Note: The spellings of some words in this and other quotes from *Real Christianity* have been updated to their modern English equivalents.)

14. Eric Metaxas, *Seven Men and the Secret of Their Greatness* (Nashville: Thomas Nelson, 2013), 53.

15. Wilberforce, *Real Christianity* (1797), 19.

16. Ibid., 10.

17. Ibid., 10.

18. John 10:10 (*Note*: This does not imply that becoming a Christian solves our every problem. We still live in a sin-broken world. But following Jesus does enable us to navigate each problem with the one who has overcome the world [John 16:33]. Jesus also provides us the standard, foundation, and empowerment to love others and overcome evil with good [Romans 12:21].)

19. 1 Samuel 17:29

20. 1 Samuel 17:37

21. Anna Warner, "Jesus Loves Me" (hymn), 1859.

22. If you're not sure whether there's a particular giant God is calling you to fight, you can ask him. See if he impresses you with a growing burden for one and then pray for ideas about how to begin fighting it. It's okay, however, if you don't sense a strong, specific calling to fight a certain giant right now, just be faithful and obedient in whatever task God *has* set before you today.

23. As Psalm 37:4 indicates, when we delight in God, he implants in our hearts the desires he wants us to have.

24. Ephesians 6:17

25. Edward Bulwer-Lytton, *Richelieu; or The Conspiracy: A Play, in Five Acts. To Which Are Added, Historical Odes on The Last Days of Elizabeth; Cromwell's Dream; The Death of Nelson by the Author of the "Lady of Lyon," "Eugene Aram" & c.* (Saunders and Otley, 1893), 39.

26. This isn't to say that words *themselves* exert such change, as God is sovereign over history (Proverbs 21:1). But words are often the tools through which these processes unfold.

27. Esther 4:14

28. Some studies overflow with jargon which might not make sense to anyone who is unfamiliar with the research topics. But many studies will be fairly understandable.

29. 2 Timothy 4:7

Appendixes

PRACTICAL APPLICATION RESOURCES

A

RESOURCE LIST

Here are just some of the resources available through Answers in Genesis, which can help you find alternative explanations to faith-challenging "facts" and follow up on remaining questions.

ANSWERSINGENESIS.ORG

You can browse hundreds of articles, research papers, and online book chapters by topic at AnswersInGenesis.org/answers or type specific questions into the website's search box.

ANSWERS TV

Subscribing to Answers TV lets you stream documentaries, conferences, presentations, and video series about multiple apologetics, science, and worldview topics—along with wholesome entertainment for study breaks.

Note—You can learn more about many of the specific topics addressed in this book through the video series *Critical Thinking Scan*, along with associated study guides and "Dig Deeper" resources available on Answers TV.

BOOKS BY TOPIC

The following books are normally available from AnswersInGenesis.org. You can also read a number of them online for free at AnswersInGenesis.org/answers/books

General Apologetics

- *The New Answers Book 1*. Edited by Ken Ham. Green Forest: Master Books, 2006.
- *The New Answers Book 2*. Edited by Ken Ham. Green Forest: Master Books, 2008.
- *The New Answers Book 3*. Edited by Ken Ham. Green Forest: Master Books, 2010.
- *The New Answers Book 4*. Edited by Ken Ham. Green Forest: Master Books, 2013.

- Lisle, Jason. *The Ultimate Proof of Creation: Resolving the Origins Debate*. Green Forest: Master Books, 2009.

Genesis Relevance and Worldview

- Ham, Ken. *The Lie: Evolution/Millions of Years, 25th Anniversary Edition*. Green Forest: Master Books, 2012.
- Ham, Ken, and A. Charles Ware. *One Race, One Blood: The Biblical Answer to Racism*. Rev. ed. Green Forest: Master Books, 2019.
- Hodge, Bodie, and Roger Patterson. *World Religions and Cults* Book Set. Green Forest: Master Books, 2016.
- Bergman, Jerry. *How Darwinism Corrodes Morality*. Kitchener: Solo Scriptura International Ministries, 2017.
- Ham, Ken. *How Could A Loving God . . .? Powerful Answers on Suffering and Loss*. Green Forest: Master Books, 2006.
- Bergman, Jerry. *Hitler and the Nazi-Darwinian Worldview*. Peterborough: Joshua Press, 2012.

Theistic Evolution and Other Compromises

- Ham, Ken. *Six Days: The Age of the Earth and the Decline of the Church*. Green Forest: Master Books, 2013.
- Chaffey, Tim, and Jason Lisle. *Old-Earth Creationism on Trial*. Green Forest: Master Books, 2008.
- *Searching for Adam: Genesis and the Truth About Man's Origins*. Edited by Dr. Terry Mortenson. Green Forest: Master Books, 2016.

The Bible

- *How Do We Know the Bible Is True?* Volume 1. Edited by Ken Ham and Bodie Hodge. Green Forest: Master Books, 2011.
- *How Do We Know the Bible Is True?* Volume 2. Edited by Ken Ham and Bodie Hodge. Green Forest: Master Books, 2012.
- *Demolishing Supposed Bible Contradictions*, Volume 1. Edited by Ken Ham. Green Forest: Master Books, 2010.
- *Demolishing Supposed Bible Contradictions*, Volume 2. Edited by Ken Ham, Bodie Hodge, and Tim Chaffey. Green Forest: Master Books, 2012.
- *Coming to Grips with Genesis: Biblical Authority and the Age of the Earth*. Edited by Terry Mortenson and Thane Urey. Green Forest: Master Books, 2008.

- VanDoodewaard, William. *The Quest for the Historical Adam: Genesis, Hermeneutics, and Human Origins*. Grand Rapids: Reformation Heritage Books, 2015.
- Anderson, Clive, and Brian Edwards. *Evidence for the Bible*. Green Forest: Master Books, 2018.
- Hodge, Bodie. *Tower of Babel: The Cultural History of Our Ancestors*. Green Forest: Master Books, 2013.

Biology

- Patterson, Roger. *Evolution Exposed: Your Evolution Answer Book for the Classroom*. Hebron: Answers in Genesis, 2007.
- Ham, Ken, and Bodie Hodge. *Glass House: Shattering the Myth of Evolution*. Green Forest: Master Books, 2019.
- Jeanson, Nathaniel. *Replacing Darwin: The New Origin of Species*. Green Forest: Master Books, 2017.
- Gitt, Werner. *In the Beginning Was Information: A Scientist Explains the Incredible Design in Nature*. Green Forest: Master Books, 2006.
- Sanford, John. *Genetic Entropy*. 4th edition. Canandaigua: Feed My Sheep Foundation, 2014.

Geology, Fossils, and the Flood

- Ham, Ken, and Bodie Hodge. *A Flood of Evidence*. Green Forest: Master Books, 2016.
- Patterson, Roger. *Evolution Exposed: Earth Science*. Hebron: Answers in Genesis, 2008.
- Snelling, Andrew. *Earth's Catastrophic Past, Volumes 1 & 2*. Green Forest: Master Books, 2010.
- Froman, Craig. *How Many Animals Were on the Ark?* Green Forest: Master Books, 2016.
- DeYong, Don. *Thousands, Not Billions*. Green Forest: Master Books, 2005.
- Lubenow, Marvin. *Bones of Contention: A Creationist Assessment of Human Fossils*. Grand Rapids: Baker Books, 2004.
- Morris, John, and Frank Sherwin: *The Fossil Record: Unearthing Nature's History of Life*. Dallas: Institute for Creation Research, 2010.

VIDEOS BY TOPIC

The following full-length videos are available through AnswersInGenesis.org/store or on Answers TV.

General Apologetics

- *The New Answers* DVDs
- *The Ultimate Proof of Creation: Resolving the Origins Debate* with Dr. Jason Lisle
- *Debunking Evolution: What Every Christian Should Know*

Genesis Relevance and Worldview

- *Genesis, Foundations, and How to Impact the Culture* with Ken Ham
- *Genesis: The Missing Piece of the Puzzle* with Calvin Smith

The Bible

- *Is the Bible True? How Do We Know?* with Bodie Hodge
- *The Genetics of Adam and Eve* with Dr. Georgia Purdom

Biology

- *Could Life Evolve by Chance? Science Says No* with Dr. Alan White
- *Genetics, Evolution, and Creation* with Dr. Georgia Purdom
- *Replacing Darwin: The New Origin of the Species* with Dr. Nathaniel Jeanson
- *The Wonder of DNA* with Dr. Georgia Purdom
- *Evolution: Not a Chance* with Dr. David Menton
- *Determining the Ark Kinds: How Many Animals Were on the Ark?* with Dr. Jean Lightner

Geology, Fossils, and the Flood

- *Three Ways to Make an Ape-Man* with Dr. David Menton
- *Lucy: She's No Lady* with Dr. David Menton
- *Circular Reasoning in Dating Methods* with Dr. Andrew Snelling
- *The Age of the Earth* with Dr. Andrew Snelling
- *Millions of Years: Where Did the Idea Come From?* with Dr. Terry Mortenson
- *Fossils and Rock Layers: The Flood, Not Evolution and Millions of Years* with Dr. Andrew Snelling
- *Radioactive and Radiocarbon Dating: Turning Foe into Friend* with Dr. Andrew Snelling

CATALOG OF LOGICAL FALLACIES

B

Below, you'll find alphabetical listings of common fallacies discussed in this book, complete with descriptions, examples, and tips for catching each fallacy. Every entry also references relevant *Critical Thinking Scan* videos on Answers TV, where you can learn more about these (or similar) fallacies.

PART 1: FALLACIES OF IRRELEVANT PREMISES

Ad Hominem

Description

Attacks the source of a message rather than arguing logically against the message itself.

Example

"Creationists are nothing but wild-eyed, dunderheaded, pseudo-intellectual conspiracy theorists."

How to Catch It

Ask, "Is this message true (or false) because . . . people who disagree (or agree) are ridiculed?" Not necessarily.

Related Video

Critical Thinking Scan, Season 2, Episode 1, "Catch Countless Fallacies with 1 Critical Thinking Hack."

Appeal to Emotion (Ad Passiones)

Description

Tries to persuade mainly by evoking an emotional reaction rather than presenting a logical, well-supported argument.

Examples

- Appeal to fear
  "Unless we quickly censor creationists, their destructive messages will continue to poison the minds of innocent children, threaten human rights, and endanger free societies."

- Appeal to pity
  "You wouldn't snatch the hard-earned pennies from a young person's personal education fund by forcing a hungry, cash-strapped student like me to pay for this speeding ticket, would you judge?"

How to Catch It

Ask, "Is this message true or false because . . . it makes me feel a certain way?" Not necessarily.

Related Videos

Critical Thinking Scan, Season 2, Episode 1, "Catch Countless Fallacies with 1 Critical Thinking Hack," and Season 5, Episode 5, "Emotions and Persuasion."

Appeal to Ignorance

Description

Argues that a message is true or false based on a lack of evidence to the contrary.

Examples

- "No one has ever disproved the existence of life on other planets, so aliens must be out there somewhere."
- "We know that humans and dinosaurs did not live at the same time because their fossils have not been found together."

How to Catch It

Ask, "Is this message true (or false) because . . . there's no evidence against (or for) it?" Not necessarily.

Related Videos

Critical Thinking Scan, Season 2, Episode 1, "Catch Countless Fallacies with 1 Critical Thinking Hack," and Season 2, Episode 3, "Appeals to Ignorance and Incredulity."

Appeal to Nature

Description

Argues that something is "good" or "bad" based only on whether it is natural or unnatural.

Example

"Nature itself attests to the advantages of cannibalism. Organisms ranging from lowly insects to great apes are known to devour members of their own species. Therefore, cannibalism is morally appropriate for humans, as well."

How to Catch It

Ask, "Is this message true (or false) because . . . it relates to something natural (or unnatural)?" Not necessarily.

Related Video

Critical Thinking Scan, Season 2, Episode 1, "Catch Countless Fallacies with 1 Critical Thinking Hack."

Appeal to Novelty

Description

Argues that something is "good" (or "bad") based only on whether it's modern (or old).

Examples

- "You should definitely buy a newer version of your phone because the latest technology is always the most useful."
- "You can't seriously believe a book that was written thousands of years ago."

How to Catch It

Ask, "Is this message true (or false) because . . . of its age?" Not necessarily.

Related Video

Critical Thinking Scan, Season 2, Episode 1, "Catch Countless Fallacies with 1 Critical Thinking Hack."

Appeal to Possibility

Description

Implies that what *might* be the case really is the case.

Examples

- "The Miller-Urey experiment showed that amino acids can form under natural conditions. So we know that a similar process must have occurred at the origin of life."
- "It's possible that a nefarious secret society is running the local pizza parlor. So that's probably exactly what's happening."

How to Catch It

Ask, "Is this message true because . . . it might be true?" Not necessarily.

Related Video

Critical Thinking Scan, Season 2, Episode 1, "Catch Countless Fallacies with 1 Critical Thinking Hack."

Appeal to Repetition (Ad Nauseum)

Description

Persuades people to believe a message by repeating it often rather than presenting a logical case for it.

Example

"Some humans aren't real persons. They're just tissue, objects, or animals. They don't really have minds or feelings." (Message is then repeated numerous times until it becomes mainstream.)

How to Catch It

Ask, "Is this message true because . . . it's repeated often?" Not necessarily.

Related Video

Critical Thinking Scan, Season 5, Episode 4, "The Power of Repetition."

Appeal to the People (Ad Populum)

Description

Argues that a message is true or false based on the number of people who believe so.

Examples

- "Of course earth is millions of years old—everybody says so!"
- "Come on, nobody really believes all those teachings in the Bible anymore."

How to Catch It

Ask, "Is this message true or false because . . . many people think so?" Not necessarily.

Related Videos

Critical Thinking Scan, Season 2, Episode 1, "Catch Countless Fallacies with 1 Critical Thinking Hack," and Season 5, Episode 3, "The Power of Conformity."

Appeal to Tradition

Description

Claims that something is good, right, or true only because it is old or traditional.

Examples

- "What do you mean we need to 'update our corrections system'? We've been locking criminals in that pillory for the last 300 years. There's no sense in changing the way it's done now."
- "Of course life can arise from nonlife—people have believed so for hundreds of years. Even Aristotle said that worms originate from rotten matter."

How to Catch It

Ask, "Is this message true because . . . it's been believed for a long time?" Not necessarily.

Related Video

Critical Thinking Scan, Season 2, Episode 1, "Catch Countless Fallacies with 1 Critical Thinking Hack."

Argument from Fallacy (Ad Logicam)

Description

Claims a message is false only because some people try using fallacies to defend it.

Example

"Some creationist writings contain fallacies or outdated arguments. So, clearly, creationism is nothing but pseudoscience."

How to Catch It

Ask, "Is this message false because . . . someone can try using flawed logic to argue for it?" Not necessarily.

Related Video

Critical Thinking Scan, Season 2, Episode 2, "Don't Creationists Use Fallacies?"

Argument from Incredulity

Description

States that a message is true or false only because the arguer finds it difficult to imagine otherwise.

Example

"There's no such thing as hell; I can't believe that a loving God would really condemn people to eternal death."

How to Catch It

Ask, "Is this message true or false because . . . someone has trouble believing otherwise?" Not necessarily.

Related Video

Critical Thinking Scan, Season 2, Episode 3, "Appeals to Ignorance and Incredulity."

Inflation of Conflict

Description

States that a message is false because people may disagree about it or debate different aspects of it.

Example

"There are so many separate church denominations which have different ideas about teachings in the Bible. With so much disagreement about its teachings, the Bible can't possibly be true."

How to Catch It

Ask, "Is this message false because . . . people can disagree about it?" Not necessarily.

Related Video

Critical Thinking Scan, Season 2, Episode 1, "Catch Countless Fallacies with 1 Critical Thinking Hack."

Genetic Fallacy

Description

Argues that a message is true or false based only on the type of source communicating it.

Examples

- Appeal to authority: "My paleontology professor said dinosaurs evolved into birds, so it must be true."
- Appeal to celebrity: "My favorite athlete wears snazzy, white tennis shoes, so I should wear them, too."
- Appeal to intelligence: "Some incredibly brilliant people have been atheists, so they must have been right when they said that God does not exist."
- Appeal to motive: "My dentist said I need to have my wisdom teeth removed. But he'll make a lot of money from me if I agree to the surgery, so of course he'd tell me to have my wisdom teeth removed. Therefore, I don't think I need to have them removed after all."
- Appeal to wealth: "A well-dressed evangelist wearing more gold than you could fit in a pirate's dentures is telling me that Jesus came to grant me earthly riches. So it must be true."
- Argument by personal charm: "An impossibly good-looking human is saying that the blender they're holding is the best in the world, so I should probably purchase a blender just like it."
- *Tu quoque* (you too): "People who say they believe the Bible sometimes act hypocritically. Therefore, the Bible can't really be true."

How to Catch It

Ask, "Is this message true or false because . . . of the kind of people who say so?" Not necessarily.

Related Video

Critical Thinking Scan, Season 2, Episode 1, "Catch Countless Fallacies with 1 Critical Thinking Hack."

Psychogenic Fallacy

Description

Implies that a message is false by suggesting underlying psychological reasons for why people may believe it.

Example

"You only believe in a God who holds people morally accountable for their actions because during your early childhood you experienced the punishment of an unforgiving parent."

How to Catch It

Ask, "Is this message false because . . . people may have a psychological reason for believing it?" Not necessarily.

Related Video

Critical Thinking Scan, Season 4, Episode 3, "Is Belief in God a Cognitive Bias?"

PART 2: FALLACIES OF UNACCEPTABLE PREMISES

Affirming the Disjunct

Description

Presents two options as mutually exclusive when both may be true.

Example

"If a loving God exists, then the world would not be full of suffering." (This suggests that either God exists or suffering exists. But the Bible explains that both statements are true—a loving God does exist and suffering also exists because of human sin.)

How to Catch It

Ask whether there really are only two mutually exclusive options.

Related Video

Critical Thinking Scan, Season 2, Episode 15, "Either-or Type Fallacies."

Circular Reasoning

Description

Arbitrarily assumes that an argument's conclusion is true in order to argue that the conclusion is true.

Example

"Vestigial structures in the human body represent 'leftovers' from our evolutionary ancestors, so evolution must be true."

How to Catch It

Check for circularity by asking if at least one of the argument's premises states (or presupposes) the same thing as its conclusion. Are there other good reasons to believe the conclusion, or would you have to accept the conclusion arbitrarily? If you'd need to believe the conclusion arbitrarily, the argument is informally fallacious.

(In this case, accepting the premise that "vestigial" structures are evolutionary leftovers would require us to arbitrarily believe that evolution is true—which is the argument's conclusion. To break the circularity, the argument would need other premises which support the claim that evolution is true. For information on common examples of other premises proposed to support evolution—and the problems with these arguments—see chapter 11 and the resources listed in appendix A.)

Related Videos

Critical Thinking Scan, Season 2, Episode 9, "Circular Reasoning," and Season 2, Episode 10, "Do Christians Use Circular Reasoning?"

Denying the Correlative

Description

Suggests that a third possibility may exist when there really are only two mutually exclusive options.

Example

"You don't have to choose between creation and evolution. You can believe that God used evolution to create people." (Actually, this is not a biblically feasible option—see chapter 2.)

How to Catch It

Ask whether there really are only two mutually exclusive options.

Related Video

Critical Thinking Scan, Season 2, Episode 15, "Either-or Type Fallacies."

Either-or Fallacy

Description

Presents only two options when other possibilities exist.

Example

"Either creationists are ignorant about the truth of evolution, or they're willfully suppressing the truth." (Other possibility: evolution is false, and creationists *are* communicating the truth.)

How to Catch It

Ask whether there really are only two mutually exclusive options.

Related Video

Critical Thinking Scan, Season 2, Episode 15, "Either-or Type Fallacies."

Equivocation (Bait-and-Switch)[2]

Description

Switches the definition of an important key word during an argument.

Example

"Of course all life-forms evolved from common ancestors. We observe evolution happening all the time. For example, scientists have documented populations of finches with short beaks evolving from populations of finches with long beaks."

How to Catch It

Check the definitions of key words in a message and ask if their meanings change. (In this case, the meaning of *evolution* switched from referring to historical science interpretations about *change between kinds* to the observational science of *variation within kinds*.)

Faulty Analogy

Description

States that two things are alike when, really, an important difference exists between them.

Example

"Like three blind men may seem to disagree when describing different parts of the same elephant, different religions may seem to disagree but really describe the same God."

How to Catch It

Look for an important difference between the items being compared. (E.g., different body parts can coexist on the same elephant, but contradictory statements about God cannot coexist as truth within the same reality.)

Note—You may also be able to turn the analogy around to enforce a biblical perspective by identifying a stolen biblical concept behind the analogy, like the existence of truth (see *stolen concept fallacy* on the next page). (E.g., "How would anyone know the blind men were feeling the same elephant? That person would have to have open eyes to see the big picture of truth. And God *has* revealed the big picture of truth to us through his Word.)

Related Video

Critical Thinking Scan, Season 2, Episode 4, "The Elephant, the Blind Man, and the Faulty Analogy."

Motte-and-Bailey Argument

Description

Reframes a controversial perspective to make it seem stronger than it really is.

Example

- **Person 1:** "I think we should legalize infanticide for parents who feel they lack the relevant funding and resources to care for their newborns."
- **Person 2:** "By definition, that would be murder."
- **Person 1** (commits fallacy): "I'm just trying to prevent children from being raised in impoverished environments."

How to Catch It

Bring back the discussion to what the original perspective truly stated.

Related Video

Critical Thinking Scan, Season 2, Episode 5, "Answering Straw Man Arguments."

Slippery Slope

Description

Claims that one action will inevitably set off a chain of events leading to dire consequences but does not show that those events are, in fact, logically connected with each other and likely to occur.

Example

"If you let your classmate borrow a pencil during one lecture, then he'll probably ask to borrow other school supplies, like your calculator, during another lecture. If he thinks he can take your calculator during a lecture, then he'll probably think he can also take your calculator during an exam. If he takes your calculator during an exam, then you'll answer the questions too slowly and fail the test. If you fail the test, then you'll fail the class. If you fail the class, then you won't be able to graduate. Therefore, you should never lend your classmate a pencil."

How to Catch It

Think about the actual likelihood of the final outcome by asking, "How probable is each if-then statement, and how many if-then statements are there?"

Related Video

Critical Thinking Scan, Season 2, Episode 14, "Slippery Slope Fallacies."

Stolen Concept Fallacy

Description

Presupposes the truth of the same thing being argued against.

Example

"How can you believe in the Bible when the Old Testament is so full of violence?"

How to Catch It

Ask big-picture questions to identify concepts in the argument which presuppose the existence of God, including truth, logic, knowledge, scientific reasoning, morality, and human value. (E.g., "Why are we concerned about violence?" Because it harms human life. "But why is human life valuable, and why is harming it morally wrong?" A biblical worldview, not a materialistic one, answers that.)

Related Videos

Critical Thinking Scan, Season 2, Episode 7, "Stolen Concept Fallacies," and Season 2, Episode 8, "Asking Big-Picture Questions."

Straw Man Argument

Description

Reframes an opposing perspective to make it seem weaker than it really is.

Example

- **Person 1:** "I think it's important for children to have access to good education."
- **Person 2** (commits fallacy): "Oh, so you're saying it's *not* important for *adults* to access educational opportunities? What kind of ageist, antisocial creature *are* you?"

How to Catch It

Bring the discussion back to what the original perspective truly stated.

Related Video

Critical Thinking Scan, Season 2, Episode 5, "Answering Straw Man Arguments."

PART 3: FORMAL FALLACIES

Affirming the Consequent

Description

Conditional arguments which claim that the "if" component (antecedent) of an "if-then" statement is true because the "then" component (consequent) is also true, using the structure

> If *p*, then *q*.
>
> *q*.
>
> Therefore, *p*.

Example

"If evolution is true, then humans and chimpanzees would have some DNA similarities. Humans and chimpanzees do have some DNA similarities. Therefore, evolution is true."

How to Catch It

Ask, "Are there other reasons why the consequent might be true besides the antecedent's being true?" (E.g., are there other reasons why humans and chimps may have DNA similarities, besides evolution's hypothetically being true?)

Related Video

Critical Thinking Scan, Season 2, Episode 12, "Affirming the Consequent."

Denying the Antecedent

Description

Conditional arguments which claim that the "then" component (consequent) of an "if-then" statement is false because the "if" component (antecedent) is also false, using the structure

> If *p*, then *q*.
>
> Not *p*.
>
> Therefore, not *q*.

Example

"If archaeologists have discovered the frozen remnants of Noah's ark, then Noah's ark existed. Archaeologists have not discovered the frozen remnants of Noah's ark. Therefore, Noah's ark did not exist."

How to Catch It

Ask, "Are there ways for the consequent to be true despite the antecedent's being false?" (E.g., are there other reasons why archaeologists have not discovered frozen remnants of Noah's ark besides the ark's not existing?)

Related Video

Critical Thinking Scan, Season 2, Episode 13, "Denying the Antecedent."

Endnotes

1. This is by no means an exhaustive list, and you can probably find examples of similar fallacies that haven't been given official names. But whether or not you know their names, you can recognize fallacies of irrelevant premises by asking, "Is this message true because . . .?"
2. Some authors group equivocation with the fallacies of irrelevant premises, but in this list, I've restricted fallacies of irrelevant premises to those which can be identified by asking, "Is this message true or false because . . .?"

CRITICAL THINKING PRACTICE EXERCISES

C

Try applying the 7 Checks of Critical Thinking to the following paragraphs from real textbooks, research papers, and popular media. Example answers related to each exercise can be found in the referenced *Critical Thinking Scan* videos available on Answers TV.

1. MESSAGE: THE HUMAN BODY CONTAINS "BAD DESIGNS," WHICH PROVIDE EVIDENCE FOR EVOLUTION.

Sample Quote

"The 'accidents' of evolutionary history explain many features that no intelligent engineer would be expected to design. For example, the paths followed by food and air cross in the pharynx of terrestrial vertebrates, including humans, so that we risk choking on food. The human eye has a 'blind spot,' which you can find at about 45° to the right or left of your line of sight. It is caused by the functionally nonsensical arrangement of the axons of the retinal cells."

Source

Douglas Futuyama, *Evolution*, 3rd ed., (Sunderland: Sinauer Associates, 2013), 54.

Related Video

Critical Thinking Scan, Season 7, Episode 9, "Thinking About 'Bad Designs.'"

2. MESSAGE: LIVING THINGS SHARE THE SAME GENETIC LANGUAGE, PROVIDING EVIDENCE FOR EVOLUTION.

Sample Quote

"All forms of life use the same genetic language of DNA and RNA, and the genetic code is essentially universal. Thus, it is likely that all species descended from common ancestors who used this code."

Source

Jane Reece et. al., *Campbell Biology*, Canadian ed. (Don Mills: Pearson Canada, 2014), 495.

Related Video

Critical Thinking Scan, Season 8, Episode 6, "The Not-So-Universal Genetic Code."

3. MESSAGE: RELIGIOUS BELIEFS RESULTED DIRECTLY OR INDIRECTLY FROM EVOLUTIONARY PROCESSES.

Sample Quote

"There are two major perspectives on why [all societies seem to have religions of some sort]. One is called functionalism, or adaptationism: the idea that religion brings positive evolutionary benefits, which are most often framed in terms of its contribution to group living. . . . Others take the view that religion is a spandrel, or by-product, of evolutionary processes."

Source

Brandon Ambrosino, "How and Why Did Religions Evolve?" *BBC Future*, accessed from bbc.com, April 18, 2019.

Related Videos

Critical Thinking Scan, Season 10, Episode 2, "Did Religious Beliefs Result from Evolution?" and Season 2, Episode 15, "Either-or Type Fallacies."

4. MESSAGE:
NOT ONLY IS IT POSSIBLE THAT ALIENS EXIST, BUT IT'S ALSO LIKELY THAT THEY EVOLVED IN SIMILAR WAYS TO HUMANS.

Sample Quote

"For the first time, researchers show how evolutionary theory can be used to support alien predictions and better understand their behavior. They show that aliens are potentially shaped by the same processes and mechanisms that shaped humans, such as natural selection. The theory supports the argument that foreign life-forms undergo natural selection and are like us, evolving to be fitter and stronger over time."

Source

University of Oxford, "Aliens may be more like us than we think: What evolutionary biology tells us about how aliens could look," *ScienceDaily*, October 31, 2017, www.sciencedaily.com/releases/2017/10/171031202151.htm.

Related Video

Critical Thinking Scan, Season 10, Episode 5, "Aliens and UFOs."

5. MESSAGE:
LIVING THINGS CAN BE CLASSIFIED INTO NESTED CATEGORIES, LIKE MAMMALS, TETRAPODS (FOUR-LIMBED CREATURES), AND VERTEBRATES (CREATURES WITH BACKBONES), BASED ON THE SIMILARITIES THEY SHARE. THESE NESTED HIERARCHIES PROVIDE EVIDENCE FOR EVOLUTION.

Sample Quote

"All tetrapods have limbs with digits . . . whereas other vertebrates do not. Thus, homologous characteristics form a nested pattern: all life shares the deepest layer, and each successive smaller group adds its own homologies to those it shares with larger groups. This nested pattern is exactly what we would expect to result from descent with modification from a common ancestor."

Source

Jane Reece et. al., *Campbell Biology*, Canadian ed. (Don Mills: Pearson Canada, 2014), 496.

Related Video

Critical Thinking Scan, Season 8, Episode 7, "Do Evolutionary Trees Show Evolution?"

6. MESSAGE: THE HORSE FOSSIL RECORD IS INCOMPATIBLE WITH BIBLICAL CREATION MODELS.

Sample Quote

"The evolution of the horse is known in exquisite detail from *Hyraoctherium* [Eohippus] to the modern horse. Scientific creationists have been forced to claim that the series is but allowed variation within a created 'kind.' If so, then rhinoceroses, tapirs, and horses are all the same 'kind,' as they can be traced to ancestors nearly identical to *Hyracotherium*. All these fossils lie in the correct order by both stratigraphic and radioisotope dating."

Source

Chris MacDonald and Lewis Vaughn, "Judging Scientific Theories," *The Power of Critical Thinking,* 4th Canadian ed. (Don Mills: Oxford University Press, 2016), 409.

Related Video

Critical Thinking Scan, Season 7, Episode 14, "Are Horse Fossils Evidence for Evolution?"

7. MESSAGE:
LIVING THINGS CONTAIN HIGH PROPORTIONS OF RELATIVELY USELESS "JUNK DNA," WHICH PROVIDES EVIDENCE FOR EVOLUTION.

Sample Quote

"Because genomes are products of natural processes rather than 'intelligent design,' all genomes contain functional and nonfunctional parts. The fraction of the genome that has no biological function is called 'rubbish DNA.'"

Source

Dan Graur, "Rubbish DNA: The Functionless Fraction of the Human Genome," *Evolution of the Human Genome I*, ed. Naruya Saitou (Tokyo: Springer Japan, 2017): 19–60.

Related Videos

Critical Thinking Scan, Season 8, Episode 2, "The 'Junk DNA' Debate," and Season 8, Episode 3, "The Onion Test."

8. MESSAGE:
LIVING THINGS CONTAIN NONFUNCTIONAL GENES, WHICH PROVIDE EVIDENCE FOR EVOLUTION.

Sample Quote

"An interesting additional line of evidence supporting evolution involves sequences of DNA known as 'pseudo-genes.' Pseudo-genes are remnants of genes that no longer function but continue to be carried along in DNA as excess baggage. Pseudo-genes also change through time, as they are passed on from ancestors to descendants, and they offer an especially useful way of reconstructing evolutionary relationships.

With functioning genes, one possible explanation for the relative similarity between genes from different organisms is that their ways of life are similar—for example, the genes from a horse and a zebra could be more similar because of their similar habitats and behaviors than the genes from a horse and a tiger. But this possible explanation does not work for pseudo-genes, since they perform no function. Rather, the degree of similarity between pseudo-genes must simply reflect their evolutionary relatedness. The more remote the last common ancestor of two organisms, the more dissimilar their pseudo-genes will be."

Source

National Academy of Sciences, *Science and Creationism: A View from the National Academy of Sciences*, 2nd ed. (Washington: National Academy Press, 1999), 20.

Related Video

Critical Thinking Scan, Season 8, Episode 4, "Pseudo-Genes."

9. MESSAGE:

HUMAN CHROMOSOME 2 RESULTED FROM A FUSION OF TWO CHROMOSOMES THAT ARE SEPARATE CHROMOSOMES IN THEIR SHARED ANCESTOR WITH THE APES, PROVIDING EVIDENCE FOR EVOLUTION.

Sample Quote

"The cells of all great apes, like chimpanzees, gorillas, and orangutans, contain 24 pairs of chromosomes. If humans share a common ancestor with apes, you'd expect us to have the same number. But surprisingly, human cells contain only 23 pairs. Now if we share a common ancestor, what happened? . . . In the line that led to us, two chromosomes that were separate in other primates became fused to form a single chromosome."

Source

Ken Miller, "Ken Miller Human Chromosome 2 Genome," YouTube video, 3:28, November 28, 2007, https://www.youtube.com/watch?v=8FGYzZOZxMw.

Related Video

Critical Thinking Scan, Season 8, Episode 9, "Human Chromosome 2 'Fusion.'"

10. MESSAGE:
JESUS WAS NOT SUPERNATURAL, SO THERE MUST BE NATURAL EXPLANATIONS FOR ANY HISTORICALLY BASED ACCOUNTS OF HIS MIRACLES RECORDED IN SCRIPTURE—INCLUDING HIS WALKING ON WATER.

Sample Quote

"The New Testament story describes Jesus walking on water in the Sea of Galilee, but according to a study led by Florida State University Professor of Oceanography Doron Nof in Tallahassee, FL, it's more likely that he walked on an isolated patch of floating ice."

Source

Florida State University, "Jesus Walked on Ice, Says Study," *ScienceDaily*, April 17, 2006, www.sciencedaily.com/releases/2006/04/060417105522.htm.

Related Videos

Critical Thinking Scan, Season 1, Episode 5, "Critical Thinking Check #1: Check Scripture," and Season 11, Episode 5, "False Teaching Lie #4: Jesus Isn't Who Scripture Says He Is."

D

WRITING TIPS

Here are a few ideas, tips, and reminders for honing your communication slingshot to glorify God, love others, and overcome evil with good (Romans 12:21). These pointers are meant for nonfiction writing, but many of them apply to crafting fiction, too.

Remember to be a stickler for structure, sandwiching all your main points between a strong introduction and conclusion.

- The introduction invites readers into your material and offers a road map of your manuscript's content. To make introductions especially effective, try kickstarting your papers with sentences that spark the readers' curiosity.
- The conclusion summarizes the points which you'd like readers to remember from your message—and the actions which those readers can take in response.
- When possible, try to write in a "circle." Bring readers back to your piece's beginning by making the conclusion a reflection of the introduction. For instance, you could reference a story you shared in your introduction or simply reintegrate some of the introduction's key words into the conclusion.

Harness the power of storytelling. Jesus communicated with stories all the time. And being the Creator (John 1:1–3), he certainly understood how stories connect with the human mind.

A word of classic storytelling advice is "show, don't tell." For example:

- Telling: I was nervous before the exam.
- Showing: I didn't bother trying to stop my knee from shaking under the desk as I waited, clutching my pencil. Hopefully, I would be able to hear the examiner's next words above the pounding of my own pulse.

Create analogies and metaphors which are fresh, relevant, and (potentially) humorous within your topic's context. For inspiration, notice all the ways other authors craft intriguing comparisons.

Pay attention to the rhythm and poetic meter of your words so that their syllables "sound right" together when they're spoken (even in readers' minds). Meter helps explain why the line when the sunlight

pierced the heavens sounds that much more compelling than the line when the sun's light pierced the clouds.

End sentences with the strongest word. For instance:

- Weaker ending: Defending the gospel is what we're all about around here.
- Stronger ending: Around here, we're all about defending the gospel.

Cut unnecessary adverbs, adjectives, and modifying phrases, which only serve to clutter. Instead, use descriptive nouns and verbs for panache and concision. For example:

- Cluttered: Bravely mustering all of his courage, he walked very slowly toward the door, which was actually standing open.
- Concise: Mustering his courage, he crept toward the open door.

Utilize "power words" that convey emotion or engage the senses, like glimmer (sight), sizzle (sound), prick (touch), and tang (taste/smell).

Add pizzazz with poetic techniques, including alliteration, consonance, and repetition.

Vary your sentence structure and length. For readability, err on the side of shorter sentences.

Remember your target audience. Are you writing in a way that connects with the readers you're trying to reach?

Read the best writing you can and think about why it's strong. Jot down specific techniques you notice the authors using for masterful communication. As you read, write down words or sentences that stand out to you.

Like mastering a slingshot, honing communication skills requires time, practice, dedication, and the humble realization that there will always be more to learn. We may never see results we deem "impressive" from our efforts. But we're not called to see results—we're called to be faithful. When we offer ourselves and our slingshots to God, he will use us in the way he knows is best.

RESEARCH TIPS

E

Here's a five-part crash course in how to find, read, and report findings from scientific studies. Along the way, remember that the authority for truth is not fallible human reasoning but the Word of our infallible God.

PART 1: TYPES OF INFORMATION SOURCES

You can learn about scientific research findings from two types of information sources:

1. Primary sources are the original articles where researchers report their findings. Typically, these articles appear in academic journals like *Science*, *American Psychologist*, *Biblical Archaeology Review*, *Answers Research Journal*, and countless others. Such journals require studies to be screened by a panel of experts (peer-reviewed) before publication. While theses and independent studies also count as primary sources, they do not undergo peer review.
2. Secondary sources talk about information from primary sources. Secondary sources include news reports and magazine articles about researchers' discoveries, along with formal papers called literature reviews, which combine information from multiple researchers.

Tip for students: research assignments usually require you to reference peer-reviewed, primary sources. However, literature reviews are handy for pointing you to primary sources, providing useful insights, and presenting overviews of a topic.

PART 2: ANATOMY OF AN ARTICLE

Whether primary or secondary sources, most formal papers begin with an *abstract*—a short summary of the paper's information. After the abstract, primary articles usually contain the following sections:

- The *introduction* explains why the study matters, presents relevant information from previous experiments, and outlines the study's hypothesis.[1]
- The *methods section* outlines how the study was conducted.
- The *results section* describes the experiment's outcomes.
- The *discussion* summarizes the study, interprets the results, compares them to findings from previous studies, and offers suggestions for future research or actions.

PART 3: FINDING RELEVANT RESEARCH ONLINE

With these basics in mind, how do you find primary studies? Here are five general steps:[2]

1. Head to an online database.

Database websites are like online libraries, stocked with articles from different academic journals. Some databases you can search for free, like PubMed, Google Scholar, or Science Direct. Others, like EBSCO or Web of Science, allow you access if you're part of a subscribing university or corporation. For research from a biblical perspective, you can also search creation databases like AnswersInGenesis.org, which features studies published in the peer-reviewed *Answers Research Journal*. (When writing assignments, however, note that not even rigorous peer-reviewed research from a biblical perspective may be considered "acceptable" for citation by secular universities due to the worldview differences.)

2. Set your search filters.

Different databases include different search features. Most have a "year" filter where you can look for studies published within a specific date range, allowing you to focus on the latest research. Many databases also include a "full text" filter, which lets you only see articles which are open access, meaning you can read them for free without being part of a university. Depending on the database, you can also choose what types of sources you search for, including books, studies, literature reviews, papers from specific journals, or articles by certain authors.

3. Enter your key words.

Once you've set your filters, the next step is typing your key words into the search bar. Some databases (or advanced search options) let you look up specific key word combinations by inserting the word *and* between the key words; search multiple key words by inserting *or*; or exclude results with a certain key word by inserting *not*. You can also search for specific key words or word combinations by placing quotation marks around them.

4. Pick a study.

Once you hit "enter," a list of article titles should pop up, showing a link to the article, author, and publishing information, along with a text preview. If the article is open access, you may see a link to a free-text version near the preview, or you may need to click the article title to see free text links. Even for studies that aren't open access, you can usually read the gist of their findings in the abstract.

Research papers are usually so long that the writers know many of their readers won't take time to examine the whole article. That's why the abstract is your best friend, providing a glimpse into the article's key content. Your second-best friend is likely the discussion section, which typically restates the study's purpose, methods, and results. These two friends will let you know if the study's content is relevant enough for you to take a closer look at the methods and results.

5. Find related studies.

On the article's page or near its text preview in your original search results, you may see *related articles* or *citing articles* links. The related articles page lists other studies on the same or similar topics. However, some of those studies may be much older than the original article (unless you reset your date filters).

While there's nothing necessarily wrong with old research, new studies may overturn or reinterpret older findings—especially in fields like biology. To see whether later researchers have other reinterpretations of a study, click the "citing articles" button present on some databases. The linked page lists all the studies which referenced the original article. Not all these studies may be 100% relevant to your topic of interest, but they *will* be newer.

On the citing article page, you may be able to check a box labeled "search within citing articles." Once you've checked this box, you can use the page's search box to look for key words in articles which cited the original study. This feature lets you see what other researchers have said about specific concepts within the paper, potentially revealing another side of the story.

PART 4: A WORD OF CAUTION: BEWARE OF WOOZLES

When reporting information from research papers, remember this immortal warning: beware of woozles. I don't mean the fictitious kind that romp with heffalumps in the Hundred Acre Wood (although spotting one of those would raise some critical thinking red flags, too). Rather, a woozle is an unsubstantiated claim which, when cited often enough, becomes treated as fact. Researchers have a name for this process—the woozle effect.

For example, let's say while researching high school violence, you encounter a statistic that 95% of teenagers report being punched at school. That's a remarkable figure, but—being an astute critical thinker—you want to make sure it's accurate. Applying Critical Thinking Check #3, you check the source by looking up the reference article provided for the statistic. Upon reading it, you realize the statistic didn't come from that article but from another, even earlier study. You finally track down the original study only to realize the real statistic states, "95% of teenagers *from one particular school in a high-violence neighborhood* report being punched at school."

This statement may well be accurate. But over the course of multiple citations, important qualifiers disappeared from the original statistic, leaving the dubious "fact" that 95% of *all teenagers* experience physical violence at school. Congratulations. You have successfully captured a woozle.

PART 5: POINTS TO REMEMBER FOR READING RESEARCH PAPERS

- Even researchers, being human, can make mistakes.
- Studies may be misled by faulty methods, instrument errors, or other confounding factors.
- Many researchers will be interpreting their observations through a secular worldview.
- Researchers' worldview assumptions can influence studies on multiple levels, including the data they choose to analyze, the methods they use to analyze it, and the conclusions they reach when interpreting their results.
- Our final authority is not fallible researchers but the infallible Word of God—the foundation which makes scientific reasoning possible.

Endotes

1. The hypothesis is the claim which the researchers are experimentally testing. For instance, researchers might hypothesize, "Students remember more information when taking notes by hand rather than typing." The experimental results will then confirm or disconfirm the hypothesis.
2. Internet tutorials and your nearest librarian can help you learn the specifics of navigating certain databases.

ACKNOWLEDGMENTS

Behind the making of this book lies a story that stretches back more than a decade, intersecting numerous lives whose contributions made *Prepare to Thrive* possible. Here are just some of the individuals I'd like to thank in the order they appeared along the journey.

To my family—thank you for discipling me with the foundations I needed to thrive at my university, encouraging my adventures with God wherever he led, and providing me with awesome writing hideouts.

To Ken Ham—thank you for proclaiming the message of biblical authority, which rocked my world at age 14.

To Dr. Margaret Helder—thank you for opening your door to a wide-eyed teenager seeking apologetics answers and being my mentor ever since.

To the many other Christians who supported me through mentorship, friendship, prayer, or places to stay during my university years—thank you for being part of my interpersonal foundations and showing me what it means to help Christian students thrive.

To the Christian writing community I joined as a student—thank you for encouraging me to create the blog that proved vital for 360° in 180, leading to my connection with Answers in Genesis–Canada.

To the students, campus ministers, and other Christians I interviewed or stayed with during 360° in 180—thank you for sharing your insights, offering your friendship, and opening your homes to a vagabond blogger (Matthew 25:35).

To Calvin Smith and Dr. Georgia Purdom—thank you for your significant roles in reviewing this book and making its publication a reality.

To the team at Answers in Genesis–Canada and friends of the ministry—thank you for your support and encouragement as this project unfolded.

To the publishing, design, and editing team members at Answers in Genesis, including Dan Zordel, Jenn Reed, Michaela Duncan, Mike Matthews, Ryan Freeman, Evonne Krell, Shonda Snelbaker, and others involved with *Prepare to Thrive*—thank you for the hours you invested in preparing this book to become a polished tool ready for use.

To the reader (yes, you!)—thank you for picking up this tool and journeying through its pages. I pray that God would use the words you've read to equip and encourage you to the fullest extent of his purposes.

Most of all, I thank God, the author of salvation, to whom all glory belongs.